THE EUROPEAN UNDERSTANDING OF INDIA

General Editors of the Series

K. A. BALLHATCHET

P. J. MARSHALL

D. F. POCOCK

European attempts to understand India have been pursued in a variety of fields. Many of the books and articles that resulted are still of great historical importance. Not only do they provide valuable information about the India of the time; they are also of significance in the intellectual history of Europe. Each volume in the present series has been edited by a scholar who is concerned to elucidate both its Indian and its European relevance.

Bishop Heber in northern India

Bishop Heber

BISHOP HEBER IN NORTHERN INDIA

Selections from Heber's Journal

Edited by
M. A. LAIRD

Lecturer in History at the Portsmouth Polytechnic

CAMBRIDGE
AT THE UNIVERSITY PRESS
1971

Published by the Syndics of the Cambridge University Press
Bentley House, 200 Euston Road, London NW1 2DB
American Branch: 32 East 57th Street, New York, N.Y.10022

Library of Congress Catalogue Card Number: 70–123673

ISBN: 0 521 07873 3

Printed in Great Britain
at the University Printing House, Cambridge
(Brooke Crutchley, University Printer)

Contents

Illustrations

These illustrations are all from sketches by Bishop Heber

Maps

Preface

Bishop Heber's Journal was first published in 1828, in two volumes, and it is from this edition that the following selections have been made. The Journal was originally edited by Heber's wife Amelia, out of material in the form of notes and letters which he wrote to her during his tour.

These selections represent about half of the original edition. As so much of that very lengthy work has had to be omitted for reasons of space, it seemed best to concentrate on the main north Indian section, starting in Calcutta and ending in Bombay; and the scope of the Introduction is limited accordingly. The chapter on Ceylon in the original was in any case based on Amelia Heber's Journal, while that on Madras is a mere fragment owing to the Bishop's untimely death only a month after the start of his tour through the southern presidency. Otherwise I have tried to present a fair sample of the original Journal, to illustrate Heber's own attitudes and the condition of the country in 1823-5.

For the spelling of Indian place-names, I have as a rule used the form in current use in India in my annotations. In the text I have left the 1828 spelling—of names and other words—unchanged.

I am very greatly indebted to Professor K. A. Ballhatchet, Dr P. J. Marshall, Miss M. E. Gibbs and Dr T. G. P. Spear for many helpful comments and suggestions.

M.A.L.

Portsmouth, February 1971

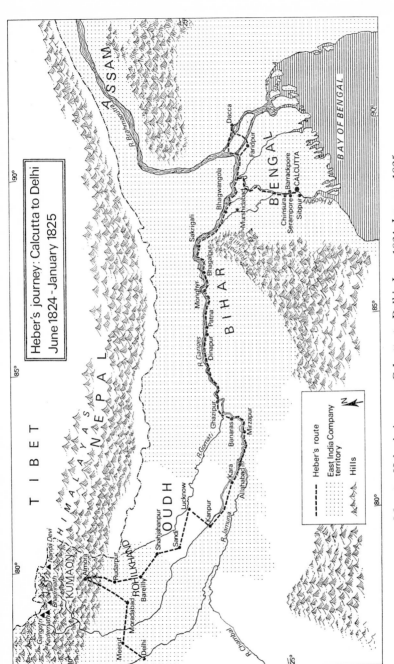

Map 1   Heber's journey: Calcutta to Delhi, June 1824–January 1825

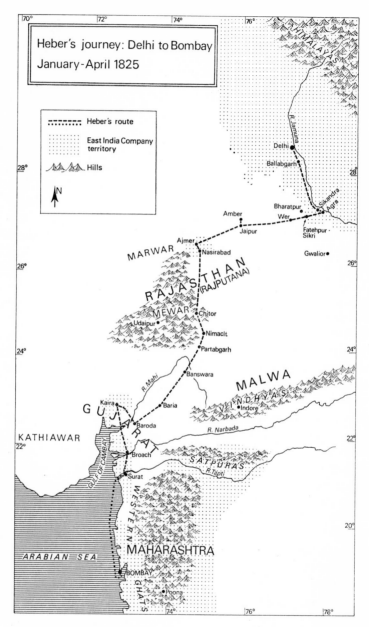

Map 2   Heber's journey: Delhi to Bombay, January–April 1825

Introduction

I

Reginald Heber is remembered now mainly as a missionary
bishop of Evangelical tendencies,[1] and although his talents and
interests were much more varied than this description might
suggest, it does contain a significant truth. His life indeed helps
to illustrate a basic shift in British attitudes towards India
which began to take place at the end of the eighteenth century.
Until then there had been little sign of British concern for
Indian missions apart from a financial contribution from the
Society for Promoting Christian Knowledge to a Lutheran
mission in the south; on the other hand, between about 1760 and
1790 at any rate the most influential writers on Hinduism
tended to interpret it in deistic terms and to argue that there was
much that was admirable in Hindu philosophy and ethics, that
Hindus worshipped the Supreme Being, polytheistic cults notwithstanding, and—by implication at least—that Christian
missionary activity was unnecessary and useless.[2] But after
about 1785 an increasingly effective challenge to this view was
mounted by British Evangelicals, who had little sympathy for
Hinduism or any other non-Christian religion—or indeed for
non-Evangelical Christianity; they believed that salvation was
only to be found through a personal belief in Christ and his
Atonement, and that they had an urgent responsibility to labour
for the conversion of a people which had fallen under British
control.

Heber's lifetime thus coincided with the beginning of a new
phase of missionary activity in India—one that was carried on
more intensively and on a wider scale than ever before. The
first Christian missionary to reach the country had been, reput-
edly, St Thomas the Apostle; at any rate there is no doubt that

---

[1] G. Smith, *Bishop Heber*. London, 1895, 55; G. D. Bearce, *British attitudes
towards India 1784–1858*, Oxford, 1961, 85.

[2] P. J. Marshall, *The British discovery of Hinduism in the eighteenth century*, Cambridge, 1970.

a church was firmly established in Malabar during the early centuries of the Christian era. Then in the sixteenth century came Roman Catholic missionaries, operating mainly in the areas under Portuguese control around the coasts but also far beyond: there were, for example, three Jesuit missions to the courts of the Mughal Emperors Akbar and Jahangir. But by the eighteenth century the Roman Catholic missionary endeavour had lost its vigour, although the churches which it had brought into being remained—especially along the west coast, in south India, and in lower Bengal. By then however the Protestants were starting in the south: from 1706 onwards the Tamilnad was the scene of a remarkable international and ecumenical mission, manned largely by German Lutherans, based on the Danish settlement of Tranquebar, and financed by the English S.P.C.K. There was however virtually no Protestant missionary work in northern India until the last decade of the century, when it was started by the Baptist Missionary Society—the first of a 'new wave' of societies founded in Britain under the influence of the Evangelical Movement. William Carey, who had played a major part in its foundation, arrived in Bengal in 1793; Joshua Marshman and William Ward joined him subsequently, and in 1800 this famous 'Trio' established itself at Serampore—like Tranquebar, a Danish colony. Their evangelistic methods included vernacular preaching and the circulation of tracts and portions of the Bible, which they translated into over 30 Indian languages. They compiled dictionaries and grammars of Bengali and other languages, and their work helped to create the conditions for the subsequent development of Bengali prose literature. Carey also took an interest in plants and animals, and was one of the founders of the Agri-Horticultural Society of India (1820). They established schools, and they investigated and agitated against some of the 'dreadful practices' which existed in contemporary Hinduism, including infanticide and especially *sati*, the burning of widows, which was then common in Bengal.[1]

Meanwhile India had become an important subject of concern to William Wilberforce and other leading Anglican Evangeli-

[1] E. D. Potts, *British Baptist missionaries in India 1793–1837*, Cambridge, 1967.

cals—the 'Clapham Sect'. The individual mainly responsible for directing their attention to India was Charles Grant, who served the East India Company in Bengal for twenty-two years before his final return to England in 1790, and subsequently in London as a Director and Chairman. While in Bengal he had experienced conversion, in the Evangelical sense, and in 1792 he wrote his pamphlet *Observations on the state of society among the Asiatic subjects of Great Britain*. He painted a gloomy picture of Indian social life, which he believed had been fundamentally corrupted by Hinduism and Islam and could only be reformed by the introduction of Christianity. Grant's thesis was readily accepted by his fellow-Evangelicals, and when the Company's Charter became due for renewal by Parliament in 1793, Wilberforce took the opportunity to introduce a clause which would have committed it to sending 'schoolmasters and missionaries' to India. It passed through a thinly-attended House of Commons, but was subsequently withdrawn as a result of violent criticism in the Court of Proprietors of East India Stock.[1] Most of the speakers argued that it was hopeless to try to convert the Indians, as they were too strongly attached to their existing religions; in any case the commitment would burden the Company with too great an expense. Randle Jackson thought that the American desire for independence had been stimulated by the spread of education there, and he warned the Company against making the same mistake in India; while Montgomery Campbell expressed a common late eighteenth-century opinion when he said that upper-class Indians at least 'were people of the purest morality and the most strict virtue'. Several speakers thought that attempts to spread Christianity would arouse Indian resentments and therefore endanger British rule, and it was this question which was to become central in the arguments over missions during the twenty years leading up to the next renewal of the Charter, in 1813.

Meanwhile, however, successive Governors-General came to view the work of the Serampore Baptists with considerable sympathy and allowed them to extend it into British territory;

[1] W. Woodfall (ed.), *Debate at East-India House, on the renewal of the Company's Charter, 23 May 1793*, London, 1793.

and some of the Company's Anglican chaplains were also beginning to take an active interest in missionary work. The Company had provided chaplains for its settlements in India since the early seventeenth century: they were essentially for the benefit of its European servants, and though the Charter of 1698 encouraged them to give some attention also to the Indians in its employment they showed little interest in missionary work until long after that date. During the eighteenth century the chaplains in fact reflected the attitudes of the clergy in contemporary England: they tended to have an easy-going existence redeemed by philanthropic activities such as organising schools and orphanages for British and Eurasian children; but by the end of the century, in India no less than in England, the Evangelical Movement had begun to have its effect. The first of the Evangelical chaplains was David Brown, who arrived in Calcutta in 1787 and set about his duties with the vigour and earnestness characteristic of his party. At that time religious observances did not weigh heavily on the British community in Calcutta, but during the next generation a remarkable 'reformation of manners' was accomplished. This was due partly to the example and exhortations of Brown and his fellow-Evangelicals, but also to the general revival of religious orthodoxy which was one aspect of the reaction against the later stages of the French Revolution. It was confirmed at the highest level: Wellesley,[1] in contrast to his predecessors, was determined to show that Christianity was the religion of the Government; he issued orders for the better observance of Sunday, attended church regularly, and after his victory over Mysore he appointed 6 February 1800 as a day of general thanksgiving. There was a procession through the streets of Calcutta to the church, where a solemn *Te Deum* was sung; and 'the inauguration of the Christian religion, as the religion of the rulers of British India, was announced by the booming of cannon and the parade of two thousand troops'[2]—an appropriate beginning for the nineteenth century.

Wellesley appointed David Brown and Claudius Buchanan—

[1] Governor-General 1798–1805.

[2] J. C. Marshman, *The life and times of Carey, Marshman and Ward*, London, 1859, I, 127.

Introduction

another Evangelical chaplain—respectively Provost and Vice-provost of Fort William College, which he founded in 1801 for training the young civil servants of the East India Company. He also appointed William Carey lecturer in Bengali, to which Sanskrit and Marathi were later added; and thus the new generation of Company officials came under religious and even missionary influences in their formative years. More generally, the Evangelical chaplains—and the Serampore missionaries—exercised an influence on the British community which ensured that there would be a substantial group of laymen ready to give their support to missionary work.

A committee of the Church Missionary Society—an Anglican Evangelical body—was formed in Calcutta in 1807, and an auxiliary to the British and Foreign Bible Society four years later. Meanwhile, with Charles Grant using his influence in the Court of Directors to appoint more Evangelicals as chaplains, the movement was spreading up the Ganges valley. The zealous and emotional Henry Martyn, who has been aptly described as 'a missionary in the guise of a chaplain',[1] arrived in 1806 and during the next four years ministered first at Dinapur and then at Kanpur (Cawnpore), where he preached a series of addresses to large crowds. One of those who heard him and was subsequently baptised was Abdul Masih, who afterwards worked as an evangelist with considerable effect. Martyn was also a talented linguist who embarked on translations of the Bible into Hindustani, Arabic and Persian; it was in order to perfect the latter that he undertook the journey to Persia and Turkey that ended with his death at Tokat in 1812.

Of still more importance than Martyn as a founder of the Anglican Church in Hindustan was Daniel Corrie. He also arrived in 1806, and after working at Chunar and Kanpur was transferred to Agra, whither he went early in 1813 together with Abdul Masih as catechist and Scripture-reader. This was a most effective partnership, and during a stay of 16 months Corrie baptised 71 converts from Hinduism and Islam.[2] Then after

[1] T. G. P. Spear, *The Nabobs*, London, 1963, 108.
[2] *Memoirs of the Right Rev. Daniel Corrie, LL.D.*, by his brothers, London, 1847, 275.

a long furlough in England he returned to India and spent the year 1818 in Banaras, before being transferred to Calcutta, which was to be his base for the next fifteen years. Meanwhile David Brown had died, in 1812, but his place in Calcutta was filled by Thomas Thomason, perhaps the most amiable and generous-minded of all the early Evangelical clergy. Corrie and Thomason proved to be the mainstays of the work of the C.M.S. in northern India during the early nineteenth century.

The twenty years between 1793 and 1813 thus saw considerable missionary and quasi-missionary work in north India, but it was still with the connivance rather than the official permission of the East India Company. As 1813 approached, therefore, a vigorous interdenominational campaign was organised, under Evangelical leadership, to ensure that the position of the missionaries should be regularised. By then the fear that missionary work would antagonise Indians and endanger British rule in India had been sharpened by a mutiny of sepoys at Vellore in 1806, which, it was suggested, had been caused by apprehensions that the British authorities were planning to convert them to Christianity; and also by some of the publications of the Serampore missionaries' press, which had reflected most uncharitably on Muhammad and the Hindu gods—much to the distaste, as well as the anxiety, of Lord Minto.[1] In 1813, however, the religious pressure on the Company was much stronger and better-organised than it had been twenty years earlier; and Wilberforce did not this time require the Company to bestow its official patronage on missions. A clause was therefore successfully introduced into the Charter Bill[2] which in effect permitted missionaries to function under the auspices of their societies, the Government adopting a policy of religious neutrality. 'It is the duty of this country', its preamble declared, 'to promote the interests and happiness of the native inhabitants of the British Dominions in India; and such measures ought to be adopted as may tend to the introduction among them of useful knowledge, and of religious and moral improvements; and in furtherance of the above objects, sufficient facilities ought to be afforded by law to persons desirous of accomplishing those

---

[1] Governor-General 1807–13. [2] 53 Geo. III, c. 155, sec. xxxiii.

Introduction

benevolent designs.' The tempo of missionary activity increased immediately: during the next decade the Baptist, London and Church Missionary Societies, the S.P.C.K., Americans and Scots all extended or began operations—in Bengal, Hindustan and Orissa in the north-east; Bombay, Gujarat and the Konkan in the west.

Not the least of their contributions was in the field of education. They concentrated at first on teaching the elements of Western learning and Christianity through the medium of the local vernaculars, though English was also taught in a few of their schools; they also started some schools for girls. The Government, on the other hand, had only just begun to modify its policy of trying, in a very half-hearted way, to revive traditional Muslim and Hindu learning. Warren Hastings,[1] who had a genuine interest in Indian culture, had founded a *madrasa*—a college for Muslims—at Calcutta in 1781, and in 1791 a Sanskrit College was established for Hindus at the holy city of Banaras by Jonathan Duncan, the British Resident. The patronage of traditional learning had been one of the functions of Indian rulers, but such attempts to continue it encountered increasing criticism in Britain, especially from Evangelicals and—a little later—from Utilitarians also: both wanted an education designed not to revive past glories, of which they were highly sceptical, but radically to transform India. Some concessions were made to the reformers in the 1813 Charter Act, which empowered the Government to spend a lakh of rupees per year out of its surplus revenues on education, on the modern Western as well as the traditional Oriental pattern. In fact however the wars which preoccupied Lord Hastings' administration (1813–23) left nothing by way of surplus revenue until its last years, so little was done by the Government until 1823, when the General Committee of Public Instruction was established to deal with educational matters in the Bengal Presidency. It hoped that Western studies might be grafted on to traditional Oriental learning, but its patronage was mainly directed towards the latter in practice.

Under Lord Hastings it was the non-governmental educational agencies which registered the most notable advances.

---

[1] Governor-General 1772–85.

7

Introduction

Apart from the mission schools there were institutions such as the Calcutta School and School Book Societies, which were founded in 1817–18 to improve the indigenous schools of Calcutta and to publish textbooks; to them missionaries, British laymen and Indians all contributed. Then there was the opening of the Hindu College, Calcutta, in 1817—the first Indian initiative for education after a Western pattern. Its founders were a group of Bengalis who were beginning to realise the potentialities of modern European learning for India. Some of them also wished to purge Hinduism of what they believed to be the degenerate social practices which had marred its original purity. The greatest leader of the reformers was Ram Mohan Roy (1772–1833), who was influenced by Muslim and Christian ideas: he had a deep admiration for the teachings of Christ, opposed idolatry and sacrifices, and evolved a monotheistic position which might be roughly summarised as Hindu–Unitarian. Further than that he would not go, much to the disappointment—indeed the annoyance—of the missionaries. As a social reformer he was mainly concerned to vindicate the rights of women: he was able to find supporting texts for his campaigns in the Hindu Scriptures, and thus played an important part especially in the agitation against *sati*, which was finally prohibited by Lord William Bentinck in 1829. But while the Hindu reformers had an importance out of proportion to their numbers, their attitudes were not shared by the majority of the 'learned natives' of northern India—a fact which was reflected in the fundamentally cautious education policy of the Government.

The Charter Act of 1813 not only smoothed the way for missionaries and committed the Government to support for education, but it provided also for the establishment of a bishop in Calcutta and three archdeacons for the Presidency cities of Calcutta, Madras and Bombay; to be maintained out of the Indian revenues.[1] The most influential advocate of an episcopate was Claudius Buchanan, a man after Wellesley's own heart, who shared that extreme reverence for the institutions of the Anglican Church which seems to have characterised most of its Scottish members. 'An Archbishop is wanted for India', he pronounced in

[1] 53 Geo. III, c. 155, sec. xlix.

1805, 'a sacred and exalted character, surrounded by his Bishops, of ample revenue and exalted sway... We want something royal, in a spiritual or temporal sense, for the abject subjects of this great Eastern empire to look up to.'[1] Buchanan's idea, though in a more modest form, was taken up and successfully pursued by Anglican Evangelicals and also by a group of High Churchmen who from about 1810 onwards were putting new life into the two old-established Anglican missionary societies, the S.P.C.K. and the S.P.G.[2]

Thomas Fanshaw Middleton, Vicar of St Pancras, was appointed as the first Bishop of Calcutta, where he arrived in November 1814. His episcopate was not however a happy one: from the first he found himself beset with problems of a kind which his rather unimaginative mind had never conceived. To begin with, the establishment of chaplains—never generous—was now quite inadequate for the vastly extended British dominions in India, and even that was never at full strength. Church buildings also were few. Still more serious, there was a host of vexatious juridical problems involving the Government, C.M.S. missionaries, and the ordination of converts. His Letters Patent gave him the authority to license the chaplains, but they also contained the provision that nothing in them should restrict the powers of the Company, which was interpreted to mean that it should continue to be responsible for their appointment, stationing, and transfer. Lord Hastings sympathised with the Bishop's desire to assume the last two of these functions, but the Court of Directors insisted on maintaining the Company's powers intact.[3] Middleton also had lengthy and vexatious disputes with the secular authorities concerning the granting of marriage-licences, the establishment of his consistory courts, and even the consecration of churches. Then there was the problem of the ordained Anglican missionaries—in effect of the C.M.S. only, as the two other societies were not yet sending such men to India. As Anglican clergymen they might have been expected to

---

[1] H. Pearson, *Memoirs of the life and writings of the Rev. Claudius Buchanan, D.D.*, London, 1817, I, 377.

[2] Founded in 1699 and 1701 respectively.

[3] C. W. Le Bas, *The life of the Right Reverend Thomas Fanshaw Middleton, D.D.*, London, 1831, I, 141–4.

Introduction

fall within the episcopal jurisdiction, and indeed the C.M.S. wanted Middleton to license them; but in fact he felt unable to do so. Nothing had been said about missionaries in the Letters Patent; indeed the bishopric, as established in 1813–14, was officially for the benefit only of the Christian population of India, and every precaution was taken not to 'alarm the natives' into thinking that it was an agency intended to pressure them into conversion. Middleton had shown considerable interest in missionary work before he had left for India; he was a member of the S.P.C.K. and had in 1813 preached the valedictory sermon for one of their German missionaries whom they were sending to south India;[1] but at least for the first two years of his episcopate he concentrated entirely on his work among Christians. A further reason for his hesitations about the C.M.S. missionaries was that they were in the habit of ministering also to the Europeans in the vicinity of their stations if there were no Company chaplains within reach, and Middleton feared that if he licensed them the Company would have an excuse to send out even fewer chaplains in the expectation that the missionary clergy would supply their place.[2] Finally, Middleton was distinctly identified with the High Church party, with the S.P.C.K. and the S.P.G.—of which the latter at least could well have been offended by any signs of undue cordiality towards the C.M.S.[3] In fact they had little need for anxiety: Middleton's relations with this society—including Thomason and Corrie, the chaplains most sympathetic to it—were marked by mutual suspicion and irritation. His refusal to ordain their converts did not help; this was another question which bristled with legal difficulties. He was supposed to administer the ecclesiastical law of England; but were Indians to be regarded as 'His Majesty's loving subjects', and what oaths were they to take on ordination? Furthermore, there were no officially-authorised translations of the Book of Common Prayer for them to use.[4]

Although Middleton always insisted that his primary duty was towards the existing Christian population,[5] he evinced

---

[1] S.P.C.K. *Report*, 1813, 58 ff. [2] Le Bas, *Middleton*, I, 400–2.
[3] H. Cnattingius, *Bishops and societies*, London, 1952, I, 91–2.
[4] Le Bas, *Middleton*, II, 269–75. [5] *Ibid.* 337–8.

Introduction

increasing interest in missionary work from about 1817 on-wards—a change in attitude to which a number of factors probably contributed. The Indians had not shown any alarm at his appearance among them—inasmuch as a reaction was forthcoming it was rather of relief that the British were not after all completely indifferent to religion. Then there was the rapid development of missionary activity by other denominations: Middleton was anxious that his Church 'should never be left behind by any other Christian society in India, but should rather take a decided lead in the career of religious enterprise'.[1] Finally there was his visit to the Tamilnad in 1816, when he was greatly impressed by much of what he saw of the work of the S.P.C.K.-supported mission there. So he wrote to the Archbishop of Canterbury early in 1817 suggesting that the S.P.G. should enter the Indian mission-field.[2] A decision to this effect was taken by the society in the following year; £5000 was immediately put at Middleton's disposal, and he was asked to formulate a plan for its Indian operations. Middleton replied with a proposal for the institution which became known as Bishop's College, whose foundation-stone he laid at Sibpur near Calcutta in 1820 and which, after various modifications of the original plan, developed primarily as a seminary for prospective Anglican priests and school-teachers. Meanwhile, in 1818, the Bishop had encouraged the Diocesan Committee of the S.P.C.K. to start some elementary schools for Bengalis. This committee had been founded three years earlier, but had hitherto confined its activities to Christians—in effect to Europeans and Eurasians: it had concentrated on such things as the circulation of Christian literature among them in cantonments, schools and hospitals. Middleton thought that education was essential to prepare Hindus and Muslims for more direct means of evangelism, and was particularly anxious for the spread of English,[3] which was duly introduced into some of the S.P.C.K. schools. Apart from this he did little to commend Christianity to the people of north India at any rate—or to promote general Indo-British understanding: in contrast to his successor he had no affection for the

[1] *Ibid.* II, 231.   [2] *Ibid.* I, 387, 480.
[3] *Ibid.* 154–5, 277.

Indians, and he managed to offend Ram Mohan Roy in the course of a clumsy attempt to convert him.[1]

In addition to south India, Middleton also visited Bombay— the city only: he did not venture as far as Poona, or to Gujarat— and the crown colony of Ceylon, which was officially added to his diocese in 1817, with its own archdeacon. He even went to Penang, but he did not visit the upper provinces of the Bengal Presidency, writing ' till the Company will build churches in those parts, I should be able to effect but little ';[2] indeed he showed a concern for formalities which was generally regarded as excessive, if not ludicrous, in the India of the early nineteenth century. He felt that he was not accorded his rightful status in Indian official society, and was particularly vexed at being ranked beneath the Chief Justices of the Presidencies[3]—though it is fair to assume that he was anxious for the honour of his Church rather than of himself personally. He regarded the achievements of the Dissenting missionaries with jealousy rather than with admiration, but he appeared at his worst in his relationship with James Bryce, the Church of Scotland chaplain in Calcutta. The Court of Directors had decided in 1813 to provide Scottish chaplains for the three Presidency cities; this was in itself resented by Middleton, who apparently felt that the English Establishment had the sole right to official recognition in British India. Bryce's activities were a continual source of irritation to the Bishop—not least because the newly-founded kirks in Calcutta and Madras were 'ornamented with conspicuous and lofty spires' far superior to anything possessed by the English churches.[4] While it is true that Middleton faced many real problems, some of which could have been averted by more foresight on the part of the authorities in 1813–14, there is no doubt that his difficulties were increased by his own attitudes. He was a man of integrity, hard-working and scholarly—he had to his credit a treatise on the Greek Article—but even his warmest admirers found him unduly haughty and pompous.[5] British society in India was much more liberal-minded in ecclesi-

---

[1] S. D. Collet, *The life and letters of Raja Rammohun Roy*, ed. D. L. Biswas and P. C. Ganguli, Calcutta, 1962, 125–6.
[2] Le Bas, II, 139.
[3] *Ibid.* 278–85.
[4] *Ibid.* I, 126–34; II, 247–8.
[5] *Ibid.* II, 322–43.

astical matters than in England, while Middleton for his part never came to terms with the fact that his situation was quite unlike that of a bishop in a well-ordered English diocese. In India, he sighed, 'every thing is anomalous'.[1] As the years went by he felt his vexations increasing; and the circumstances of his death seem appropriate for such a man. On 3 July 1822 a ray of the evening sun 'shone full upon him' when out for a drive. 'He immediately declared that he was struck by the sun, and returned home', where he developed a fever and became very irritable and restless. Then during the evening of 8 July he fell into 'a state of the most appalling agitation', shortly after which he expired.[2]

Historians have admitted Middleton's failings as a man but have tended to take the view that his insistence on the prerogatives of his Church was essential to provide it with a solid foundation. In fact, however, his episcopate was a record of almost unrelieved failure which provided an object-lesson rather than an example, at least as regards northern India. Inter-church and even inter-mission relations were worsened rather than improved by him; he did little for the missionary movement, which had achieved a momentum of its own by the time of his arrival; he was unable to solve the juridical problems which plagued him; he did nothing on balance to improve the relationship between Europeans and Indians; and even his most enduring monument—Bishop's College—was badly planned and proved a continual source of concern subsequently. It was indeed fortunate for the Indian Church that his successor was a totally different kind of man.

II

Reginald Heber was born on 21 April 1783. His family were Yorkshire gentry with estates in that county and at Hodnet in Shropshire. His half-brother Richard was for a few years M.P. for Oxford University, but was probably better known as an enthusiastic book-collector.

Reginald was educated at Whitchurch grammar school and, after 1796, at a small private school at Neasden in Middlesex.

---

[1] *Ibid.* I, 374.   [2] *Ibid.* II, 320–2.

Introduction

He was an amiable and clever boy who early revealed his life-long skill and interest in natural history, drawing, religion, and romantic tales. His school friend John Thornton—a nephew of Henry Thornton, banker and prominent Evangelical—subsequently recalled 'In the long winter evenings, a group of boys was frequently formed round him, whilst he narrated some chivalrous history, or repeated ancient ballads, or told some wild tale, partly derived from books, and partly from his own invention. For the exact sciences, or for critical knowledge, Reginald had no taste.'[1] In 1800 he proceeded to Brasenose College, Oxford; his undergraduate career reached its climax three years later with his recitation of the poem *Palestine* which he had written for the Seatonian prize. It was received with great enthusiasm by the audience in the Sheldonian Theatre and indeed proved to be one of the very few prize poems to achieve any lasting fame. In 1812 it was set to music as an oratorio by William Crotch.

The invasion scare of 1803–4 evoked some more poetry, this time of a suitably martial and patriotic nature:

'Swell, swell the shrill trumpet clear sounding afar,
Our sabres flash splendour around . . .'[2]

Heber also turned his hand to drilling a corps of volunteers at the family estate of Hodnet. Then in July 1805 he and John Thornton set out on what was, thanks to the war, a somewhat unconventional Grand Tour—through the northern and eastern fringes of the Continent. They explored Norway, admiring the mountain scenery, the lakes and the waterfalls; then they proceeded through Sweden and Finland to St Petersburg in Russia. By the middle of the winter—January 1806—they were in Moscow, where Heber's romantic soul was greatly excited by the old Kremlin building, a relic of the days of Tartar rule. 'As I walked up its high staircase', he wrote to his mother, 'and looked around on the terraces and towers, and the crescents which yet remain on their gilded spires, I could have fancied myself the hero of an eastern tale, and expected, with some impatience, to

[1] *The life of Reginald Heber, D.D.*, by his widow, London, 1830, I, 9.
[2] *Ibid.* 34.

see the talking-bird, the singing-water, or the black slave with his golden club.'[1] But the houses of the city, 'with the exception of some vast palaces belonging to the nobility, are meanness itself. The shops are truly Asiatic, dark, small, and huddled together in long-vaulted bazars, and the streets ill-paved and lighted.'[2] Heber indeed showed as much interest in the social conditions of the lands through which he passed as in their more romantic features: his journal included observations on Russian peasant life[3] and on the manufactures of the towns through which he passed.

By the spring of 1806 Heber and his friend had moved south to the lands around the Sea of Azov which had only recently been annexed by Russia, and where the 'Asiatic' influences were still stronger; indeed one can regard this Russian journey as Heber's introduction to Asia. There they encountered Armenians, Jews and Greeks; Nogays and Kalmuks—Mongolian peoples, with tents, camels and mares' milk—and the Cossacks, of whom Heber came to think very highly: even the beggars were 'manly and dignified',[4] and they celebrated Easter with 'solemn and magnificent' services.[5] A little later Heber and Thornton found themselves riding down the north bank of the Kuban River (to the east of the Sea of Azov), which then marked the frontier between the Russian Empire and the lands of the still independent Circassian tribes. In this turbulent region they had an escort of armed Cossack cavalry: 'We...travelled with our swords ready, our pistols primed, and enjoying all the novelty and dignity of danger', Heber wrote in a letter to his brother.[6] The Cossacks' clothes were 'made nearly in the Persian manner...of the most glowing colours, and the richer sort have red or yellow boots...We pass our time among these fine fellows very pleasantly', he continued, 'We teach them the Hungarian broadsword exercise, and they teach us the exercise of the lance'.[7] South of the river was a 'land of romance', with wooded hills rising steeply to the great ridge of the Caucasus, whose snow-clad peaks could be seen in the far distance; and Heber ended this letter with a story fit for such a land. A Circassian prince had

[1] *Ibid.* 151.   [2] *Ibid.* 152.   [3] *Ibid.* 140–5.
[4] *Ibid.* 245.   [5] *Ibid.* 240–4.   [6] *Ibid.* 246–7.   [7] *Ibid.* 247–8.

recently swum the Kuban to seek refuge in Russia from his enemies.

He had been in love, he said, with a girl whose relations asked a thousand rubles for her price, a sum which he could not pay. Unable, however, to live without her, he carried her off with an armed force from her home, and killed four of her father's retainers who attempted to resist him. His retreat to his own fortress was, however, cut off; his party put to the sword, and his mistress retaken. The girl would, he said, (and he cried bitterly as he spoke) be sold to the Turks, and be lost to him forever.[1]

On 22 April 1806 Heber and Thornton crossed the Strait of Kertch to the Crimea, where they travelled down the coast to the ancient port of Kaffa—which by then consisted largely of ruins—before turning inland to the mountains. There they found themselves among the Crimean Tartars, a Muslim people of whom Heber wrote, 'Nothing could be more interesting... than... the appearance of every one we met. A mirza, or noble, one of the few who still remain in the country, overtook us, and I was delighted at being addressed for the first time by the oriental salam.'[2] In the lowlands in the north of the peninsula they encountered shepherds; and Heber wrote, 'Both mountaineers and shepherds are amiable, gentle, and hospitable, except where they have been soured by their Russian masters.'[3] In fact he thought the imposition of Russian rule had been a misfortune for the area, especially as they had 'established their abominable code of slavery.'[4] At the Isthmus of Perekop the travellers 'with great regret quitted the Crimea and its pleasing inhabitants; it was really like being turned out of paradise, when we abandoned these beautiful mountains' for the endless Ukrainian plain.[5] They arrived back in England in October 1806, after passing through Hungary, Austria and Germany.

Heber's account of his travels in southern Russia gives a foretaste of his north Indian journal of twenty years later. The facility and elegance of his literary style had not yet fully matured, but the essentials were already there: shrewd observations and sympathetic interest in the habits of Eastern peoples; delight in beautiful scenery, colourful dress and romantic tales;

---

[1] *Ibid.* 249.   [2] *Ibid.* 266–7.   [3] *Ibid.* 274–5.
[4] *Ibid.* 270.   [5] *Ibid.* 274.

and a generous readiness to think well of the people whom he encountered, which no doubt helps to explain the welcome which he received almost everywhere. His interest in the East had been awakened before he went to Russia—while at Oxford he had been impressed by the work of Sir William Jones[1]—but it was greatly strengthened and confirmed by his tour. After his return home he started—but did not complete—a *History of the Cossacks*,[2] and subsequently he contributed articles on eastern Europe to the *Quarterly Review*; while extracts from the journal of his Russian tour were used as notes by E. D. Clarke in his *Travels in Russia Tartary and Turkey* (1810). Heber's north Indian journal contains many references to Russia; he certainly came to regard his experiences of 1806 as a foretaste of India.

Shortly after his return to England Heber took orders and was presented in 1807 by his brother to the family living of Hodnet, where he remained until his departure for Calcutta sixteen years later. He described his position in a letter to Thornton as 'a sort of half-way station, between a parson and a squire';[3] but in an age when many of the clergy took a very casual attitude towards their work Heber proved to be a most conscientious parish priest, determined not to neglect his pastoral duties for the sake of his many other interests. He preached regularly and effectively; he comforted the sick and the dying; he gave to the poor and the unfortunate with liberality and also with tact—which he showed not least towards 'those whose humble rank in life is too often thought to exempt their superiors from all need of mingling courtesy with kindness'.[4] This talented and versatile man found a deep satisfaction in the work of a country parson: he was not above deriving moral inspiration from the lives of some of his parishioners, and not surprisingly became greatly beloved by them.

In 1809 Heber married Amelia Shipley, daughter of the Dean of St Asaph, and a niece of Anna Maria, Sir William Jones' wife. Through the influence of his father-in-law Heber was in 1817 appointed a prebendary of St Asaph's Cathedral.

In his general ecclesiastical and theological outlook Heber

---

[1] *Ibid.* 39.
[2] *Ibid.* 563–684.
[3] *Ibid.* 392.
[4] *Ibid.* 357.

stood in the centre of the Anglican spectrum, if anything inclining to the Evangelical side. Since about 1785 Evangelicals had become increasingly influential in the Anglican and Dissenting churches alike: they had been responsible for among other things the foundation of the Baptist, London and Church Missionary Societies between 1792 and 1799, and also of the British and Foreign Bible Society, an interdenominational body, in 1804. Many of the national leaders of the movement, such as Wilberforce, were Anglicans, and by the second decade of the nineteenth century there was considerable support for it among the lower clergy, but it was as yet scarcely represented in the episcopate. At the other extreme of the Church of England were the High Churchmen, who had come to dominate the S.P.G. and—to a lesser extent—the S.P.C.K. Unlike their descendants in the Tractarian Movement after 1833 they were strongly Protestant; but whereas the Evangelicals stressed the authority of personal religious experience, confirmed by the test of scripture, High Churchmen emphasised the apostolic succession, the episcopal order, and the need for a strict observance of the discipline, liturgy and sacraments of the Church of England; also the alliance of Church and State.

In the early nineteenth century, Evangelicals and High Churchmen regarded one another with deep and unconcealed aversion; it was a time when it was not altogether easy to remain a moderate, let alone a reconciler; which gives an additional interest to Heber's position. G. D. Bearce described Heber as 'closely connected with the Evangelical wing of the Anglican Church',[1] but this is misleading. It is true that he was an active member of both the Bible Society and the C.M.S., but it was characteristic of him that in 1818, when the S.P.G. made its somewhat belated decision to enter the Indian mission-field, he should have made a proposal for the C.M.S. to merge with it so that the task of evangelisation could go forward unhampered by inter-party rivalry.[2] He disapproved of those who restricted 'the name of "Evangelical and Religious"' to the limits of their own

[1] G. D. Bearce, *British attitudes towards India 1784–1858*, 85. George Smith more accurately described him as 'broadly evangelical'—*Bishop Heber*, 55.
[2] *Reginald Heber*, I, 491–8.

Shibboleth, and of accounting all their brethren who disagreed
with them on particular topics, as secular, at least, or careless,—
if not altogether profane and carnal'.[1] He disagreed especially
with Evangelicals such as Thomas Scott who accepted the
Calvinist doctrine of predestination: in a critique of Scott's
Force of Truth he declared that he was 'an Arminian from conviction', and after pointing out that election implies reprobation—
that God foreordains the majority of men to everlasting punishment—he exclaimed 'God forgive those who hold doctrines
which lead to a conclusion so horrible!' Typically, however, he
continued that he did not wish

> to reflect on the personal character and personal holiness of those who
> hold the doctrine of election...I believe them to be men as holy, as
> humble, and as charitable as men, in our present state, can hope to be...
> I am...inclined to bless God for the riches of His grace, which has kept
> the good men from those snares which their opinions laid for them, and
> forbidden them to trust their salvation to doctrines which they do not act
> upon, though they fancy that they believe them.[2]

In India he was to take a basically similar view of Hinduism and
its effects—or lack of them—on its followers. Meanwhile Heber's
general attitude to High Churchmen and Evangelicals was
summed up in a letter of 1820, in which he referred to them as
'the two fiercest and foolishest parties that ever divided
a Church'.[3]

Heber thus did not shrink from controversies in defence of
what he believed to be true Anglican principles, but he pursued
such matters not only with resolution but with a courtesy and
moderation unusual at that period; another example was his
letter to a Roman Catholic who had married the daughter of one
of his parishioners, in which he set out the points of agreement
and difference between the two churches lucidly and temperately.[4]
He was in favour of Roman Catholic Emancipation.[5] As for the
Dissenters, he summarised his attitude in 1819: 'Though perfect
charity should be observed towards dissenters, and though we
should be ready to cooperate with them in any good work, by
which the peculiarities of our Creed or Church discipline are not

---

[1] *Ibid.* 526, cf. 359. [2] *Ibid.* 539–46. [3] *Ibid.* II, 5–6.
[4] *Ibid.* I, 407 ff. [5] *Ibid.* II, 47–8.

compromised, this amiable principle should not lead us to support
their missions, or attend their places of worship.'[1] The 'good
work' which provided the most notable focus for Anglican–
Dissenter cooperation at that period was the British and Foreign
Bible Society, which was accordingly an object of particular dislike and suspicion to High Churchmen. Heber however defended
it against their attacks in a sermon which he preached on its
behalf at Shrewsbury in 1813,[2] and six years later he wrote
a long letter to the *Christian Remembrancer* defending the participation in it of Anglican clergy.[3]

Heber's less controversial achievements included over fifty
hymns, of which several attained a lasting popularity with
English-speaking congregations—especially *Holy, holy, holy,
Lord God Almighty*; *Brightest and best of the sons of the morning*;
God that madest earth and heaven, which he set to a Welsh folk-
tune; and the missionary hymn *From Greenland's icy mountains*,
which he wrote in 1819 at the request of his father-in-law the
Dean of St Asaph, in connexion with a service in aid of the S.P.G.
at Wrexham. He delivered the Bampton Lectures at Oxford in
1815, on *The personality and office of the Christian Comforter*; and
subsequently he embarked upon a Dictionary of the Bible: he
was no textual critic, but he had a detailed knowledge of the
history, geography, and customs of the people connected with it.
His most notable scholarly achievement, however, was his
monumental edition of the works of Jeremy Taylor, the seven-
teenth-century Anglican divine with whose poetical temperament,
generally moderate views, and 'chaste and consecrated spirit of
devotion' Heber felt much in common.[4] Indeed it was with the
Anglican Fathers of the late sixteenth and seventeenth centuries,
the divines whose spiritual insights and literary grace had
developed the Anglican *via media* as a permanent creative force,
that Heber's affinities really lay—rather than with any of the
ecclesiastical partisans of his own time.

In his political views Heber was a moderate Tory; if they help
to illustrate the continuing association between that party and

[1] *Ibid.* I, 550.
[2] R. Heber, *Sermons preached in England*, London, 1829, 211 ff.
[3] *Reginald Heber*, I, 519 ff.
[4] *Quarterly Review*, Mar. 1827, 455; *D.N.B.*, 'Jeremy Taylor'.

the Anglican clergy, they are also a reminder of the genuine conscientiousness which could inform Tory paternalism. He thought that Parliamentary reform would do little good, and in the troubled years after Waterloo expressed his apprehensions in letters to friends about radicalism in the Press and the popularity of the works of Tom Paine among the poor. But he admitted that there was an excuse for widespread popular unrest 'where great real want is contrasted with great real or apparent prodigality' among the upper classes,[1] and he thought it essential that the latter should 'make some more considerable sacrifices than they are now inclined to do, for the sake of public tranquillity';[2] in particular he wanted them to relax the game laws, to live on their property, and to improve 'the condition of the cottager'.[3]

Heber was a frequent contributor to the *Quarterly Review*, which was founded in 1809 as a counterblast to the reformist *Edinburgh Review*. Apart from some articles on central and east European affairs, he contributed one on Byron's plays (July 1822). He approached this controversial figure with his customary fair-mindedness; if he shared the general disapproval of *Don Juan* and *Cain*, he praised *Childe Harold* and some of the later plays.[4] The conscientious and scholarly churchman was indeed very evidently a man of the Romantic era: as we have already seen, Heber's imagination was stirred by exotic splendours, by mountains and other things which readily evoked Romantic enthusiasm; and he was friendly with some of the leading Romantic writers of the day, including Scott, Southey and Coleridge. Scott had breakfast with him at Oxford when he was in the process of writing *Palestine*, to which he contributed some suggestions;[5] and the recitation itself was suffused with Romantic atmosphere—at least in the eyes of Charles Edward Grey, who was then one of the audience and subsequently a Chief Justice of Bengal. Recalling the occasion at a later date he wrote that the young Heber's recitation

was altogether untrammelled by the critical laws of elocution, which were...either by the poet unknown or forgotten; and there was a charm

---

[1] *Reginald Heber*, I, 445.   [2] *Ibid.* 434.   [3] *Ibid.* 446
[4] An edition of Byron's poems was published in 1859 with footnotes by Heber among others.   [5] *Reginald Heber*, I, 30.

in his somewhat melancholy voice, that occasionally faltered, less from a feeling of the solemnity and even grandeur of the scene, of which he was himself the conspicuous object—though that feeling did suffuse his pale, ingenuous, and animated countenance—than from the deeply felt sanctity of his subject, comprehending the most awful mysteries of God's revelations to man.[1]

Of Southey's poems, Heber particularly enjoyed *The curse of Kehama*, which had an Indian mythological theme; during the long voyage to India he recommended it to his fellow-passengers, to whom he also recited Coleridge's *Ancient Mariner*.[2] Southey's affection and admiration for Heber is apparent in the poem which he wrote after his death, *On the portrait of Reginald Heber*.[3] And Heber himself wrote some secular poetry which had considerable vogue during the nineteenth century: at least nine editions of his collected poems were published between 1841 and 1883. They included a series of affectionate birthday sonnets addressed to his lifelong friend Charlotte Dod; she had been born in December, and one year he apostrophised her as his

'Dear Snowdrop of the shorten'd day,
Fann'd by the wild and wintry wind!'[4]

One of his more serious poems had an Asian theme:

Timour's Councils

Emirs and Khans in long array,
To Timour's council bent their way;
The lordly Tartar, vaunting high,
The Persian with dejected eye,
The vassal Russ, and, lured from far,
Circassia's mercenary war.
But one there came, uncalled and last,
The spirit of the wintry blast!
He mark'd, while wrapt in mist he stood,
The purpos'd track of spoil and blood;
He mark'd, unmoved by mortal woe,

[1] *Ibid.* 32.
[2] *Journal—Letters*, 285–6. (These references are to Vol. II of the 2-volume edition of Heber's *Journal*, 1828.)
[3] *Reginald Heber*, II, 514–20.   [4] G. Smith, *Bishop Heber*, 68.

Introduction

That old man's eye of swarthy glow;
That restless soul, whose single pride,
Was cause enough that millions died;
He heard, he saw, till envy woke,
And thus the voice of thunder spoke:
'And hop'st thou thus, in pride unfurl'd,
To bear those banners thro' the world?
Can time nor space thy toils defy?
Oh king, thy fellow-demon I!
Servants of death, alike we sweep
The wasted earth, or shrinking deep.
And on the land, and o'er the wave,
We reap the harvest of the grave.
But thickest then that harvest lies,
And wildest sorrows rend the skies,
In darker cloud the vultures sail,
And richer carnage taints the gale,
And few the mourners that remain,
When winter leagues with Tamerlane!
But on, to work our lord's decree;
Then, tyrant, turn, and cope with me!
And learn, though far thy trophies shine,
How deadlier are my blasts than thine!
Nor cities burnt, nor blood of men,
Nor thine own pride shall warm thee then!
Forth to thy task! We meet again.
On wild Chabanga's frozen plain!'[1]

Heber's Oriental interests, stimulated by his travels in Russia in 1806, widened and deepened subsequently, so that by the time of his appointment as Bishop of Calcutta he had become well-read in Asian history and travels and to some extent in Asian literature, in translation. In 1816 for example he contributed a long review of Sir John Malcolm's *History of Persia* to the April *Quarterly*, and he also read Firdausi's *Shah Nama*.[2] He was capable of introducing Asian analogies in the most un-

[1] *Reginald Heber*, i, 441–2.
[2] Ibid. 437.

expected circumstances: after a visit to Oxford in 1818 he wrote that whereas Christ Church was formerly 'an absolute monarchy of the most ultra-oriental character, [now] the reigning dean [C. H. Hall] is as little attended to, to all appearance, as the peishwah of the Mahrattas'.[1]

At the same time he was developing an active interest in missionary work, as was evinced by the sermons he preached on behalf of the Bible Society, the S.P.C.K. and especially the C.M.S.[2]—not to mention *Greenland's icy mountains*. He used to tell his wife that he felt attracted to missionary work himself, especially in India, a country which, as she wrote, 'had a romantic charm in his mind'. 'It was with this knowledge of her husband's feelings' that she first heard of Bishop Middleton's death, while on a visit to her father in north Wales late in 1822; 'and the conviction that her husband's inclinations would lead him to accept of the office should it be offered to him, immediately flashed on her mind'.[3] By that time their old friend Sir Charles Watkin Williams Wynn, whose country seat was in nearby Denbighshire, had been appointed President of the Board of Control for India; and on 2 December 1822 he duly wrote to Heber hinting that the bishopric might be his for the asking, but adding 'I cannot expect...that, with your fair prospects of eminence at home, you should go to the Ganges for a mitre'.[4] Heber replied 'I will confess that (after reading missionary reports and some of Southey's articles in the Quarterly) I have sometimes been tempted to wish myself Bishop of Calcutta, and to fancy that I could be of service there...As it is, I am, probably, better at home, so far as my personal happiness is concerned, than in a situation...which involves so many sacrifices of health, home, and friendship.'[5] But after a month of hesitation Heber finally sent Wynn his letter of acceptance, on 12 January 1823.

Subsequent letters illustrate further the unique combination of missionary and romantic motives which took Heber to India. On 18 January he told a friend 'I hope I am not an enthusiast'— a word which at that time was used by Anglicans in a pejorative

---

[1] *Ibid.* 499. [2] *Sermons preached in England*, IX, X, XI.
[3] *Reginald Heber*, II, 95–6. [4] *Ibid.* 97. [5] *Ibid.* 98.

sense, especially in connexion with Methodists—'but I am and have long been most anxious for the cause of Christianity in India; and I have persuaded myself that I am not ill-adapted to contribute to its eventual success'.[1] A few weeks later he wrote that his appointment would bring 'many, very many, advantages in an extended sphere of professional activity, in the indulgence of literary curiosity, and, what to me has many charms, the opportunity of seeing nature in some of its wildest and most majestic features'.[2] An old friend of his mother's 'very warmly opposed his plan of going to India, and added, laughingly, "your's is the Quixotism of religion, and I almost believe you are going in search of the ten lost tribes of Israel". He replied "Perhaps your joke may have truth in it; at any rate, I think I can be of use among the natives; it will be my earnest endeavour, and I am very zealous in the cause."'[3]

In the various sermons and addresses which Heber gave before his departure for India he achieved the unusual feat of pleasing men of the most diverse opinions. The news of his appointment did not at first give much satisfaction to High Churchmen, but his reply to the Bishop of Bristol's valedictory address at a meeting of the S.P.C.K., in which he paid graceful tribute to its work in south India and promised to do what he could to further it,[4] was very well received, Archbishop Manners-Sutton commenting 'It was perfect'.[5] On the other hand his appointment was warmly welcomed by the C.M.S.;[6] and after his last sermon at Lincoln's Inn (of which he was the official preacher) a leading Methodist could only exclaim 'Thank God for that man!'[7] It was therefore with some reason that he could tell Charlotte Dod that he was 'on good terms with and well thought of both by the Evangelicals and High Churchmen'.[8] His earlier suggestion for a merger between the C.M.S. and the S.P.G. had not of course borne fruit, but one of the things which he hoped to do as Bishop of Calcutta was to 'moderate' between the two rival societies

[1] *Ibid.* 116.   [2] *Ibid.* 124.   [3] *Ibid.* 120.
[4] S.P.C.K. *Report*, 1823, 70–5.
[5] E. Churton, *Memoir of Joshua Watson*, Oxford, 1863, 134–5.
[6] C.M.S. *Report*, 1823–4, 112–4.
[7] *Reginald Heber*, II, 134.
[8] Smith, *Bishop Heber*, 125.

so as to ensure that their activities could go forward without friction;[1] a task for which the omens were favourable as he set out.

III

Heber was consecrated at Lambeth on 1 June 1823, sailed on the 16th, and arrived in Bengal in October; by which time Lord Hastings had been succeeded as Governor-General by Lord Amherst. During his administration Hastings had inflicted decisive defeats on the Gurkhas and the Marathas and had suppressed the Pindari bands which had been ravaging central India, so that from 1818 the authority of the East India Company reigned supreme over the greater part of the sub-continent—all the lands to the south and east of the Thar Desert and the Sutlej River. Amherst's record proved comparatively undistinguished, though Heber had good relations with him and defended him against his critics in his letters.[2] The main event of his administration was the first Anglo-Burmese War, which broke out in February 1824 and continued for two years, thus coinciding almost exactly with Heber's episcopate. Before it started, the Burmese had annexed much of Assam and laid claim to east Bengal; the Company's forces captured Rangoon without much difficulty in May 1824, but were unable to advance into the centre of the country until the following year. By the peace treaty of 1826 the Burmese surrendered Assam and also the coastal provinces of Arakan and Tenasserim, while the princely state of Manipur became virtually a British protectorate. Meanwhile, in 1824, there had been a mutiny of some sepoys at Barrackpore, and signs of unrest appeared in north and central India when it seemed that the British were in difficulties. A crisis actually occurred in the state of Bharatpur in 1825, only a few weeks after Heber had passed through: Sir David Ochterlony, the Agent in Rajputana, wanted to intervene to enforce the claim of a boy prince against a usurper; Amherst disagreed, so Ochterlony resigned. But Sir Charles Metcalfe, who then returned to Delhi for the second time as Resident, persuaded

---

[1] *Reginald Heber*, II, 100.
[2] *Ibid.* 311, 332–3; *Journal—Letters*, 393.

Amherst that the operation was necessary after all, and the Bharatpur fortress was captured the following year. No general revolt actually took place, and Amherst's rule drew peacefully to its close in 1828; nevertheless Heber needed some courage for his travels—first to visit Dacca in July 1824 when a Burmese invasion was a possibility, and thereafter to proceed through the barely-pacified principalities of northern India.

Heber spent the eight months after his arrival—from October 1823 to June 1824—in Calcutta dealing with the business which had accumulated since the death of Middleton over a year before. There had not even been an archdeacon to hold the fort, as the first incumbent of that office had died a few weeks after the first bishop; one of Heber's first acts therefore was to appoint Daniel Corrie Archdeacon of Calcutta. In one respect Heber's task was even more formidable than that of his predecessor: the diocese, which already included the whole of the Company's territories, together with South Africa and Ceylon, was now further enlarged to include Australia; for which a separate archdeaconry was established in 1824. It thus extended from St Helena in the South Atlantic eastwards to Canton and Sydney on the shores of the Pacific Ocean. On the other hand some of the questions which had so troubled Bishop Middleton were cleared up at the outset of Heber's episcopate; especially through the Indian Bishops and Courts Act of 1823[1] which stipulated that the Bishop should be given a travel allowance and a house in Calcutta—points which Heber had brought to Wynn's attention before his departure.[2] More important, it empowered him to ordain Indians for service within the diocese of Calcutta without requiring them to take the oaths which were customary in England. Heber's episcopate therefore saw the first Anglican ordination of Indians—including the Tamil Christian David, the north Indian Abdul Masih, and the Eurasian Bowley, the last two of whom had already received Lutheran ordination from the German missionaries in the service of the C.M.S. The question of the validity (or otherwise) of Lutheran orders in Anglican eyes is a very complicated one, especially as the Scandinavian Lutheran churches had retained bishops but the Germans had not; here we must simply note that

---

[1] 4 Geo. IV, c. 71.   [2] *Reginald Heber*, ii, 131.

Introduction

Heber stood in the moderate Anglican tradition in this as in other matters. While he refused to say that a non-episcopal church was no true church, and was glad to receive the sacraments from the hands of non-episcopally-ordained ministers where none other were within reach—as in Germany in 1806—he believed episcopacy to have the authority of apostolic tradition and to belong to the perfection of a church; to be the *via tutissima*. He did not require Abdul Masih and Bowley to renounce their Lutheran orders, but he maintained that Anglican ordination would have the practical advantage of making the two men more useful in an Anglican Church and missionary society.[1]

The other problem which had tormented Bishop Middleton, but which Heber was able to solve before he left England, was that of the licensing of Anglican missionaries; he secured a definite legal opinion that they were subject to the episcopal authority.[2] But although such a regularisation of their missionaries' position had long been wanted by the C.M.S., when Heber reached Calcutta he encountered some opposition from the lay members of the newly-founded Calcutta Auxiliary C.M.S.—the local branch of the Society—who objected when he proposed to license and station the missionaries. Heber stood firm on his main point, but the assignment of stations was subject in effect to a sensible compromise in the shape of consultations between the bishop and the local society.[3] After this problem had been solved, Heber's relations with the C.M.S. were excellent. There was never any such difficulty with the S.P.G., whose High Church principles made them positively yearn for episcopal direction. It was during Heber's episcopate that the S.P.G. took over the Indian missionary work of the S.P.C.K.

Heber—like Middleton—was very cordially disposed towards the various non-Roman episcopal churches of the East, of which he came into contact in India especially with the Armenians and, in the south, the Syrians. He hoped that Anglican influence would stimulate a revival of 'learning and scriptural knowledge among

---

[1] *Journal—Letters*, 426–9; cf. Cnattingius, *Bishops and societies*, 130–4. Anglican attitudes to Lutheran orders have been most usefully analysed by this scholar.

[2] *Reginald Heber*, II, 174.

[3] *Ibid.* 175–6; Cnattingius, *Bishops and societies*, 118–21, 175.

their clergy',[1] and made arrangements for the admission of their divinity students at Bishop's College. As regards the Protestant Dissenters he combined a genuine admiration for their missionary efforts—especially in the case of the Baptists—with an insistence on the duty of Anglicans to support their own in preference. Some sense of rivalry continued, but its spirit was transformed—from one of jealousy and vexation, as it had been for Middleton, to mutual respect and generosity of feeling. The Dissenters soon began to join in the general chorus of praise which Heber evoked wherever he went: William Carey thought him 'a man of very liberal principles and a very catholic spirit',[2] and the Baptist historian John Clark Marshman—Joshua Marshman's son—wrote that he 'always appeared more anxious to promote the general good than the interests of his own section of the church'.[3] As for the Scots, Middleton's old adversary James Bryce paid a warm tribute to Heber's memory at a meeting shortly after his death;[4] and a writer in the *Edinburgh Review* described his character as 'singularly amiable and exalted', continuing 'if we could persuade ourselves that bishops in general were at all like Bishop Heber, we would tremble for our Presbyterian orthodoxy'.[5] In short Heber successfully erased, for the duration of his episcopate at least, the painful impression which Middleton had made on the C.M.S., the English Dissenters and the Scots alike.

Heber left Calcutta for his visitation of northern India on 15 June 1824. At first he travelled eastwards by boat through the waterways of the Ganges delta, arriving at Dacca on 3 July. This city had been the capital of the Mughal province of Bengal during the seventeenth century and an important trading centre, but Heber found it 'merely the wreck of its ancient grandeur': its political importance had been lost first to Murshidabad and then to Calcutta, and its textile industry had been virtually ruined by competition from British manufacturers. Heber's stay in Dacca

[1] *Reginald Heber*, ii, 377.
[2] National Library of Wales MS 1207 E—Carey to Ryland, 6 July 1824.
[3] J. C. Marshman, *Carey, Marshman and Ward*, ii, 292.
[4] D. Corrie, *A sermon preached in...Calcutta, on Sunday, April 23, 1826, on...the death of the Right Reverend Reginald, Lord Bishop of the diocese*, Calcutta, 1826, Appendix, 37–8.   [5] *E.R.*, Dec. 1828, 312.

was further saddened for him by the death of his chaplain and friend, Martin Stowe. After this rather melancholy start to his journey he sailed up the Ganges through Bihar, where he showed great interest in the Paharis—one of the tribes that inhabited the hills of central India and which, in contrast to the plainsmen around, was neither Hindu nor Muslim. Heber thought they might be particularly receptive to a missionary. By early September he had reached the holy city of Banaras, where he spent a week, and subsequently, after passing through Allahabad and Kanpur, he left the East India Company's territory and entered the state of Oudh, whose sovereigns had been allied to the Company since 1765 and increasingly subject to its control. By 10 November he was back in British territory—in Rohilkhand, a land which had fallen under the control of Afghan chiefs in the 1740s and which the Company had finally secured in 1801. On its northern border was the swampy malarial forest of the Terai, a dismal tract through which Heber had to pass before he reached the mountains of Kumaon, where he was rewarded with views 'most sublime and beautiful. . . my eyes filled with tears, everything around was so wild and magnificent that man appeared as nothing, and I felt myself as if climbing the steps of the altar of God's great temple'. This region had been ceded to the Company by the Gurkhas in 1816.

Heber spent the new year of 1825 in Delhi, where he explored the ruins of the buildings of the mediaeval sultans and had an audience with the Emperor—'the poor old descendant of Tamerlane'—now merely a pensionary of the Company, shorn of political power. Proceeding southwards, Heber admired the memorials of Mughal greatness at Sikandra, Agra and Fatehpur Sikri, and then embarked upon a two-month ride through the desert and semi-desert of Rajasthan. The princes of this region had suffered greatly during the anarchic years prior to 1818, when they had entered into treaties with the Company. They had been ravaged by the Maratha princes Sindhia and Holkar, by the Pindaris and Amir Khan the Afghan leader, and Heber thought that the peace which Hastings' success had made possible was generally appreciated. He reached Gujarat in the middle of March; after visiting the court of the Maharaja of Baroda, a

Maratha prince, he made his way down to the old port of Surat
and took a ship for Bombay, where he arrived on 19 April.

The main interest of Heber's Journal of this tour has always
been his impressions of the land and the people, and the self-
revelation of his own most attractive character that it provided.
But before becoming engrossed in these aspects one should
remind oneself that it was undertaken not just out of curiosity
but as a professional duty: it was essentially a visitation of the
Anglican Christian communities which had by then come into
existence in all the important centres of northern India—civilian
and military; British, Eurasian and Indian; in East India Company territory and in the princely states. Heber tried whenever
possible to be in some such centre on a Sunday, so that he would
be able to conduct services and to preach; other functions which
he often performed were the consecration of churches and burial-
grounds, confirmation, and the inspection of Christian schools.
Having said this, it remains true that the bishop had by no means
completely displaced the romantic-minded traveller who twenty
years previously had been so pleased to find himself within sight
of the peaks of the Caucasus among the martial and picturesque
peoples of southern Russia. Heber the bishop found the military
escort which the unsettled state of much of the country made
essential rather an embarrassment and reduced it to the minimum
that was needed; but Heber the romantic could write 'I enjoy
very much this sort of wild travelling',[1] and a little earlier he
had reported to some friends 'My life has been that of a Tartar
chief, rather than an English clergyman'[2]—a remark in which a
certain relish is detectable. With his extreme susceptibility to the
beauty of rivers and mountains it is natural that the most charming
descriptive passages of the Journal should be those evoked by the
experience of sailing up the Ganges through Bengal and Bihar,
and by crossing the mountains of Kumaon. As for buildings,
Heber was suitably impressed by the magnificence of Lucknow
and Agra, by Banaras and Delhi, but perhaps most deeply moved
by the deserted castellated palace of Amber outside Jaipur—the
Romantic vision again.

Heber believed that, on balance, British rule would prove to

---

[1] *Journal—Letters*, 364.   [2] *Ibid.* 358.

be a benefit for India, and he thought highly of the officials whom he encountered during the course of his travels. But he believed nevertheless that it was unpopular in north India at least, especially among Muslims, in spite of the peace that it had brought, and that attempts at rebellion were possible. The reasons for this included the judicial system, of which he was very critical; and he thought that the Government should spend a higher proportion of its Indian revenues on public works for the benefit of the local people. He also disagreed with the policy of excluding even upper-class Indians from participation in government; and more generally of the haughtiness and lack of consideration for the feelings of the people of which he thought most of the British in India were guilty.[1] For his part Heber refused to let his judgement be warped by the prejudices against Indians which were common among the British community especially in Calcutta; and in fact it is evident from his Journal that as he travelled around he developed a warm liking for the people from his personal observations of their manners and habits. Frequently he relates some anecdote or incident which reveals them as intelligent, loyal, hard-working, brave, affection-ate and cheerful—indeed with as full a share of human virtues as were to be found among people in any part of the world, including Europe. Perhaps the most attractive feature of Heber's Journal is the strong sense of the fundamental one-ness of mankind which he conveys; he does not give the impression that in passing from England to India he encountered a completely different order of human beings. Not that the picture is idealised; but again he viewed what he regarded as the shortcomings of the people he met in the context of general human failings. Nor did he reserve his approval for those customs or artistic creations which approxi-mated closest to those of Europe: like other Romantics Heber was always ready to appreciate the exotic, believing that there is a natural and healthy diversity as well as a basic one-ness of humanity. One is not surprised that the Bishop became very well liked by the members of his various escorts, and indeed by virtually all the Indians whom he encountered.

[1] See *infra*, 144–5, 155–6, 198, 249, 305; also *Journal—Letters*, 341, 371–2; *Reginald Heber*, ii, 265, 270, 280–93, 334, 413–14.

Introduction

Heber's affection for the people of India did not however extend to their religion; indeed he thought that their likeable qualities had developed in spite of rather than because of Islam and especially Hinduism. He wrote in his Journal 'Of the natural disposition of the Hindoo, I . . . see abundant reason to think highly. . . All that is bad about them appears to arise either from the defective motives which their religion supplies, or the wicked actions which it records of their gods, or encourages in their own practice.' In making these unfavourable comments on Indian religion Heber was expressing the general attitudes of the new missionary movement, and if the manifestations of his missionary zeal were in fact comparatively restrained while he was in India it was from prudence, and a recognition of the complexity of the difficulties in the way of evangelism, rather than any doubts about its basic validity. He did not indeed believe that non-Christians were necessarily destitute of the grace of God, or that they might not 'please him and obtain a seat in one of those many mansions which our Father's house contains';[1] and in his charges to the clergy of the Calcutta diocese he condemned in uncharacteristically violent language those missionaries who taught that non-Christians were 'under the sentence of reprobation from God', still more one who apparently maintained that Indians had a 'moral incapacity' to receive the Gospel.[2] He thus believed that the mercy of God could save a Hindu from the fatal consequences of his religion; he wrote that even in the 'aweful and besotted darkness' of Banaras, 'God may have much people in this city'; but there is little sign in Heber's writings of that profound respect for the great non-Christian religions as manifestations—in whatever degree—of the spirit of God in different cultures, which was early articulated by German Romantics, was taken up by F. D. Maurice in mid-nineteenth-century England, and became increasingly evident in theological and missionary circles in the early twentieth century.

Heber's basic approach to missionary work was most clearly illustrated in the sermon that he preached in aid of the C.M.S. at

---

[1] *Reginald Heber*, I, 544. Heber argued this view at length in his sixth Bampton Lecture, 391–416.

[2] R. Heber, *A charge delivered to the clergy of the diocese of Calcutta*, London, 1827, 18–19.

Whittington in 1820. Although virtuous men exist among the
heathen who may attain salvation through the mercy of God, the
majority were not 'innocent and conscientious followers of the
law of nature'—as many eighteenth-century writers had suggested—but were guilty of dishonest and cruel practices to a
greater extent than was usual in Christian countries. He then
went on to paint a glowing picture of the temporal blessings, no
less than the spiritual, that could be expected to follow the spread
of Christianity: slavery would be mitigated, the position of
women improved, and the wealth and happiness of the country
in question would increase. He then referred to the special
responsibility incumbent upon the British to support missionary
work in view of the fact that so many countries had fallen under
their political and commercial influence—not to mention the debt
that Britain had incurred to peoples whom that influence had so
far only harmed, among whom he included the Africans and the
Pacific Islanders.[1] These arguments—the conventional stock-in-
trade of contemporary missionary addresses—recur in a sermon
which he preached at Bombay on Whit Sunday 1825—but the
last one was elaborated into a very personal appeal which
deserves to be quoted at some length, not least as a moving
expression of his feelings at the end of his journey across northern
India. He asked:

Can it really be maintained with any semblance of truth, or reason, or
humanity, that [the people of India] who toil for us; who shed their blood
in our defence; whose wealth contributes so largely to the prosperity of
Britain, and their valour (their faithful and invincible valour and allegiance)
so essentially promotes our security and renown; that these men, with
whom we live and converse, distinguished by so many estimable and
amiable qualities of intelligence, of bravery, of courteous and gentle
demeanour, are devoid of a claim on all the good which we can render or
obtain for them, on our affections, our bounties, our services, and, I will
add, our prayers? Can we petition their Father and our's that His glorious
kingdom may come, without desiring...that they may be partakers in
it with us? Or can we forget that such prayers and desires are no other
than a mockery of God, unless our actions follow our lips, and we endeavour,
in God's strength and help, to forward that triumph of His mercy for
which we profess ourselves solicitous.[2]

[1] *Sermons preached in England*, 201–4.
[2] *Sermons preached in India*, 193–4.

Hitherto, missionaries had more often tried to justify their work by emphasising the apparent shortcomings of the Indians, and it had been left to their opponents to defend them; but Heber at least showed that there was no need for missionaries to be ungenerous.

Heber's Journal was very well received by contemporaries, and it must have helped to counteract the generally unfavourable impressions of India conveyed by several other publications of that period, such as Grant's *Observations* and Mill's *History*. Three editions were published in 1828 alone, a fourth followed in 1829, and a fifth in 1844. The *Edinburgh Review* called it 'the most instructive and important publication that has ever been given to the world, on the actual state and condition of our Indian empire';[1] and the *Quarterly* thought it 'one of the most delightful books in the language'.[2] F. J. Shore, writing in 1834, praised Heber's 'accuracy of observations, extent of information, and above all, penetration beyond the surface' of Indian affairs.[3] Much more recently, a leading authority has described the Journal as 'quite the best description of India in the twenties'.[4] Such enthusiasm does not seem excessive: the Journal provides, among other things, a good impression of the changing economic circumstances of the country, which had led to the collapse of the manufactures of Dacca and Surat and increased emphasis on the cultivation of cash crops such as indigo, sugar and opium; also to the decline of the Muslim aristocracy and the rise of Hindu *nouveaux riches*. Heber comments not only on the corruption of petty Indian officials but also on the smallness of their salaries, which he suggests is the root of the problem. In Oudh he describes at length the tangle of political and administrative difficulties that the Company's system of subsidiary alliances could lead to, the upstart magnificence of Lucknow notwithstanding. As on many other questions he gives both sides of the argument between the Resident and the King concerning methods of revenue-collection, and on the basis of his own observations comes tentatively to the conclusion that 'the misfortunes and

[1] *E.R.*, Dec. 1828, 314. [2] *Q.R.*, Jan. 1828, 104.
[3] F. J. Shore, *Notes on Indian affairs*, London, 1837, I, 517.
[4] T. P. G. Spear, *The twilight of the Mughals*, Cambridge, 1951, 69.

Introduction

anarchy of Oude are somewhat overrated'. At Delhi we are given a memorable description of Akbar II trying pathetically to maintain at least an outward show of Imperial authority amid the dilapidated splendour of Shah Jahan's palace; and Heber's attitude towards the 'poor humbled potentates' whom he encountered at several points in his tour—combining sympathy for fallen greatness with an authentic nineteenth-century note of disapproval for courtly vices—was an index of a general change in British opinion which was beginning to take place by then. The Journal also illustrates the transitional stage which had been reached in the evolution of Indian education and culture: at Banaras, for example, Heber visited both Jai Narayan's school, recently founded to provide an education on Western lines, and Duncan's Sanskrit College; and he noted that many Brahmins had come to feel 'a degree of weariness of their own system, and a disposition to enquire after others'. We are also reminded of India's continuing contacts with the Near and Middle East, especially through Heber's encounters with Muslims who knew something of Iran or the Ottoman lands. His meeting with Swami Narayan in Gujarat is of particular interest as an early example of something that was to occur frequently during the following century: Hindus with monotheistic and social-reformist tendencies had a natural appeal for missionary-minded Christians, but Heber was not the only one whose more sanguine hopes were disappointed. And finally there are the innumerable vignettes which convey an authentic flavour of the everyday realities of north Indian life in the mid-1820s: pilgrims, village scenes, cows crossing the Ganges. Heber's interest in fact encompassed every aspect of that life: the local people from Emperor to peasant; British governors, soldiers and missionaries; religion and economics, cities and countryside, painting and architecture, crops, birds and animals—his Journal is a great panorama depicted with sympathy and artistry in lucid and graceful prose, by one imbued with the central traditions of Anglican Christianity together with the spirit of the early nineteenth-century Romantic and missionary movements.

It was moreover an expression of what the *Quarterly Review* called 'a noble and cultivated mind, pouring itself out with openness and candour, in the confidence of the most tender affection'[1]—for Heber wrote his Journal originally for the benefit of his wife, who much to his regret could not accompany him on his tour. The adjectives most frequently used to describe Heber's character have been 'gentle' and 'moderate'. These are accurate enough as far as they go, but in themselves they do not do him full justice. If he was gentle—and indeed courteous, tactful and unassuming—he could also be firm when he believed an important principle to be at stake, for example in licensing and stationing C.M.S. missionaries, or in urging on the officers of the Dinapur cantonment the need for a lending-library and better church-attendance; while the physical courage and resourcefulness required to bring his journey to a successful conclusion also has ample illustration. And while Heber was pre-eminently a man of moderation, it was not the moderation that springs from colour-lessness, uncertainty or undue caution. Rather was it the product of a Romanticism disciplined and directed by Anglican Christi-anity, of a tension between personal and institutional religion, heart and mind; clothed with good taste and a kind of unassuming dignity; salted with common sense and wit; and sanctified by a readiness to recognise goodness wherever it showed itself—in Hindus and Christians, Dissenters as well as Anglicans.

Heber was not a profound or original thinker; in his attitudes he was generally rather conventional—except for his sensitive humanity, which is what above all won him the affection of his contemporaries. Archdeacon Barnes of Bombay, who had been one of Middleton's few admirers, met him in Gujarat in March 1825 and wrote subsequently:

The Bishop's manner everywhere is exceedingly popular; and though there are some points, such as his wearing white trowsers and a white hat, which I could wish were altered with more regard to his station, and which, perhaps, strike me the more after being accustomed to the par-ticular attention of Bishop Middleton in such points, yet really I feel compelled to forgive him, when I observe his unreserved frankness, his anxious and serious wish to do all the good in his power, his truly amiable and kindly feelings, his talents and piety, and his extraordinary powers of conversation, accompanied with so much cheerfulness and vivacity.[2]

[1] *Q.R.*, Jan. 1828, 104.
[2] *Reginald Heber*, ii, 298–9.

Indeed there could not have been a greater contrast than between the first and the second bishops of Calcutta: where Middleton was vexed and irritable, Heber was cheerful and good-tempered; where Middleton was pompous and haughty, Heber was unassuming; where Middleton groaned for the well-ordered routine of an English diocese, Heber relished the thought of being the first Protestant bishop to penetrate the mountains of Kumaon and the deserts of Rajputana. The contrast might be explained to some extent in terms of their respective social origins and early careers: Middleton, the son of a country rector and dependent in the early stages of his career on the patronage of Bishop Pretyman of Lincoln—a prominent High Churchman— would have felt more of a compulsion to emphasise the dignity of his office than Heber, who belonged to a gentry family and owed his appointment to Calcutta to one who was a friend rather than a patron in the usual sense of the term.

Heber left Bombay by sea in June 1825 and arrived back in Calcutta in October, visiting Ceylon on the way. In February 1826 he was off again, this time to Madras, on what proved to be his last journey. During March he travelled southwards through the Tamilnad to Tiruchchirappalli (Trichinopoly), where on 3 April he spent a characteristically busy morning: he confirmed fifteen local people, preached a sermon, examined the mission schools, and received a deputation of Christians who wanted a pastor; like Middleton before him he was greatly impressed with what he saw of the mission in that part of India. After all that he decided to refresh himself with a cold bath—from which however he never emerged alive; after waiting for half an hour his servant looked in and found his corpse.[1] He was buried in St John's Church, Tiruchchirappalli—still a few weeks short of his forty-third birthday.

Brief as Heber's episcopate proved to be, it was longer than that of his two successors. Bishop J. T. James arrived in Calcutta in January 1828, only to die in August of the same year; he was followed by J. M. Turner, who survived from December 1829 until 7 July 1831. Thus during a period of exactly nine years no less than four bishops of Calcutta had followed one another into

[1] *Ibid.* 436–7.

premature graves. The fifth, Daniel Wilson, arrived towards the end of 1832 at the unpromising age of 54; but it was this tough old Evangelical who broke the unhappy tradition by surviving for a quarter of a century. His task was eased by the long-overdue division of the diocese into its component parts: Daniel Corrie's long Indian career was crowned by his appointment as the first Bishop of Madras, to which he proceeded in 1835; Australia got its first bishop the following year, and Bombay in 1837.

Heber's Journal

Part I

BENGAL

Bishop Heber arrived off the mouth of the River Hooghly on 3 October 1823. During the following week he proceeded slowly up the river to Fort William on the southern outskirts of Calcutta, and on 11 October he entered the city itself.

The approach to the city from the fort is striking;—we crossed a large green plain, having on the left the Hooghly, with its forest of masts and sails seen through the stems of a double row of trees. On the right-hand is the district called Chowringhee, lately a mere scattered suburb, but now almost as closely built as, and very little less extensive than, Calcutta. In front was the esplanade, containing the Town Hall, the Government House, and many handsome private dwellings,—the whole, so like some parts of Petersburgh, that it was hardly possible for me to fancy myself any where else. No native dwellings are visible from this quarter, except one extensive but ruinous bazar, which occupies the angle where Calcutta and Chowringhee join. Behind the esplanade, however, are only Tank-square, and some other streets occupied by Europeans,—the Durrumtollah and Cossitollah are pretty equally divided between the different nations, and all the rest of Calcutta is a vast town, composed of narrow crooked streets, brick bazars, bamboo huts, and here and there the immense convent-like mansion of some of the more wealthy 'Baboos' (the name of the native Hindoo gentleman, answering to our Esquire) or Indian merchants and bankers. The Town-hall has no other merit than size, but the Government-house has narrowly missed being a noble structure; it consists of two semi-circular galleries, placed back to back, uniting in the centre in a large hall, and connecting four splendid suites of apartments. Its columns are, however, in a paltry style, and instead of having, as

it might have had, two noble stories and a basement, it has three
stories, all too low, and is too much pierced with windows on
every side. I was here introduced to Lord Amherst; and afterwards went to the Cathedral,[1] where I was installed. This is a
very pretty building, all but the spire, which is short and clumsy.
The whole composition, indeed, of the Church, is full of architectural blunders, but still it is in other respects handsome. The
inside is elegant, paved with marble, and furnished with very
large and handsome glass chandeliers, the gift of Mr M'Clintoch,
with a light pulpit, with chairs on one side of the chancel for the
Governor-General and his family, and on the other for the Bishop
and Archdeacon. We dined to-day at the Government-house;
to a stranger the appearance of the bearded and turbaned waiters
is striking.

October 12.—This was Sunday. I preached, and we had a good
congregation.

October 13.—We drive out twice a day on the course; I am
much disappointed as to the splendor of the equipages, of which
I had heard so much in England; the horses are most of them
both small and poor, while the dirty white dresses and bare limbs
of their attendants, have to an unaccustomed eye an appearance of
any thing but wealth and luxury. Calcutta stands on an almost
perfect level of alluvial and marshy ground, which a century ago
was covered with jungle and stagnant pools, and which still
almost every where betrays its unsoundness by the cracks conspicuous in the best houses. To the East, at the distance of four
miles and a half, is a large but shallow lagoon of salt water, being
the termination of the Sunderbunds,[2] from which a canal is cut
pretty nearly to the town, and towards which all the drainings of
the city flow, what little difference of level there is, being in
favour of the banks of the river. Between the salt lake and the
city, the space is filled by gardens, fruit trees, and the dwellings
of the natives, some of them of considerable size, but mostly
wretched huts, all clustered in irregular groupes round large
square tanks, and connected by narrow, winding, unpaved streets

[1] At that time St John's Church was being used as the Cathedral. The present
Cathedral—St Paul's—was consecrated in 1847.
[2] A wide belt of low-lying swampy forest, which extends inland from the coast
of Bengal and forms part of the Ganges delta.

and lanes, amid tufts of bamboos, coco-trees, and plantains, picturesque and striking to the sight, but extremely offensive to the smell, from the quantity of putrid water, the fumes of wood smoke, coco-nut oil, and above all the ghee,[1] which is to the Hindoo his principal luxury. Few Europeans live here, and those few, such as the Missionaries employed by the Church Missionary Society in Mirzapoor,[2] are said to suffer greatly from the climate. Even my Sircar,[3] though a native, in speaking of the neighbouring district of Dhee Intally, said that he himself never went near the 'bad water' which flows up from the salt water lake, without sickness and head-ache.

To the South, a branch of the Hooghly flows also into the Sunderbunds. It is called, by Europeans, Tolly's Nullah, but the natives regard it as the true Gunga, the wide stream being, as they pretend, the work of human and impious hands, at some early period of their history. In consequence no person worships the river between Kidderpoor and the sea, while this comparatively insignificant ditch enjoys all the same divine honours which the Ganges and the Hooghly enjoy during the earlier parts of their course. The banks of the Tolly's Nullah are covered by two large and nearly contiguous villages, Kidderpoor and Allypoor, as well as by several considerable European houses, and are said to be remarkably dry and wholesome. To the North is a vast extent of fertile country, divided into rice-fields, orchards and gardens, covered with a thick shade of fruit trees, and swarming with an innumerable population, occupying the large suburbs of Cossipoor, Chitpoor, &c. This tract resembles in general appearance, the eastern suburb, but is drier, healthier, and more open; through it lie the two great roads to Dum Dum and Barrackpoor. Westward flows the Hooghly, at least twice as broad as the Thames below London Bridge,—covered with large ships and craft of all kind, and offering on its farther bank the prospect of another considerable suburb, that of Howrah, chiefly inhabited by ship-builders, but with some pretty villas interspersed. The road

---

[1] Clarified butter.

[2] The C.M.S. station in north-central Calcutta. It included a boys' school and a printing press.

[3] This word had many different meanings. In this context it denotes a servant who carried out the functions of steward and accountant.

Bengal

which borders Calcutta and Chowringhee, is called, whimsically enough, 'the circular road', and runs along nearly the same line which was once occupied by a wide ditch and earthen fortification, raised on occasion of the Maharatta war.[1]

From the North-west angle of the fort to the city, along the banks of the Hooghly, is a walk of pounded brick, covered with sand, the usual material of the roads and streets in and near Calcutta, with a row of trees on each side, and about its centre a flight of steps to descend to the river, which in the morning, a little after sun-rise, are generally crowded with persons, washing themselves and performing their devotions, of which indeed, ablution is an essential and leading part. The rest consists, in general, in repeatedly touching the forehead and cheeks with white, red, or yellow earth, and exclamations of Ram! Ram![2] There are some Brahmins however, always about this time seated on the bank under the trees, who keep counting their beads, turning over the leaves of their banana-leaf books, and muttering their prayers with considerable seeming devotion, and for a long time together. These are 'Gooroos', or Religious Teachers, and seem considerably respected. Children and young persons are seen continually kneeling down to them, and making them little offerings, but the wealthier Hindoos seldom stop their palankeens for such a purpose. Where the esplanade walk joins Calcutta, a very handsome quay is continued along the side of the river; resembling in every thing but the durability of material, the quays of Petersburgh. It is unhappily of brick instead of granite, and is as yet unfinished, but many houses and public buildings are rising on it, and it bids fair to be a very great additional ornament and convenience to Calcutta. Vessels of all descriptions, to the burden of 600 tons, may lie almost close up to this quay, and there is always a crowd of ships and barks, as well as a very interesting assemblage of strangers of all sorts and nations to be seen. Of these, perhaps the Arabs, who are numerous, are the

[1] The East India Company constructed the 'Maratha Ditch' in 1742, to protect Calcutta at a time when the Marathas were ravaging the territories of the Nawab of Bengal, Alivardi Khan.

[2] A god-king of Hindu mythology; the hero of the epic *Ramayana* (see also *infra*, pp. 159–61).

most striking, from their comparative fairness, their fine bony and muscular figures, their noble countenances and picturesque dress.

Though no slavery legally exists in the British territories at this moment,[1] yet the terms and gestures used by servants to their superiors, all imply that such a distinction was, at no distant date, very common. 'I am thy slave',—'Thy slave hath no knowledge', are continually used as expressions of submission and of ignorance. In general, however, I do not think that the Bengalee servants are more submissive or respectful to their masters than those of Europe. The habit of appearing with bare feet in the house, the manner of addressing their superiors by joining the hands as in the attitude of prayer, at first gave them such an appearance. But these are in fact nothing more than taking off the hat, or bowing, in England; and the person who acts thus, is as likely to speak saucily, or neglect our orders, as any English footman or groom. Some of their expressions, indeed, are often misunderstood by new comers as uncivil, when nothing less than incivility is intended. If you bid a man order breakfast, he will answer, 'Have I not ordered it?' or, 'Is it not already coming?' merely meaning to express his own alacrity in obeying you. They are, on the whole, intelligent, and are very attentive to supply your wishes, even half, or not at all expressed. Masters seldom furnish any liveries, except turbans or girdles, which are of some distinctive colour and lace; the rest of the servant's dress is the cotton shirt, caftan, and trowsers of the country, and they are by no means exact as to its cleanliness. The servants of the Governor-General have very handsome scarlet and gold caftans.

Capital punishments are described as far from frequent, and appear to be inflicted for murder only; for smaller crimes, offenders are sentenced to hard labour, and are seen at work in the public roads, and about the barracks, in groupes more or less numerous, each man with fetters on his legs, and watched by policemen, or sepoys. These poor creatures, whatever their original crimes may have been, are probably still more hardened

[1] In fact slavery did exist. It was abolished by law in 1843.

by a punishment which thus daily, and for a length of time together, exposes them in a degraded and abject condition, to the eyes of men. I never saw countenances so ferocious and desperate, as many of them offer, and which are the more remarkable as being contrasted with the calmness and almost feminine mildness which generally characterizes the Indian expression of features. What indeed can be expected in men who have neither the consolations of Christianity, nor the pity of their brethren,—who are without hope in this world, and have no just idea of any world but this!

November 20.—The Botanic Garden[1] is a very beautiful and well-managed institution, enriched, besides the noblest trees and most beautiful plants of India, with a vast collection of exotics, chiefly collected by Dr Wallich himself, in Nepaul, Pulo Penang, Sumatra, and Java, and increased by contributions from the Cape, Brazil, and many different parts of Africa and America, as well as Australasia, and the South Sea islands. It is not only a curious, but a picturesque and most beautiful scene, and more perfectly answers Milton's idea of Paradise, except that it is on a dead flat instead of a hill, than any thing which I ever saw. Among the exotics I noticed the nutmeg, a pretty tree, something like a myrtle, with a beautiful peach-like blossom, but too delicate for the winter even of Bengal, and therefore placed in the most sheltered situation, and carefully matted round. The Sago-palm is a tree of great singularity and beauty, and in a grove or avenue produces an effect of striking solemnity, not unlike that of gothic architecture. There were some splendid South American creepers, some plantains from the Malayan Archipelago, of vast size and great beauty; and, what excited a melancholy kind of interest, a little wretched oak, kept alive with difficulty under a sky and in a temperature so perpetually stimulating, which allowed it no repose, or time to shed its leaves and recruit its powers by hybernation. .... Dr Wallich has the management of another extensive public establishment at Titty-ghur, near Barrackpoor, of the same nature with this, but appropriated more to the intro-

---

[1] This garden was at Sibpur, on the Hooghly, a few miles downstream from Calcutta. It had been established in 1786.

duction of useful plants into Bengal. He is himself a native of Denmark, but left his country young, and has devoted his life to Natural History and Botany in the East. His character and conversation are more than usually interesting; the first all frankness, friendliness, and ardent zeal for the service of science; the last enriched by a greater store of curious information relating to India and the neighbouring countries, than any which I have yet met with.[1]

These different public establishments used to be all cultivated by the convicts in chains, of whom I have already spoken. In the Botanic Garden their labour is now supplied by peasants hired by the day or week, and the exchange is found cheap, as well as otherwise advantageous and agreeable; the labour of free-men here, as elsewhere, being infinitely cheaper than that of slaves.

December 12.—I attended, together with a large proportion of the European Society of Calcutta, an examination of the Native Female Schools, instituted by Mrs Wilson,[2] and carried on by her together with her husband and the other Missionaries of the Church Missionary Society. The progress which the children as well as the grown pupils had made, was very creditable; and it may show how highly we ought to appreciate Mrs Wilson's efforts, when I mention, that when she began her work there was no known instance of an Indian female having been instructed in reading, writing, or sewing; and that all those who knew most of the country regarded her attempt to bring them together into schools as idle as any dream of enthusiasm could be.[3] She is a sensible and amiable young woman, with patience and good temper sufficient to conquer most obstacles, and who has acquired an influence over these poor little girls and their parents, as well as over her grown pupils, which at first sight seems little less than magical. It was very pretty to see the little swarthy children come

[1] Nathaniel Wallich was Superintendent of the Botanical Garden from 1817 to 1846. He was the author of *Plantae Asiaticae Rariores* and other works.

[2] This was Mary Ann Cooke, who had arrived in Calcutta in 1821 and subsequently married the C.M.S. missionary Isaac Wilson.

[3] In fact there had been individual examples of literate Indian women, but they had been taught by private tutors in their homes rather than in schools.

forward to repeat their lessons, and show their work to Lady Amherst,[1] blushing even through their dark complexions, with their muslin veils thrown carelessly round their slim half-naked figures, their black hair plaited, their foreheads specked with white or red paint, and their heads, necks, wrists, and ancles loaded with all the little finery they could beg or borrow for the occasion. Their parents make no objection to their learning the catechism, or being taught to read the Bible, provided nothing is done which can make them lose caste. And many of the Brahmins themselves, either finding the current of popular opinion too strongly in favour of the measures pursued for them to struggle with, or really influenced by the beauty of the lessons taught in Scripture, and the advantage of giving useful knowledge, and something like a moral sense to the lower ranks of their country-men and countrywomen, appear to approve of Mrs Wilson's plan, and attend the examination of her scholars. There is not even a semblance of opposition to the efforts which we are now making to enlighten the Hindoos; this I had some days ago an excellent opportunity of observing, in going round the schools supported by the Society for Promoting Christian Knowledge with Mr Hawtayne,[2] and seeing with how much apparent cordiality he was received, not only by the children themselves and the schoolmasters, though all Hindoos and Mussulmans, but by the parents and the neighbouring householders of whatever religion.

December 25.—This being Christmas-day I had a large congregation and a great number of communicants, I think about 300. Now, and at Easter-day, it is the custom in Calcutta to give very splendidly to the communion collection, which is the fund for the support of the European poor (for there are no poor's rates), and is managed with great judgement and attention by a body of gentlemen, calling themselves the select vestry of the Cathedral. There is a good deal of distress among the Europeans and half-castes here, arising from various causes, especially from the multitude of speculations which have been tried of late years in

---

[1] Lady Amherst did much to encourage girls' schools.

[2] One of the Anglican chaplains in Calcutta. He had played an active part in the management of the S.P.C.K. schools since their foundation in 1818.

Indigo and other establishments. If a man once begins falling so far as to borrow money, it is hardly possible for him to recover himself, the interest of loans is so high, and the necessary expences of living so great, while a return to England, except in forma pauperis and at the Company's cost, is too expensive to be thought of by persons under such circumstances. Nor are they luxuries only that ruin the colonist in Calcutta. House-rent is enormous, and though the poorer classes of Europeans and half-castes live in wretched dwellings, in very unwholesome parts of the town, they are often obliged to pay for these as much as would rent an excellent house in most of the market towns of England, and would furnish them with very tolerable dwellings even in London. Clothes too are dear. On the other hand provisions, by those who will stoop so low, are to be had for almost nothing from the remains of the dinners of the principal European families, which the climate will not suffer to be kept till another day, and are therefore disposed of by the Khânsamans[1] at a very low rate indeed. Still there is much real want, and I apprehend that a man who gives as a Christian ought to give, will in Calcutta find little opportunity for saving, and still less for amusement and needless luxury.

December 28.—I went this morning to return a visit which I had received from Colonel Krefting, the Danish Governor of Serampoor,[2] a fine old veteran who has been above 40 years resident in Bengal, yet still preserves the apparently robust health and florid old age of Norway, of which country he is a native.

Serampoor is a handsome place, kept beautifully clean, and looking more like an European town than Calcutta, or any of its neighbouring cantonments. The guard, which was turned out to receive me, consisted of perhaps a dozen Sepoys in the red Danish uniform; they were extremely clean and soldier-like looking men, and the appearance of the place flourishing. During the long war in which England was engaged, and so long as the Danes remained neutral, it was really so, and a vast deal of commerce was

---

[1] House-steward.
[2] The Danes occupied Serampore from 1755 to 1845.

carried on under the benefit of its flag. At the time of the Copenhagen rupture, Lord Minto sent two or three companies of infantry to take possession of it.[1] Since that period the settlement has grievously declined, and so much the faster, because no stipulation was made by the Danish Government at home at the time of the general pacification, for the continuance of a grant of 200 chests of opium yearly, which, previous to the rupture, the English East India Company were accustomed to furnish to the Danish Government of Serampoor at the cost price, thereby admitting them to share in the benefits of this important monopoly. This grant has been earnestly requested since by Colonel Krefting, but hitherto without success, and in consequence he complains that the revenues of the settlement do not meet its current expences, and that the Government have been utterly unable to relieve the sufferers by the late inundation.[2] Of Colonel Krefting every body speaks highly; and I have found great sympathy expressed in his misfortunes and those of his colony. I fear, however, that Government will not be able to grant his petition without authority from England, though they shew him in other respects what kindness and favour they can.

The administration of Serampoor, as it respects the police, is extremely good, and does much credit to Colonel Krefting and his Danish magistrates. During the late inundation he was called on for more vigorous measures than usual, since a numerous band of 'Decoits', or river-pirates, trusting to the general confusion and apparently defenceless state of the place, attacked his little kingdom, and began to burn and pillage with all the horrors which attend such inroads in this country. The Colonel took the field at the head of his dozen Sepoys, his silver-sticks,[3] policemen, and sundry volunteers, to the amount of perhaps 30, killed some of the ruffians, and took several prisoners, whom he hanged next morning, without deigning to ask aid from his powerful neighbours at Barrackpoor.

[1] In 1808.

[2] At the end of the rainy season of 1823 there had been widespread flooding in much of lower Bengal.

[3] Attendants of senior officials and Indian aristocrats, who carried silvered staffs (*chobdars*).

Bengal

From Serampoor I proceeded to Chandernagore, where I had also to return a visit to Monsieur Pelissier, the French Governor. It is, I think, a smaller town than the former, and with a less striking appearance from the river; the houses are mostly small, and the streets presented a remarkable picture of solitude and desertion. I saw no boats loading or unloading at the quay, no porters with burdens in the streets, no carts, no market people, and in fact only a small native bazar, and a few dismal looking European shops. In the streets I met two or three Europeans smoking segars, and apparently with little to do, having almost all the characteristic features and appearance of Frenchmen.

I had half an hour's very agreeable conversation with the Governor, and promise myself much pleasure from his acquaintance. He is only just arrived at this place from Pondicherry,[1] where he had passed several years, and of which he seems very fond; of the climate of Bengal he complains as being too hot and too cold, and says that his family have suffered in their healths during their residence here.

January 1, 1824.—Most of the Hindoo idols are of clay, and very much resemble in composition, colouring, and execution, though of course not in form, the more paltry sort of images which are carried about in England for sale by the Lago di Como people. At certain times of the year, great numbers of these are in fact hawked about the streets of Calcutta in the same manner, on men's heads. This is before they have been consecrated, which takes place on their being solemnly washed in the Ganges by a Brahmin Pundit. Till this happens, they possess no sacred character, and are frequently given as toys to children, and used as ornaments of rooms, which when hallowed they could not be, without given offence to every Hindoo who saw them thus employed. I thought it remarkable that though most of the male deities are represented of a deep brown colour, like the natives of the country, the females are usually no less red and white than our porcelain beauties as exhibited in England. But it is evident from the expressions of most of the Indians themselves, from the style of their amatory poetry, and other circumstances, that they

---

[1] The main French settlement in India, on the coast south of Madras.

consider fairness as a part of beauty, and a proof of noble blood. They do not like to be called black, and though the Abyssinians, who are sometimes met with in the country, are very little darker than they themselves are, their jest books are full of taunts on the charcoal complexion of the 'Hubshee'. Much of this has probably arisen from their having been so long subjected to the Moguls, and other conquerors originally from more northern climates, and who continued to keep up the comparative fairness of their stock by frequent importation of northern beauties. India too has been always, and long before the Europeans came hither, a favourite theatre for adventurers from Persia, Greece, Tartary, Turkey, and Arabia, all white men, and all in their turn possessing themselves of wealth and power. These circumstances must have greatly contributed to make a fair complexion fashionable. It is remarkable, however, to observe how surely all these classes of men in a few generations, even without any intermarriage with the Hindoos, assume the deep olive tint, little less dark than a Negro, which seems natural to the climate. The Portuguese natives[1] form unions among themselves alone, or if they can, with Europeans. Yet the Portuguese have, during a three hundred years' residence in India, become as black as Caffres.[2] Surely this goes far to disprove the assertion, which is sometimes made, that climate alone is insufficient to account for the difference between the Negro and the European. It is true that in the Negro are other peculiarities which the Indian has not, and to which the Portuguese colonist shews no symptom of approximation, and which undoubtedly do not appear to follow so naturally from the climate, as that swarthiness of complexion which is the sole distinction between the Hindoo and the European. But if heat produces one change, other peculiarities of climate may produce other and additional changes, and when such peculiarities have 3 or 4000 years to operate in, it is not easy to fix any limits to their power. I am inclined after all, to suspect that our European vanity leads us astray in supposing that our own is the primitive complexion, which I should rather suppose was that of the Indian, half way

[1] Heber was referring to Eurasians of Portuguese-Indian descent, of whom there were substantial communities, especially in the coastal provinces of India.
[2] Kaffirs.

between the two extremes, and perhaps the most agreeable to the eye and instinct of the majority of the human race. A colder climate, and a constant use of clothes, may have blanched the skin as effectually as a burning sun and nakedness may have tanned it, and I am encouraged in this hypothesis by observing that of animals the natural colours are generally dusky and uniform, while whiteness and a variety of tint almost invariably follow domestication, shelter from the elements, and a mixed and unnatural diet. Thus while hardship, additional exposure, a greater degree of heat, and other circumstances with which we are unacquainted, may have deteriorated the Hindoo into a Negro, opposite causes may have changed him into the progressively lighter tints of the Chinese, the Persian, the Turk, the Russian, and the Englishman....

We went on the 7th of January, 1824, to Titty-ghur, a convenient and comfortable house, in a beautiful situation, most kindly lent to us for a couple of months, by Dr Wallich. It is on the banks of the river, about two miles from Barrackpoor, and in the middle of the Company's experimental botanic garden. The weather is now very delightful, and we are comparatively free from the dense fogs which at this season beset Calcutta and Chowringhee.

Returning one day from Calcutta, I passed by two funeral piles, the one preparing for a single person, the other nearly consumed, on which a Suttee had just taken place. For this latter purpose a stage had been constructed of bamboos about eighteen inches or two feet above the ground, *on* which the dead body had been laid, and *under* which, as my native servants told me, the unhappy widow had been stretched out, surrounded with combustibles. Only a heap of glowing embers was now seen here, besides two long bamboos, which seemed intended to keep down any struggles which nature might force from her. *On* the stage was what seemed a large bundle of coarse cotton cloth, smoking, and partially blackened, emitting a very offensive smell. This my servants said was the husband's body. The woman they expressly affirmed had been laid *below* it, and ghee poured over her to hasten her end, and they also said the bamboos had been laid *across her.* I notice these particulars, because they differ from the account of a similar and recent ceremony, given by the Baptist missionaries, in which it is said that the widow is laid by the side of her husband, on the platform, with her arm embracing him, and her face turned to him.[1] Here I asked repeatedly, and received a different account. Yet the missionaries have had every possible opportunity of learning, if not of actually witnessing, all the particulars of the ceremony which they describe. Perhaps these particulars vary in different instances. At all events it is a proof how hard it is to gain, in this country, accurate information as to facts which seem most obvious to the senses. I felt very sick at heart, and regretted I had not been half an hour sooner, though probably my attempts at persuasion would have had no chance of success. I would at least have tried to reconcile her to life. There were perhaps twenty or thirty people present, with about the same degree of interest, though certainly not the same merriment, as would have been called forth by a bonfire in England. I saw no weeping, and heard no lamentations. But when the boat drew near, a sort of shout was raised, I believe in honour of Brahma, which was met by a similar outcry from my boatmen.

January 15.—Dr Marshman, the Baptist Missionary from Serampoor, dined with me. Dr Carey[2] is too lame to go out. The talents and learning of these good men are so well known in Europe, that I need hardly say that, important as are the points on which we differ, I sincerely admire and respect them, and desire their acquaintance. In speaking of the Suttee of yesterday Dr Marshman said that these horrors are of more frequent occurrence within these few last years, than when he first knew Bengal; an increase which he imputes to the increasing luxury of the higher and middling classes, and to their expensive imitation of European habits, which make many families needy, and anxious to get rid, by any means, of the necessity of supporting their mothers, or the widows of their relations. Another frequent cause is, he thinks, the jealousy of old men, who having married young wives, still cling to their exclusive possession even in

---

[1] W. Ward, *A view of the history, literature, and mythology of the Hindoos,* London, 1822, iii, 312, 319.

[2] See introduction, p. 2.

death, and leave injunctions, either with their wives themselves
to make the offering, or with their heirs to urge them to it. He is
strongly of opinion that the practice might be forbidden in Bengal,
where it is of most frequent occurrence, without exciting any
serious murmurs. The women he is convinced, would all be loud
in their praises of such a measure, and even of the men, so few
would have an immediate interest in burning their wives,
mothers, or sisters-in-law, that they would not set themselves
against what those who had most influence with them would be
much interested in having established. The Brahmins, he says,
have no longer the power and popularity which they had when he
first remembers India, and among the laity many powerful and
wealthy persons agree, and publicly express their agreement,
with Rammohun Roy,[1] in reprobating the custom, which is now
well known to be not commanded by any of the Hindoo sacred
books, though some of them speak of it as a meritorious sacrifice.
A similar opinion to that of Dr Marshman I have heard expressed
by the senior Judge of the Sudder Dewannee Adawlut.[2] Others,
however, of the members of the Government think differently.
They conceive that the likeliest method to make the custom more
popular than it is, would be to forbid and make it a point of
honour with the natives; that, at present, no woman is supposed
to be burnt without her own wish certified to the magistrate, that
there are other and less public ways to die (on that account more
liable to abuse than the Suttees) which might be resorted to if this
were forbidden, and that if we desire to convert the Hindoos, we
should above all things be careful to keep Government entirely
out of sight in all the means which we employ, and to be even, if
possible, over scrupulous in not meddling with, or impeding those
customs which, however horrid, are become sacred in their estimation, and are only to be destroyed by convincing and changing
the popular mind. When Christian schools have become universal
the Suttee will fall of itself. But to forbid it by any legislative
enactment would, in their opinion, only give currency to the
notion, that we mean to impose Christianity on them by force,
and retard its progress to an almost indefinite period.

[1] See Introduction, p. 8.
[2] *Sadr Diwani Adalat*—the highest civil Court of Appeal.

Bengal

February 5.—I had a curious visit a few days ago from a person who previously announced himself by letter as the Rev. Jacob Mecazenas, lately arrived from Rome, and anxious to wait upon me. I asked him to dinner two days after, but to my dismay, about 10 o'clock on the morning of the appointed day, instead of the smooth well-spoken Jesuit I had made up my mind to expect, I heard a thundering voice in the portico, and was greeted by a tall stout ecclesiastic with a venerable beard, a long black cassoc, a calotte, and a triangular hat, who announced himself as Father Mecazenas of the Dominican order, and come to pass the day with me! I found he was a native of Teflis,[1] but brought up in one of the Roman Catholic Armenian Convents established in Asia, and that he had passed his later years at Rome. He spoke wretched Italian, a very little French, and no English or Hindoostanee, and scarcely more than a few words of Latin. I had an engagement at the Government House during a part of the morning, which I pleaded, and hunted about to find if I had any books which would enable the poor man to pass his time rather less irksomely in my absence, but I found that the few Latin books which I had un-packed were in Calcutta, that I had no Italian of any kind, and that the only French books which I could get at, were the Tragedies of Voltaire,—a harmless work certainly, but bearing so formidable a name that I doubted whether, even if he could, he would read them. I was not mistaken, the name was enough for him, and though he made no objection in my presence, I was told that no sooner was my back turned than with a deep groan he laid them down, and desired a servant to take them away. Accordingly he passed the greater part of the morning in walking up and down the room, and looking out at the boats on the Hooghly. I pitied the poor man, and when I had finished my necessary business, on my return renewed my conversation with him, which got on better than I at first expected. I asked him some questions about Georgia and Armenia, but the most which I got was a list of the different tribes of Caucasus, a specimen of the Georgian vocabulary for the most common articles, and the Georgian alphabet, which he wrote out for me, and which I was surprised to find differ very materially from the Slavonic, the Armenian, and every other

[1] Tbilisi, in Georgia.

58

with which I am acquainted. At last dinner came to his relief as well as mine, and he soon began to display the appetite of a hardy mountaineer. I have seldom seen any one make such quick dispatch with whatever was put on his plate, and he made a no less good use of the three French words with which he seemed most familiar, 'a votre santé!' tossing down one bumper of wine after another, laughing all the time with the voice of a lion, till I began to fear some exhibition would follow, not very creditable either to the Church of Rome or to the table of a Protestant Bishop. He was, however, too strong to be affected by what he drank, except that it a little increased his fluency and noisy hilarity; and as soon as the cloth was fairly off the table, I thought it high time to call for coffee. I had been all this time expecting to be asked to subscribe to something or other, since, the dinner always excepted, I could not perceive why else the good man should have shewn so much anxiety for my acquaintance; and accordingly at length he rose, brought out an immense paper book, and after a short complimentary speech, solicited my patronage to a fund he was employed in collecting, to repair the temple of Fortuna Virilis, in Rome, which was, he said, appropriated as a hospital and place of instruction for Armenian and other youths, and pilgrims, but had been grievously injured by certain excavations which the French made while in Rome, in order to examine the nature of its substruction and foundations. His paper was to the same effect, but was written in English, and evidently the composition of some of the Calcutta native writers. He then talked of credentials from Rome; but though I asked for them, both in Latin and Italian, he produced none, but evaded the question. However, had he produced them, he would not have been at all more likely to gain his object with me, since I neither quite believed the story of the French having committed an outrage at variance with their general conduct, nor did I conceive myself called on to build up churches for the members of a different communion in Rome, when all which I can do is likely to fall so far short of the claims of charity in India. If the poor man, who was very pressing, had asked me for himself, and in the capacity which I suspect really belonged to him, of a mendicant, he would have fared better. As it was I was unrelenting, though civil; and we parted, with at least the satisfaction on my part, that I had given him a good dinner.

February 7.—I went down to Calcutta this morning, to attend a 'Durbar', or native levee of the Governor's, which all the principal native residents in Calcutta were expected to attend, as well as the vakeels[1] from several Indian princes. I found on my arrival the levee had begun, and that Lord Amherst, attended by his Aides-du-camp and Persian secretary,[2] had already walked down one side, where the persons of most rank, and who were to receive 'khelâts', or honorary dresses, were stationed. I therefore missed this ceremony, but joined him and walked round those to whom he had not yet spoken, comprising some persons of considerable rank and wealth, and some learned men, travellers from different eastern countries, who each in turn addressed his compliments, or petitions, or complaints to the Governor. There were several whom we thus passed who spoke English not only fluently but gracefully. Among these were Baboo Ramchunder Roy and his four brothers, all fine, tall, stout young men. . .

After Lord Amherst had completed the circle, he stood on the lower step of the throne, and the visitors advanced one by one to take leave. First came a young Raja of the Rajapootana district, who had received that day the investiture of his father's territories, in a splendid brocade khelât and turban; he was a little, pale, shy-looking boy, of 12 years old. Lord Amherst, in addition to these splendid robes, placed a large diamond aigrette in his turban, tied a string of valuable pearls round his neck, then gave him a small silver bottle of attar of roses, and a lump of pawn, or betel, wrapped up in a plantain leaf.[3] Next came forwards the 'vakeel', or envoy of the Maharaja Scindeah, also a boy, not above sixteen, but smart, self-possessed, and dandy-looking. His khelât and presents were a little, and but a little, less splendid than those of his precursor. Then followed Oude, Nagpoor, Nepaul, all represented by their vakeels, and each in turn honoured by similar, though less splendid, marks of attention. The next was

[1] Ambassadors.

[2] At that time Persian was still the medium for official communications with most of the princes of India.

[3] Attar and *pan* were customarily presented at the end of a visit; the *pan* was for chewing. See also *infra*, pp. 74–5.

a Persian Khân, a fine military-looking man, rather corpulent, and of a complexion not differing from that of a Turk, or other southern Europeans, with a magnificent black beard, and a very pleasing and animated address. A vakeel from Sind succeeded, with a high red cap, and was followed by an Arab, handsomely dressed, and as fair nearly, though not so good-looking, as the Persian. These were all distinguished, and received each some mark of favour. Those who followed had only a little attar poured on their handkerchiefs, and some pawn. On the whole it was an interesting and striking sight, though less magnificent than I had expected, and less so I think than the levee of an European monarch. The sameness of the greater part of the dresses (white muslin) was not sufficiently relieved by the splendour of the few khelâts; and even these which were of gold and silver brocade were in a great measure eclipsed by the scarlet and blue uniforms, gold lace, and feathers, of the English. One of the most striking figures was the Governor-general's native Aid-du-camp, a tall, strong-built, and remarkably handsome man, in the flower of his age, and of a countenance at once kind and bold. His dress was a very rich hussar uniform, and he advanced last of the circle, with the usual military salute; then, instead of the offering of money which each of the rest made, he bared a small part of the blade of his sabre, and held it out to the Governor. The attar he received, not on his handkerchief, but on his white cotton gloves. I had on former occasions noticed this soldier from his height, striking appearance, and rich uniform. He is a very respectable man, and reckoned a good officer.

March 1.—We bade adieu to Tittyghur with regret, but just as we were on the point of setting out, a severe storm of thunder, rain, and wind came on, which detained us about an hour, being the first regular north-wester which we had seen. It fairly lashed the river into high waves, and produced a delightful effect on the air, laying the dust and refreshing vegetation, as if by magic. My wife and children went by water, and I took in the carriage with me our Sircar. He is a shrewd fellow, well acquainted with the country, and possessed of the sort of information which is likely to interest travellers. His account of the tenure of lands very closely corresponded with what I had previously heard from others. The 'Zemindars' or landholders, let their lands, sometimes in large divisions, to tenants corresponding to the Scotch tacksmen, who underlet them again, and occasionally, which generally occurs near Calcutta, to the cottagers and cultivators immediately, and in very minute portions. The lands are sometimes on lease for a good many years, sometimes from year to year only. The usual rent for rice-land in Bengal, at least in this part of it, is two rupees a begah, or about twelve or fifteen shillings an acre; for orchards five rupees, or about £1. 12s. for the acre. All rents are paid in money, and the principle of 'metairie', which I explained to him, is unknown. The tenant in most of the villages is at the expense of the buildings, but these are so cheap and frail, as probably to cost less than thatching a stack in England, and can hardly be said to last longer. Land in this neighbourhood sells at about fifty rupees the begah, but did not fetch near so much before the roads were opened, which has been a measure of exceeding utility to the landholders here. The Baboo pointed out two or three large houses which we passed, as the residences of wealthy Zemindars, but who had also still more splendid houses in Calcutta. One of these, who was dignified by Lord Wellesley with the title of Raja, has a really fine villa, surrounded with a sort of park, the borders of which are planted with a handsome myrtle-leaved tree, about as large as an English horse-chestnut, which is here very common, but which he has defaced by clipping each individual tree into a regular conical shape. This the Baboo pointed out as a piece of extreme neatness and elegance. Another gateway on the left hand, in a very picturesque wood of coco-trees and bamboos, was guarded by an immense wooden idol of a young man, having only sandals and a sash painted black, the rest being flesh-colour. It must have been I should think thirty feet high. The Sircar said smiling, 'that great idol stands sentry to all the gods and goddesses within'. It was in fact the entrance to the pagoda at Kaida, which I had previously seen from the river. A little further by the road-side was a huge tower-like structure, about sixteen feet high, supported on eight or ten massive but low wheels, of wood painted red, and adorned with a good deal of clumsy carving. 'That', he said, again smiling, 'is our god's carriage; we keep it on the main road, because it is too heavy for the lanes of the neighbouring village. It is a fine sight to see the people from all the neighbourhood come together to draw it, when the statue is put in on solemn days.' I asked what god it belonged to, and was answered 'Brahma'.[1] He added, it required between two and three hundred people to move it, which I do not believe, though I can easily suppose that number may usually assist. I asked if self-immolation ever took place here as at Juggernaut,[2] but he assured me 'never that he had heard of'. As we passed through Chitpoor, he shewed me the house of the 'Nawâb of Chitpoor'. Of this potentate I had not heard before. He now is called by Europeans the Nawâb of Moorshedabad, where he resides, and is, it seems, the descendant of the Mohammedan nobleman who was the Lord of the district before our conquest, and still retains a considerable appanage of lands and pensions, to the amount of about 100,000 S. rupees monthly, with an honorary guard of Sepoys, and many of the exteriors of royalty.[3]

While he resided in his house at Chitpoor he was always received by the Governor on state days at the head of the stairs, and conducted, after an embrace, to a sort of throne at the upper end of the room, and when he took his leave, he was distinguished by a salute from the Fort, and turning out the guard. The Baboo told me all this, and did not fail to point out the different measure which the Mussulmans in India had received from that they had given to his countrymen. 'When they conquered us, they cut off the heads of all our Rajas whom they could catch. When the English conquered them, they gave them lands and pensions!' I do not exactly know whether he said this by way of compliment or no. I have reason to believe that the sentiment is very common among the Hindoos, and I doubt even, whether they would or would not have been better pleased had we, in such cases, been

[1] In fact this would have been the carriage on which the image of the god Jagannath was pulled through the streets at the annual festival, the *Rathjatra*.

[2] This reference is to the most celebrated of the temples of Jagannath, at Puri in Orissa. Devotees sometimes used to throw themselves under the wheels of the moving carriage, getting killed or seriously injured in the process.

[3] As the Mughal Empire declined in the early eighteenth century Bengal had become in effect an independent kingdom, ruled from Murshidabad by a succession of Nawabs. Since 1765 however they had lost all real power and had become simply the pensioners of the East India Company.

less lenient and liberal. Nevertheless it is evident that in thus keeping up, even at a considerable expense, these monuments of the Mahommedan power, our nation has acted wisely as well as generously. It is desireable that the Hindoos should always be reminded that we did not conquer them, but found them conquered, that their previous rulers were as much strangers to their blood and to their religion as we are, and that they were notoriously far more oppressive masters than we have ever shewn ourselves.

We passed a sort of Sepoy, dressed very splendidly in the native style, with a beautiful Persian gun and crooked hanjar,[1] but no bayonet. My companion pointed him out with much glee, as one of the attendants of Baboo Budinâth Roy,[2] who lives in this neighbourhood, and has a menagerie of animals and birds only inferior to that at Barrackpoor. This privilege of being attended by armed men is one greatly coveted by the wealthy natives of India, but only conceded to the highest ranks. Among the Europeans no person now claims it in Calcutta, save the Chief-justice and the Commander-in-chief, each of whom is attended in public, besides his silver sticks, by four or five *spears*, very elegantly worked, the poles of silver, and the blades generally gilt, with a place for the hand covered with crimson velvet, and a fringe of the same colour where the staff and blade join. The natives, however, like to have swords and bucklers, or musquets carried before them, and some have lately ventured to mount sentries at their gates, equipped very nearly like the regular troops in the pay of Government. One of these the Baboo soon afterwards pointed out to me, at the great house of the Mullich family, near the entrance of Calcutta.[3] I had afterwards however reason to know, that this was without permission, and that Rooplaul Mullich got severely censured for it by the Persian secretary, whose functions extend to the regulation of precedence among the natives throughout India, and indeed to many of the duties of our Herald's College.

[1] Curved dagger.

[2] Baidyanath Roy was a liberal supporter of the various projects of Western education in Calcutta, including Mrs Wilson's girls' schools, to which he donated Rs.20,000 in 1825.

[3] Probably the Mullick family of Barabazar.

Bengal

March 8.—I had an interesting visit this morning from Rhadacant Deb,[1] the son of a man of large fortune, and some rank and consequence in Calcutta, whose carriage, silver sticks, and attendants were altogether the smartest I had yet seen in India. He is a young man of pleasing countenance and manners, speaks English well, and has read many of our popular authors, particularly historical and geographical. He lives a good deal with Europeans, and has been very laudably active and liberal in forwarding, both by money and exertions, the education of his countrymen. He is secretary, gratuitously, to the Calcutta School Society,[2] and has himself published some elementary works in Bengalee. With all this he is believed to be a great bigot in the religion of his country's gods,—one of the few sincere ones, it is said, among the present race of wealthy Baboos. When the meeting was held by the Hindoo gentlemen of Calcutta, to vote an address of thanks to Lord Hastings on his leaving Bengal, Rhadacant Deb proposed as an amendment that Lord Hastings should be particularly thanked for 'the protection and encouragement which he had afforded to the ancient and orthodox practice of widows burning themselves with their husbands' bodies',—a proposal which was seconded by Hurree Mohun Thakoor, another wealthy Baboo. It was lost however, the cry of the meeting, though all Hindoos, being decidedly against it. But it shews the warmth of Rhadacant Deb's prejudices. With all this I found him a pleasing man, not unwilling to converse on religious topics, and perhaps even liking to do so from a consciousness that he was a shrewd reasoner, and from anxiety, which he expressed strongly, to vindicate his creed in the estimation of foreigners. He complained that his countrymen had been much misrepresented, that many of their observances were misunderstood both by Europeans and the vulgar in India, that for instance, the prohibition of particular kinds of food, and the rules of caste had a spiritual meaning, and were intended to act as constant mementos of the duties of temperance, humanity, abstraction from the

[1] Radha Kanta Deb, 1784–1867.

[2] Established in 1818. Its main object was to improve the standard of the elementary Bengali schools of Calcutta and, secondly, to increase the facilities for learning English.

world, &c. He admitted the beauty of the Christian morality readily enough, but urged that it did not suit the people of Hindostan; and that our drinking wine, and eating the flesh of so useful and excellent a creature as the cow, would, in India, be not only shocking, but very unwholesome. I said that nobody among us was *required* to eat beef if he did not like it. He however shook his head, and said that the vulgar of India *would* eat beef readily enough if they were allowed to do so. He asked me several questions respecting the doctrines of the Church of England, on which I hope I gave him satisfactory information, (preferring to remove his prejudices against us, rather than to make any direct attack on his own principles). His greatest curiosity, however, was about the Free-masons, who had lately been going in solemn procession to lay the first stone of the new Hindoo College.[1] 'Were they Christians?' 'Were they of my Church?' He could not understand that this bond of union was purely civil, convivial, or benevolent, seeing they made so much use of prayer; and was greatly surprised when I said, that in Europe both Christians and Mussulmans belonged to the Society; and that of the gentlemen whom he had seen the other day, some went to the Cathedral, and some to Dr Bryce's[2] church. He did not, indeed, understand that between Dr Bryce and the other chaplains any difference existed; and I had no desire, on finding this, to carry my explanations on this point further. He asked, at length, 'if I was a Mason?' 'If I knew their secret?' 'If I could guess it?' 'If I thought it was any thing wicked or Jacobinical?' I answered, that I was no Mason; and took care to express my conviction that the secret, if there was any, was perfectly harmless; and we parted very good friends, with mutual expressions of anxiety to meet again. Greatly indeed should I rejoice, if any thing which I can say would be of service to him.

I have for these few days past been reading the Hindoostanee Pentateuch, with my 'Moonshee', or teacher, who has never seen it before, and is highly delighted with its beauty and eloquence, particularly with the account of Paradise, the flood, and the fall

[1] A new building for the institution opened in 1817; see Introduction, p. 8.
[2] The Church of Scotland chaplain in Calcutta, and an active Freemason; see also Introduction, pp. 12, 29.

of man. 'It must have been a delightful place', said he, when reading of Eden and its four rivers. He asked me many, and some very interesting questions, and I began almost to hope that what I had the opportunity of saying to him, would, joined to the excellence of the Scriptures themselves, have gradually some effect, when one day he manifested a jealousy of the superiority of our Scriptures over those of his countrymen, and brought me a book, which he assured me greatly resembled the work of Moses, begging me to read it, which I readily promised. It was a translation into English of the '*Supta Sati*', a portion of the 'Marcumdeya Purana',[1] and recounts the exploits of a certain goddess, named 'Maha-Maya', (Great Delusion,) produced by the combined energies of all the deities united, in order to defeat the demons and giants. Some parts of it are not unlike the most inflated descriptions in the Edda;[2] and though a strange rhapsody, it is not devoid of spirit. But it has not the most distant approach to any moral lesson, or to any practical wisdom. The translator is a Brahmin from Madras.

The external meanness of all the shops, depositories, and warehouses in this great city is surprising. The bazars are wretchedness itself, without any approach to those covered walks, which are the chief glory of the cities of Turkey, Russia, and Persia, and which, in a climate like this, where both the sun and the rains are intolerable, would be more than any where else desireable.

April 21.—I entered into my 42nd year. God grant that my future years may be as happy, if he sees good! and better, far better spent than those which are gone by! This day I christened my dear little Harriet[3]! God bless and prosper her with all earthly and heavenly blessings! We had afterwards a great dinner and evening party, at which were present the Governor and Lady Amherst, and nearly all our acquaintance in Calcutta. To the

[1] The *Markandeya Purana*. The *Puranas* are a collection of Hindu religious writings, including accounts of the creation of the universe and stories of gods and men.

[2] An Icelandic book of poems about gods and heroes, dating from the early Middle Ages.

[3] The Bishop's youngest daughter.

latter I also asked several of the wealthy natives, who were much pleased with the attention, being in fact one which no European of high station in Calcutta had previously paid to any of them. Hurree Mohun Thakoor observing 'what an increased interest the presence of females gave to our parties', I reminded him that the introduction of women into society was an ancient Hindoo custom, and only discontinued in consequence of the Mussulman conquest. He assented with a laugh, adding, however, 'it is too late for us to go back to the old custom now'. Rhadacant Deb, who overheard us, observed more seriously, 'it is very true that we did not use to shut up our women till the times of the Mussulmans. But before we could give them the same liberty as the Europeans they must be better educated.' I introduced these Baboos to the Chief-justice, which pleased them much, though perhaps they were still better pleased with my wife herself presenting them pawn, rose-water, and attar of roses before they went, after the native custom.

June 15.—This morning I left Calcutta for my Visitation through the Upper Provinces. This excursion, to which both my wife and I had long looked forwards with delightful anticipations, will now become a dreary banishment to me, as the state of her own health, and the circumstance of her having an infant, are considered as insuperable obstacles to her undertaking such a journey. Accompanied by my domestic Chaplain, Mr Stowe,[1] I embarked on board a fine 16 oared pinnace for Dacca, which was to be the first station on my Visitation. After about two hours squabbling with the owner and navigators of the vessel, we got under weigh, with a fine south breeze and the flood-tide. Archdeacon Corrie,[2] with his wife and children, accompanied us in a budgerow, and we had two smaller boats, one for cooking, the other for our baggage.

June 16.—A Bengalee boat is the simplest and rudest of all possible structures. It is decked over, throughout its whole length, with bamboo; and on this is erected a low light fabric of

---

[1] Martin Stowe had previously been Heber's curate at Hodnet.
[2] See Introduction, pp. 5, 27.

bamboo and straw, exactly like a small cottage without a chimney. This is the cabin, baggage-room, &c.; here the passengers sit and sleep, and here, if it be intended for a cooking-boat, are one or two small ranges of brick-work, like English hot-hearths, but not rising more than a few inches above the deck, with small, round, sugar-loaf holes, like those in a lime-kiln, adapted for dressing victuals with charcoal. As the roof of this apartment is by far too fragile for men to stand or sit on, and as the apartment itself takes up nearly two-thirds of the vessel, upright bamboos are fixed by its side, which support a kind of grating of the same material, immediately above the roof, on which, at the height probably of six or eight feet above the surface of the water, the boatmen sit or stand to work the vessel. They have, for oars, long bamboos, with circular boards at the end, a longer one of the same sort to steer with, a long rough bamboo for a mast, and one, or sometimes two sails, of a square form, (or rather broader above than below,) of very coarse and flimsy canvass. Nothing can seem more clumsy or dangerous than these boats. Dangerous I believe they are, but with a fair wind they sail over the water merrily. The breeze this morning carried us along at a good rate, yet our English-rigged brig could do no more than keep up with the cooking boat.

An appearance of neatness and comfort is exhibited by the native villages; and, as an Indian generally lays out some of his superfluous wealth in building or adding to a pagoda,[1] it is a strong mark of progressive and rapid improvement to say, as Mr Corrie did to-day, that *all* the large pagodas between 'Calcutta and this place have been founded, or re-built, in his memory'. This, however, I must confess, does not tell much for the inclination of the Hindoos to receive a new religion. Indeed, except in our schools, I see no appearance of it. The austerities and idolatries exercised by them, strike me as much, or I think more, the more I see of them. A few days since I saw a tall, large, elderly man, nearly naked, walking with three or four others, who suddenly knelt down one after the other, and catching hold of his foot, kissed it repeatedly. The man stood with much gravity

---

[1] Heber uses this term to denote Hindu temples.

to allow them to do so, but said nothing. He had the string ('peeta',[1]) of a Brahmin. Another man passed us on Sunday morning last, hopping on one foot. He was a devotee who had made a vow never to use the other, which was now contracted, and shrunk close up to his hams. Lately, too, I saw a man who held his hands always above his head, and had thus lost the power of bringing them down to his sides. In general, however, I must own that these spectacles are not so common, at least so far as I can yet judge, as, before I came to India, I expected to find them.

June 17.—About two o'clock this morning we had a north-wester, accompanied with violent thunder and lightening. It lasted about two hours, and was so severe, that we could not but feel thankful that it had not overtaken us the night before, while we were under sail. I have never heard louder thunder, or seen so vivid and formidable lightening. Happily, our attendant boats were close in shore, under the shelter of the high bank, while our own mariners did their work exceedingly well and quietly, letting go a second anchor, and veering out as much cable as they had on board. After having done all that under such circumstances was to be done, they gave the cry of 'Allah hu Allah!' and went to prayers, a circumstance which, unaccompanied as it was by any marks of confusion or trepidation, gave me a very favourable impression of them, though I afterwards recollected that it was in fact pretty near the hour when that call is uttered from the mosque, which used to thrill me when I heard it in the Crimea, 'Prayer is better than sleep! prayer is better than sleep!' Our boat, with this length of cable, rode well and easily, but we had some trouble-some work in closing the cabin windows, as our rooms, and all they contained, were getting a complete cold bath. Indeed, there really ran something like a sea in the channel of the river where we now lay. What passed gave me confidence in the vessel and her crew. The latter are numerous, sixteen rowers, four men accustomed to the management of the sails, and the serang,[2] all Mussulmans, and natives of Dacca, and its vicinity. They are wild

---

[1] The *poita*—tied diagonally across the upper half of the body.
[2] Skipper.

and odd-looking people, light-limbed, and lean, and very black, but strong and muscular, and all young men, with a fiercer eye and far less civil manner than the Hindoos of Calcutta, to which expression of character their dress contributes, (when they wear any, which is the case this cool morning) being old uniform jackets of the infantry and artillery, with red caps and dirty turbans wrapped round them. As they sat round the fire this morning, cooking their victuals for breakfast, they might pass for no bad representatives of Malay pirates.

During the following week the Bishop and his party sailed slowly north and east through the waterways of the Ganges delta. On 23 June he commented:

The country was extremely pretty, the high banks being fringed almost down to the water's edge with bamboos, long grass, and creepers, and the shore above covered with noble banians, palms, and peepuls, with very neat villages under their shade, while the figures of the women in coarse but white cotton mantles, walking under the trees, and coming with their large earthen jars on their heads, to draw water, gave a liveliness to the picture which was very interesting. Several indigo works[1] were on the river side, and I thought the appearance of the boats, the houses, and the peasantry, all improved as we approached the Burra Gunga.[2] We had a storm of thunder and heavy lightening to-day about noon. The Serang made fast on the lee of a small sandy point. There was no real occasion for his doing so, but he pleaded that if it came on to blow hard, he could not manage his vessel in a river of so rapid a stream, and the depth and direction of whose channel was so uncertain. This indeed was one of the points on which I had been cautioned, that I should never force a Serang to proceed when he was anxious to 'lugana' (make fast.) These people, when engaged by the trip, have no interest in needless delays, and though they may sometimes be over-cautious, they always know their own rivers, and the state of the weather, better than

---

[1] The cultivation of indigo had been developed on a large scale in Bengal since the 1780s.
[2] The main outflow of the Ganges.

we can do. Most, if not all the accidents which occur to Europeans on the Ganges, arise from their making their crew proceed against their wishes and judgement.

June 24.—We this day made a better progress, the river being deeper and wider, while the stream continued almost equally powerful. In the neighbourhood of the place where we halted for the night, which was chiefly cultivated with rice, with some patches of sunn hemp, were two villages, to one of which we walked, and found it large, populous, and beautifully embosomed in trees, some of them of a kind which I had not before met with . . . We met during our walk through the village, the brahmin of the place, a young and intelligent man, who very civilly not only answered our questions, but turned back to accompany us in our walk. He said the name of the village was Titybania, that it, with a property round it, amounting to a rental of 14,000 rupees a year, belonged to a Hindoo family, whose name I forget, and who were now engaged in a law-suit. That a muktar[1] was named to receive the rents, and that, as he shrewdly observed, 'The Company get their taxes, the poor people their receipts as usual, and all things go on as before, except the two brothers, who are rightly served for quarrelling'. I asked if indigo was cultivated; he said no, and that probably the soil might be too clayey for it; but added, 'The indigo is a fine thing to put money into the purse of the baboo, but we poor people do not want to see it. It raises the price of rice, and the rent of land.' The rent of indigo-ground, he said, was above twelves anas the begah (five shillings an acre). That of rice-ground five (about two shillings the acre). This is far less than in the neighbourhood of Calcutta, but the place is certainly very sequestered. No tygers, he said, are ever seen here. We passed by some Mussulman cottages, distinguished by the poultry which were seen round them,[2] and a very small, but new and neat Hindoo cottage, before whose door its owners were busy preparing a small garden, an unusual sight in India, and at a short distance from which a young banian tree was planted on a hillock of turf, carefully surrounded with thorns, woven into a sort of dead-hedge, with much care and neatness. I pointed out this last

---

[1] Agent.   [2] Hindus regarded chickens as unclean.

to the brahmin, who merely said it would be a great tree in time, and very beautiful in that part of the village. A handsome young woman, adorned with unusual gaiety of silver anklets, &c. went into the house, and the owner himself was a young man, so that probably the banian was a votive offering on occasion of their marriage, or the birth of their first child. At a small distance, and on the brink of the river, was a little wretched hut of straw and reeds, removed from all other dwellings, with a long bamboo and a small ragged flag, stuck into the ground, on each side of its front. It was, the brahmin said, the tomb of a Mussulman holy man. While we were passing on, several other villagers collected round us. Some of them seemed greatly amused with our unusual figures and complexion, and our imperfect Hindoostanee, but there was not the least expression of shyness, nor any real in-civility. Abdullah[1] said it was quite amazing to see how familiar the common people had become with Englishmen during the last twenty years. He remembered the time when all black people ran away from a white face, and the appearance of a single Euro-pean soldier struck consternation into a village. 'They used to them now', he said, 'they know they no harm do.' The country-people in this neighbourhood seem contented and thriving, for them, though of course their most flourishing condition would be reckoned deep poverty in England. The boats on this river are much neater than those on the Hooghly. Their straw tilts are better made, their sterns not so unreasonably high, their sails less flimsy, nay, many of them are painted, and have copper or gilded eyes fixed into their bows and on each side of the helm. We had two beggars by the boat, the one an old man with a white beard, blind, and led by two boys, who were, he said, his children. I asked how old he was, but he did not seem to understand my question, merely answering that he had been blind forty years, and had lost his eyes soon after he married. There are surprisingly few beggars in Bengal. Of those whom I have seen, the greater part have super-added some religious character to their natural claims on our pity. This old man, however, had nothing of the

---

[1] A convert to Christianity from Islam, who had travelled in the Middle East before he entered the Bishop's service. Unfortunately he proved to be an incor-rigible drunkard, and Heber had to dismiss him after his return to Calcutta in 1825.

sort, and merely asked alms as a helpless and unhappy being. I was heartily glad that I had come out provided.

June 28.—The river continues a noble one, and the country bordering on it is now of a fertility and tranquil beauty, such as I never saw before. Beauty it certainly has, though it has neither mountain, nor waterfall, nor rock, which all enter into our notions of beautiful scenery in England. But the broad river, with a very rapid current, swarming with small picturesque canoes, and no less picturesque fishermen, winding through fields of green corn, natural meadows covered with cattle, successive plantations of cotton, sugar, and pawn, studded with villages and masts in every creek and angle, and backed continually (though not in a continuous and heavy line like the shores of the Hooghly) with magnificent peepul, banian, bamboo, betel, and coco trees, afford a succession of pictures the most riants that I have seen, and infinitely beyond anything which I ever expected to see in Bengal. To add to our pleasure this day, we had a fine rattling breeze carrying us along against the stream, which it raised into a curl, at the rate of five miles an hour; and more than all, I heard from my wife. We brought to at seven near a large village, called Tynybanya. The banks near the river were cultivated in alternate quillets with rice and cotton. Then followed long ridges of pawn, which grows something like a kidney-bean, and is carefully covered above and on every side with branches of bamboo, forming a sort of hedge and roof, as high as a man's head. When these branches and leaves become withered, (which they soon do) they look exactly like a high mud wall, so like indeed, that when we first saw them in the course of the morning, we both thought they were garden walls, and that the pawn was cultivated within instead of under them. Pawn seems one of the most highly valued productions of India, if we judge either by the pains taken in its cultivation, or the price which it bears; we were told that its retail price was sixty leaves, (each as large as a bay-leaf) for an ana (1½*d*.) no contemptible rate in a country where all products of agricultural labour are so cheap, and where rice may be had at less than half an ana the seer, a weight of nearly two pounds. Yet the only use of pawn (which has a hottish spicy flavour) is to wrap up the betel-nut which the natives of India delight in chewing, and for which I should have thought many other leaves would answer as well. Our servants, indeed, have an idea that the root of the pawn is collected by the apothecaries as medicine, and sold at a high rate for exportation, but I never remember hearing of it. I tried chewing the betel to-day, and thought it not unpleasant, at least I can easily believe that where it is fashionable, people may soon grow fond of it. The nut is cut into small squares and wrapped up in the leaf, together with some chunam.[1] It is warm and pungent in the mouth, and has the immediate effect of staining the tongue, mouth, and lips, a fiery orange colour. The people here fancy it is good for the teeth, but they do not all take it. I see about half the crew without the stain on their lips, but I do not think the teeth of the others are better.

The betel is a beautiful tree, the tallest and slenderest of the palm kind, with a very smooth white bark. Nothing can be more graceful than its high slender pillars, when backed by the dark shade of bamboos and other similar foliage. A noble grove of this kind succeeded to the pawn rows at our village this evening, embosoming the cottages, together with their little gardens, and, what I see here in greater perfection than I have yet seen in Bengal, their little green meadows and home-steads. We rambled among these till darkness warned us to return. The name of this river is Chundnah. We saw a large eagle seated on a peepul tree very near us. On the peepul an earthen pot was hanging, which Abdullah said was brought thither by some person whose father was dead, that the ghost might drink....

June 29.—This morning we continued our way with a strong and favourable breeze against 'a broader and a broader stream, that rocked the little boat', and surpassing the Hooghly almost as much in width as in the richness, beauty, and cheerfulness of its banks, which makes me believe that Calcutta is really one of the most unfavourable situations in Bengal. We passed some fishing-boats of very ingenious construction, well adapted for paddling in shallow water, and at the same time not unsafe, being broad in the beam and finely shaped. They were also clinker built, the first of that kind which I have seen in India. About 12 o'clock

[1] Lime.

we passed on our left-hand a large and handsome European house, very nobly situated on a high dry bank, with fine trees round it, and immediately after, we saw before us a sheet of water, the opposite bank of which was scarcely visible, being in fact Gunga in her greatest pride and glory. The main arm which was visible, stretched away to the north-west, literally looking like a sea, with many sails on it. Directly north, though still at a considerable distance, the stream was broken by a large sandy island, and to the south, beyond some low sandy islets and narrower channels, we saw another reach, like the one to the north, with a sandy shore, looking not unlike the coast of Lancashire, as seen trending away from the mouth of the Mersey. To one of these islets we stood across with a fine breeze. There the boatmen drew ashore, and one of them came to ask me for an offering, which it was (he said) always customary to make at this point, to *Khizr*, for a good passage. Khizr, for whom the Mussulmans have a great veneration, is a sort of mythological personage, made up of different Rabbinical fables concerning Eliezer the servant of Abraham, and the prophet Elijah, on which are engrafted the chivalrous legends respecting St George! They believe him to have attended Abraham, in which capacity he drank of the fountain of youth, which gave him immortality. This is Rabbinical, but the Mussulmans also believe him to have gone dry-shod over Jordan, to have ascended to heaven in a fiery chariot, and lastly, to be a valorous knight, who helps the arms of the believers, and will return at length on a white horse, a little before the day of judgement, together with, and as the Vizier of our Lord, to destroy Dejjal or Anti-Christ, and subdue the multitudes of Gog and Magog. But as having access to the fountain of life, and as having passed Jordan, he is particularly disposed to love and cherish the waters, and all which belong to, or sail on them. Dacca, under the Mogul dynasty, was placed under his peculiar protection, and he naturally succeeded to that veneration, which in the same district, the Hindoos had previously been in the habit of paying to their Varuna, god of the seas and rivers.

July 1.—The noise of the Ganges is really like the sea. As we passed near a hollow and precipitous part of the bank, on which the wind set full, it told on my ear exactly as if the tide were coming in; and when the moon rested at night on this great, and, as it then seemed, this shoreless extent of water, we might have fancied ourselves in the cuddy of an Indiaman, if our cabin were not too near the water. About half-past five we stood across the river, which ran really high, and washed the decks handsomely, and brought to amid rice, indigo, and sugar-fields, near the native town of Jaffiergunge, and had an interesting walk, though it was too late for a long one. The people were cutting indigo, which they then packed in large bundles, and loaded in boats. It both looked and smelt something like new-made hay, though with rather a stronger flavour. . . .

July 2.—We entered the river of Jaffiergunge, called Commer-colly in Rennell's map,[1] which here, however, as in other places, probably from some alteration in the course of the stream, is utterly useless. The country all populous, highly cultivated with rice, sugar, cotton, and indigo; and though woody, the banks are not oppressed with such exuberant and heavy arborage as those of the Hooghly. We passed a considerable indigo factory, with a very pretty house attached to it. There seemed more machinery, and more activity here, than in any which we have seen. The appearance of the workmen, whose naked limbs and bodies were covered with the blue dye, was very singular.

The wind favoured our progress to-day; and though the Serang did not care to abandon his trusty tow-line,[2] the men had light work, and were in high spirits. On passing a banian tree, where were an old mat and a pitcher, one of them ran forwards without giving any notice of his intentions, drew the mat round his loins, placed the potsherd by his side according to rule, and so ridiculously imitated the gestures of a 'Yogi', (a religious mendicant,) singing all the time in the dismal tune which they use, putting his hands over his head, sprinkling earth on his face, &c. that his comrades were quite disabled from their work with laughing, and I was myself exceedingly amused. Indeed, not having seen him run forwards, I really at first supposed him to be the person he counterfeited, and wondered at the irreverent

[1] James Rennell had been appointed Surveyor-General of Bengal in 1764.
[2] Used for towing the boat from the bank.

mockery with which so holy a man was treated, till in a few minutes he sprang up, threw his mat and handful of ashes at his comrades, and catching up his truncheon of bamboo, resumed his place in the team with an agility and strength which urged all the rest into a round trot. This is only one out of twenty instances which every day offers, of the vivacity of these fellows, who are, in fact, always chattering, singing, laughing, or playing each other tricks. Yet I have met many people in Calcutta who gravely complain of the apathy and want of vivacity in the natives of India. My own observation, both of these men and of the peasants and fishermen whom we pass, is of a very different character. They are active, lively, gossiping, and laborious enough when they have any motive to stimulate them to exertion. Had I an indigo plantation, I would put them all to task-work, and I am sure that, with due inspection to prevent fraud, few labourers would surpass them in steady work, and still fewer would equal them in cheapness. Their habit of coming late to their labour, and breaking off early, arises from the variety of callings which each man at present exercises, and the time which he loses in preparing his food. Make it worth their while to establish messes, where one should cook for the remainder, and give them facilities of eating a noon-day meal on the scene of their work, and they would, I think, be easily persuaded, with far greater comfort to themselves, and advantage to their employers, to begin and leave off work at the same time with English labourers. Indeed, at some of the indigo works which we have passed, this seems the case; and I am sure that the fishermen and dandies[1] work as late and as early as any people.

The stream as we advanced became broader, and the country assumed the character of inundation. The villages, on land a little elevated, were each surrounded by its thicket of bamboos and fruit-trees. Some fine tall spreading banians and peepuls were scattered on the driest patches of the open country, but the rest was a sheet of green rice, intersected in every direction by shallow streams, which did not as yet cover the crop, but made it look like rushes in a marsh. The low banks of the river were marked out by the bushes of Datura Stramonium, and long silky

[1] Boatmen.

tufted grass, which from place to place rose above the water, and here our boatmen waded sometimes mid-leg, sometimes knee-deep. Indigo, in this low country, is confined to the banks round the villages, whence we saw several boats conveying it to the works which we had left behind us.

On 3 July Heber arrived at Dacca.

July 4.—Dacca, Mr Master[1] says, is, as I supposed, merely the wreck of its ancient grandeur. Its trade is reduced to the sixtieth part of what it was, and all its splendid buildings, the castle of its founder Shahjehanguire, the noble mosque he built, the palaces of the ancient Nawâbs, the factories and churches of the Dutch, French, and Portuguese nations, are all sunk into ruin, and over-grown with jungle.[2] Mr Master has himself been present at a tyger hunt in the court of the old palace, during which the elephant of one of his friends fell into a well, overgrown with weeds and bushes. The cotton produced in this district is mostly sent to England raw, and the manufactures of England are preferred by the people of Dacca themselves for their cheapness. There are still a few Armenians resident in the town, some of them wealthy, with a Church, and two Priests. Their Archbishop, who makes once in four or five years a journey from Nakitchvan[3] to India, is now in the place, on the same errand with me. There are also a few Portuguese, very poor and degraded. Of Greeks the number is considerable, and they are described as an industrious and intelligent people, mixing more with the English than the rest, and filling many of the subaltern situations under government. The clerk at the English Church (it happens singularly enough) is a Greek, and the Greek Priest has sent to request a permission to call on me. Of English there are none, except a few indigo planters in the neighbourhood, and those in the civil or military service. But the Hindoo and Mohammedan population, Mr

[1] G. C. Master: appointed Second Judge of the Provincial Court of Appeal at Dacca in 1821; d. 1832.

[2] The Mughal conquest of Bengal was completed during the reign of the Emperor Jahangir (1605–27), who made Dacca the capital of the province. It became an important centre for trade especially in cotton textiles.

[3] A town on the Araxes River in Armenia, then under Persian but from 1828 under Russian control.

Master still rates at 300,000, certainly no immoderate calculation, since, as he says, he has ascertained that there are above 90,000 houses and huts. The climate of Dacca, Mr Master reckons one of the mildest in India, the heat being always tempered by the vast rivers flowing near it, and the rapidity of their streams discharging the putrid matter of the annual inundation more rapidly than is ever the case in the Hooghly. The neighbourhood affords only one short ride at this season, and not many even when the ground is dry, being much intersected by small rivers, and some large and impenetrable jungles coming pretty close to the northeast of the town. Boating is popular, and they make boats very well here. Indeed I cannot conceive a situation which more naturally would lead men to take delight in sailing. No vessels, however, larger than the small country built brigs ever come to Dacca; during the rains, ships of any moderate burden might do so, but it would be attended with some risk, and the inducements to enter this branch of the Ganges are not sufficient to encourage men to endanger their vessels or themselves, though as far as Luckipoor, small European craft have been known to come. The majority prefer Chittagong, though even this last has a harbour little adapted for vessels of burthen.

July 5.—To-day I had visits from most of the civil and military functionaries of Dacca. I had also a visit from Mr Lee, a sort of secretary to his highness the Nawâb Shumsheddowlah,[1] to congratulate me on my arrival, and to appoint a day for his calling on me. This potentate is now, of course, shorn of all political power, and is not even allowed the state palanquin, which his brother (whose heir he is) had, and which his neighbour the Nawâb of Moorshedabad still retains. He has, however, an allowance of 10,000 s.rupees per month, is permitted to keep a court, with guards, and is styled 'highness'. The palanquin, indeed, was a distinction to which his brother had no very authentic claim, and which this man could hardly expect, having been very leniently dealt with in being allowed the succession at all. He had in his

---

[1] A grandson of Jasarat Khan, who had been the Naib-nazim (i.e., deputy governor) of Dacca at the time when the East India Company had taken control of Bengal. By Heber's time the title of Nawab was used purely out of courtesy. Shams-ud-daula died in 1831.

youth been a bad subject, had quarrelled with government and his own family, and been concerned in the bloody conspiracy of Vizier Ali.[1] For his share in this, he was many years imprisoned in Calcutta, during which time he acquired a better knowledge of the English language and literature than most of his countrymen possess. He speaks and writes English very tolerably, and even fancies himself a critic in Shakespear. He has been really a man, Mr Master tells me, of vigorous and curious mind, who, had his talents enjoyed a proper vent, might have distinguished himself. But he is now growing old, infirm, and indolent, more and more addicted to the listless indulgences of an Asiatic prince; pomp, so far as he can afford it, dancing girls, and opium, having in fact scarce any society but that of his inferiors, and being divested of any of the usual motives by which even Asiatic princes are occasionally roused to exertion. To such a man a strong religious feeling would (even as far as this world is concerned) be an inestimable treasure. But to inspire Shumsheddowlah with such a feeling, there are, alas! few if any facilities.

Government has seldom more than five companies of infantry at Dacca; but this number is now doubled, and they have also sent a small flotilla of gun-vessels, which are said to be on their way. Had the Burmese really possessed any considerable force of war-boats in the neighbourhood of Teak Naaf, Dacca might easily have fallen their prey;[2] and the alarm excited lately was very great, and with some better reason than I had supposed. Among other objects of fear and suspicion was the poor old Nawâb, whom the English suspected of plotting against them, and sending information to the Burmese. That the Nawâb would not weep his eyes out for any reverses of the British army, is, indeed, probable. But as to intelligence, he had none to send which was worth the carriage, and was so far from contemplating the approach of the Burmese with indifference, that he had taken means for removing his family as soon as possible, in case of serious alarm, while he himself requested leave to attach himself

[1] Wazir Ali became Nawab of Oudh in 1797, but after a few months the Governor-General, Sir John Shore, insisted that he be set aside in favour of his uncle. He was pensioned off to Banaras, where in 1799 he rose in an abortive insurrection.
[2] For the Burma war, see Introduction, p. 26.

to Mr Master, to remain or go, whenever and wherever he might think proper.

Dacca, as Abdullah truly said, is 'much place for elephant'. The Company have a stud of from 2 to 300, numbers being caught annually in the neighbouring woods of Tiperah and Cachar, which are broken in for service here, as well as gradually inured to the habits which they must acquire in a state of captivity. Those which are intended for the Upper Provinces, remain here some time, and are by degrees removed to Moorshedabad, Bogwan-golah, Dinapoor, &c. since the transition of climate from this place to Meerut, or even Cawnpoor, is too great, and when sudden, destroys numbers. I drove in the evening, with Mr Master, through the city and part of the neighbourhood. The former is very like the worst part of Calcutta near Chitpoor, but has some really fine ruins intermingled with the mean huts which cover three-fourths of its space. The castle which I noticed, and which used to be the palace, is of brick, yet shewing some traces of the plaster which has covered it. The architecture is precisely that of the Kremlin of Moscow, of which city indeed, I was repeatedly reminded in my progress through the town. The Grecian houses, whose ruined condition I have noticed, were the more modern and favourite residence of the late Nawâb, and were ruined a few years since by the encroachments of the river. The obelisk, or 'Mut'[1] which I saw, was erected as an act of piety very frequent in India, by a Hindoo, who about 25 years ago accumulated a large fortune in the service of the East India Company. Another mut of an almost similar form, was pointed out to me a little way out of the town. The pagodas, however, of Dacca, are few and small, three-fourths of the population being Mussulmans, and almost every brick building in the place having its Persian or Arabic inscription. Most of these look very old, but none are of great antiquity. Even the old palace was built only about 200 years ago, and consequently, is scarcely older than the banqueting-house at Whitehall. The European houses are mostly small and poor, compared with those of Calcutta; and such as are out of the town, are so surrounded with jungle and ruins, as to give the idea of desolation and unhealthiness. No

[1] A *matha* is in fact a Hindu monastery.

cultivation was visible so far as we went, nor any space cleared except an area of about twenty acres for the new military lines. The drive was picturesque, however, in no common degree; several of the ruins were fine, and there are some noble peepul trees. The Nawâb's carriage passed us, an old landau, drawn by four horses, with a coachman and postillion in red liveries, and some horse-guards in red also, with high ugly caps, like those of the old grenadiers, with gilt plates in front, and very ill mounted. The great men of India evidently lose in point of effect, by an injudicious and imperfect adoption of European fashions. An Eastern cavalier with his turban and flowing robes, is a striking object; and an eastern prince on horseback, and attended by his usual train of white-staved and high-capped janizaries, a still more noble one; but an eastern prince in a shabby carriage, guarded by men dressed like an equestrian troop at a fair, is nothing more than ridiculous and melancholy. It is, however, but natural, that these unfortunate sovereigns should imitate, as far as they can, those costumes which the example of their conquerors has associated with their most recent ideas of power and splendour. Stowe has been very ill ever since he arrived here; to-day he is better, but still so unwell as to make me give up all idea of leaving Dacca this week.

I met a lady to-day who had been several years at Nusseerabad in Rajpotana, and during seven years of her stay in India, had never seen a Clergyman, or had an opportunity of going to Church. This was, however, a less tedious excommunication than has been the lot of a very good and religious man, resident at Tiperah, or somewhere in that neighbourhood, who was for nineteen years together the only Christian within seventy miles, and at least 300 from any place of worship. Occasionally he has gone to receive the Sacrament at Chittagong, about as far as from his residence as York from London. These are sad stories, and in the case of Nusseerabad, I hope, not beyond the reach of a remedy.

July 6.—The Nawâb called this morning according to his promise, accompanied by his eldest son. He is a good looking elderly man, of so fair a complexion as to prove the care with which the descendants of the Mussulman conquerors have kept up their northern blood. His hands, more particularly, are nearly as white as those of an European. He sat for a good while smoking his hookah, and conversing fluently enough in English, quoting some English books of history, and shewing himself very tolerably acquainted with the events of the Spanish war, and the part borne in it by Sir Edward Paget.[1] His son is a man of about 30, of a darker complexion, and education more neglected, being unable to converse in English. The Nawâb told us of a fine wild elephant, which his people were then in pursuit of, within a few miles of Dacca. He said that they did not often come so near. He cautioned me against going amongst the ruins, except on an elephant, since tygers sometimes, and snakes always, abounded there. He asked me several pertinent questions as to the intended extent and object of my journey, and talked about the Greek priest, who, he said, wished to be introduced to me, and whom he praised as a very worthy, well-informed man. I asked him about the antiquities of Dacca, which he said were not very old, the city itself being a comparatively recent Mussulman foundation. He was dressed in plain white muslin, with a small gold tassel attached to his turban. His son had a turban of purple silk, ribbed with gold, with some jewels in it. Both had splendid diamond rings. I took good care to call the father 'his highness', a distinction of which Mr Master had warned me that he was jealous, and which he himself, I observed, was very careful always to pay him. At length pawn and attar of roses were brought to me, and I rose to give them to the visitors. The Nawâb smiled, and said, 'what has your Lordship learned our customs?' Our guests then rose, and Mr Master gave his arm to the Nawâb to lead him down stairs. The staircase was lined with attendants with silver sticks, and the horse-guards, as before, were round the carriage; this was evidently second-hand, having the arms of its former proprietor still on the pannel, and the whole shew was any thing but splendid. The Company's sepoys were turned out to present arms, and the Nawâb's own followers raised a singular sort of acclamation as he got into his carriage, reckoning up the titles of his family, 'Lion

[1] Paget served in the Peninsular War as a Lieutenant-General. He subsequently became Governor of Ceylon, and in 1823 Commander-in-chief of the forces in the East.

of War!' 'Prudent in Counsel!' 'High and Mighty prince', &c.
&c. But the thing was done with little spirit, and more like the
proclamations of a crier in an English court of justice, than a ceremony in which any person took an interest. I was, however,
gratified throughout the scene by seeing the humane (for it was
even more than good natured) respect, deference, and kindness,
which in every word and action Mr Master shewed to this poor
humbled potentate. It could not have been greater, or in better
taste, had its object been an English prince of the blood.

July 8.—In the afternoon I accompanied Mr Master to pay a
visit to the Nawâb, according to appointment. We drove a considerable way through the city, then along a shabby avenue of
trees intermingled with huts, then through an old brick gate-way
into a sort of wild-looking close, with a large tree and some bushes
in the centre, and ruinous buildings all round. Here was a company of Sepoys, drawn up to receive us, very neatly dressed and
drilled, being in fact a detachment of the Company's local
Regiment, and assigned to the Nawâb as a guard of honour. In
front was another and really handsome gateway, with an open
gallery, where the 'Nobut', or evening martial music, is performed, a mark of sovereign dignity, to which the Nawâb never
had a just claim, but in which Government continue to indulge
him. Here were the Nawâb's own guard, in their absurd coats
and caps, and a crowd of folk with silver sticks, as well as two
tonjons[1] and chahtahs,[2] to convey us across the inner court. This
was a little larger than the small quadrangle at All Souls, surrounded with low and irregular, but not inelegant buildings, kept
neatly, and all whitewashed. On the right-hand was a flight of
steps leading to a very handsome hall, an octagon, supported by
gothic arches, with a verandah round it, and with high gothic
windows well venetianed. The octagon was fitted up with a large
round table covered with red cloth, mahogany drawing-room
chairs, two large and handsome convex mirrors, which shewed
the room and furniture to considerable advantage, two common
pier-glasses, some prints of the king, the emperor Alexander,
lords Wellesley and Hastings, and the duke of Wellington, and

---

[1] A kind of sedan-chair. [2] Umbrellas.

two very good portraits, by Chinnery,[1] of the Nawâb himself, and the late Nawâb his brother. Nothing was gaudy, but all extremely respectable and noblemanly. The Nawâb, his son, his English secretary, and the Greek priest whom he had mentioned to me, received us at the door, and he led me by the hand to the upper end of the table. We sate some time, during which the conversation was kept up better than I expected; and I left the palace a good deal impressed with the good sense, information, and pleasing manners of our host, whose residence considerably surpassed my expectations, and whose court had nothing paltry, except his horse-guards and carriage. The visit ended in an invitation to dinner, but without fixing a day. I said I should be happy, and hinted that an early day would suit me best. So that it does not delay my journey, I shall like it very well.

July 22. —A—long interval has occurred, during which I have had neither time nor heart to continue my journal, having been closely occupied in attending the sick and dying bed of my excellent and amiable friend, Stowe, and in the subsequent necessary duties of taking care of his interment and property. She for whose eyes I write these pages, will gladly spare me a repetition of the sad story of his decline, death, and burial.

On Saturday, the 9th, I confirmed about twenty persons, all adults, and almost all of the higher ranks. On the following Sunday I consecrated the Church. This perhaps ought, in strictness, to have preceded the Confirmation; but the inversion afforded the Catechumens an immediate opportunity of attending the Lord's Supper, of which they all availed themselves, as well, I believe, as all the other inhabitants of the station. The whole number of communicants was 34 or 5, and I never witnessed a congregation more earnestly attentive. On this occasion poor Stowe was to have preached, but that duty now devolved on me.

In the evening I consecrated the burial ground; a wild and dismal place, surrounded by a high wall, with an old Moorish gateway, at the distance of about a mile from the now inhabited part of the city, but surrounded with a wilderness of ruins and

[1] George Chinnery, 1766–1852. Much of his work was done in India.

jungle. It is, however, large and well adapted for its purpose, containing but few tombs, and those mostly of old dates, erected during the days of Dacca's commercial prosperity, and while the number of European residents was more considerable than it is at present.

One evening I drove with Mr Master to see the prisons. The first we visited was a place of confinement for the insane, which the humanity of government provides in every district. There were altogether a considerable number, the curable and incurable, the male and female, separated in distinct wards, under the care of the Surgeon of the station and several native Doctors. The place was airy, well suited to the climate, and the prisoners seemed well treated, though when I praised their cleanliness, Mr Master observed, that he feared they knew we were coming. The patients, however, when asked it they had any complaints, only urged (which some of them did very fluently) that they were unjustly confined, and could prove themselves either to have been never mad, or now to be quite recovered. Two only seemed dangerous, and were kept in small grated cells, though several had light handcuffs on. One of these talked incessantly with violent gesticulations, menacing his keepers through his bars; the other was a gloomy and sullen wretch, stretched out on his mat, but now and then uttering a few low words, which Mr Master said were bitter curses. The first was a Brahmin schoolmaster, and had murdered his brother; the second was in a decent rank of society, and had repeatedly attempted the lives of his wife and children. Melancholy or mere fatuity seemed the most general characters which the disease assumed. Mad persons may be sent hither by their friends, on payment of a small sum, or, if poor, by the 'Daroga' of each 'pergunnah', (the superintendant of a district)[1] whose duty it is to apprehend and send to the district asylum, any dangerous or disgusting object of this kind who may be at large.

The prison was very well arranged, with roomy wards, dry and airy apartments, and permission given once a day to all the prisoners to go out on a large plain, within a low outer wall, to

[1] More precisely, the superintendent of police in the sub-division of a district.

dress their victuals. This indulgence indeed, joined to the lowness of even the main wall, makes it necessary to keep them all in irons, but that is, in this climate, a far less evil than a closer confinement, or the increased interruption of the fresh air. The prisoners complained loudly that their allowances were not sufficient. Mr Master told me that the present dearth of rice, made them, indeed, far less than they used to be, but that the original scale was too high, and more than a man could earn by labour. Some Burmans were here, and the only persons not handcuffed (except the debtors). They had been taken in the Company's territory, not in arms, but unable to give any good account of themselves, and therefore supposed to be spies. They seemed, however, poor simple peasants, and Mr Master said, he had recommended government to discharge them, since in truth, there had always been a little smuggling trade on the Munnipoor[1] frontier for salt and ivory, and these men, he verily believed had no further or more sinister views. They were middle-sized, well made men, in complexion and countenance half-way between the Indian and Chinese, and a good deal tattooed. The debtors were numerous and very miserable objects. So long as they continue here, their creditors are bound to make them the same allowance as government makes to the criminals, but a Hindoo creditor, though murmuring grievously at this expense, is generally (Mr Master said, and Dr Carey had said the same thing before,) intensely cruel, and prefers the gratification of revenge, even to that of avarice. Several of the debtors here were very old men, and some had been kept many years in prison.

July 20.—I went to pay my farewell visit to the Nawâb, who had been really more than civil. Almost every day during the last week, he had sent baskets of fruit, dressed dishes and pastry, some (which is a common eastern compliment) for my own dinner, others with a special recommendation for my sick friend. All the return I could make, and it was one which I heartily pray God in his goodness may make useful, was the present of my Hindoo-stanee prayer-book, which, being splendidly bound, and containing much which a Mussulman would not dislike, I cast 'like

---

[1] Manipur—a state in the hills between Assam and Burma.

bread on the waters', though I fear on a stormy sea, and one turbid with gross indulgences and prejudices. Poor old man! I should rejoice to learn that he had sometimes looked into its pages. This he voluntarily promised to do in his last visit, and as we were alone, we had a good deal of talk about politics and other things, in the course of which he desired I would sometimes write to him. He then said, ' I am not going to offer you a valuable present, but only trifles which are here common, but which in Europe would be curiosities. This muslin I do hope you will offer in my name to your lady, and instead of your present stick, now that you are lame (I had not quite recovered the effects of the sun on my legs)[1] that you will walk with my cane.' Of the former I am no judge, the latter is very pretty, of a solid piece of ivory, beautifully carved. It is too fine for me to walk with, but I shall always value it. I was received and dismissed on this, as on the former occasion, with presented arms.

Bishop Heber left Dacca on 22 July and started his long voyage up the Ganges to Allahabad.

July 23.—We commenced our journey this morning with unusual alertness, but ere long it was interrupted. A sudden turn of the river exposed us, about 12 at noon, to so strong a contrary wind, that after a few trials the men declared they could not proceed, and begged leave to get their dinner, in the hope that the breeze might moderate. I was not sorry for this delay, as I hoped to receive information from Dacca which might set me at liberty to go directly northward, but letters arrived which to my great sorrow established the fact that Miss Stowe[2] was on her way to Dacca, and made it adviseable for me to push on to meet her as fast as possible. I put, therefore, into immediate force the magic of my own silver sticks, and the potent talisman of brass which adorned the girdle of the Chuprassee[3] whom Mr Master had ordered to accompany me to Hajygunge, and sent to the jemaut-dar[4] of the nearest village a requisition for twenty men to drag my

[1] They had been badly sunburnt during the final stages of Heber's voyage to Dacca.
[2] The sister of the Bishop's late chaplain.
[3] Messenger.   [4] Village head-man.

boats, with the information at the same time, that the service would not be, as I fear it often is in this country, gratuitous. No sooner, however, were the messengers seen approaching, than half the village, fearing that it was some Government duty which was required, were seen running away to hide themselves, and it was not till the jemautdar had gone round to explain matters to some of their wives, that any tolerable workmen made their appearance. At last the prescribed number arrived, and we began moving with tolerable rapidity, and continued advancing prosperously till nine o'clock at night, when the twenty men were extremely well satisfied with two rupees among them! and willingly promised to attend next morning, so cheap is labour in this part of India. An event has occurred on the Matabunga since we traversed-it, which shews the low state of morality among the peasants of India, and how soon and how surely a sudden temptation will transform the most peaceable into banditti. A large boat attached to the gun-boats which arrived the other day at Dacca from Calcutta, loaded with ammunition, got aground pretty near the same place where we had the bank cut through. The country people were called in to assist in getting her off, very likely from the same village whose inhabitants we found so diligent and serviceable. The ammunition, however, was packed in cases resembling those in which treasure is usually conveyed in this country, and in consequence as is supposed of this mistake, the boat, being by the accident separated from the fleet, was attacked the following night by (as is said) near 300 people, armed with spears, bamboos, hoes, and whatever else a tumultuary insurrection usually resorts to. They were repulsed by the Sepoys with difficulty, and not till several had been shot. The affair made a great noise in Dacca, nothing of the kind having been heard of for many years in that neighbourhood. A commission had gone to the spot to enquire into the case, and one of the small neighbouring Zemindars was said to be in custody. Natives, Mr Master said, are often pillaged, and travel always in more or less danger. But Decoits[1] seldom venture on an European boat, and still more rarely on a vessel in the Company's service, and guarded by soldiers.

[1] Robbers or brigands.

Bengal

Two days later Heber arrived at Faridpur, where he met E. L. Warner, the local magistrate.

July 25.—Mr Warner I find had not heard a word of the alleged attack on the Company's boats on these waters. Such a thing might, he said, have occurred in the Kishnagur district without his hearing of it, but he conceived it must have been greatly exaggerated. He said that the Indians can never tell a story without excessive falsification one way or the other. He had frequently had cases of assault brought before him, in which the plaintiff at first stated that he had been attacked and nearly killed by above a hundred men, when it turned out that he had received a beating from one or two men, twenty or thirty others being possibly present, (as in a village or market) but taking no part in the quarrel. In the same way if a house of a boat is robbed, the complainant generally exaggerates the number of Decoits to any multitude which he may think likely to excite the magistrate's attention and pity. Nevertheless there was, he said, a great deal of gang robbery, very nearly resembling the riband-men of Ireland,[1] but unmixed with any political feeling, in all these provinces. It is but too frequent for from five to ten peasants to meet together as soon as it is dark, to attack some neighbour's house, and not only plunder, but torture him, his wife and children, with horrible cruelty, to make him discover his money. These robbers in the day-time follow peaceable professions, and some of them are thriving men, while the whole firm is often under the protection of a Zemindar, who shares the booty, and does his best to bring off any of the gang who may fall into the hands of justice, by suborning witnesses to prove an alibi, bribing the inferior agents of the police, or intimidating the witnesses for the prosecution. In this way many persons are suspected of these practices, who yet go on many years in tolerably good esteem with their neighbours, and completely beyond the reach of a government which requires proof in order to punish. Mr Warner thinks the evil has increased since the number of spirit shops has spread so rapidly. At present these places bring in a very considerable

[1] The Ribbonmen were members of a Roman Catholic secret society which flourished especially in the north of Ireland in the early nineteenth century, in rivalry with the Orangemen.

revenue to government, and are frequented by multitudes both of the Hindoo and Mussulman population. They are generally, however, resorted to at night, and thus the drunkenness, the fierce and hateful passions which they engender, lead naturally to those results which night favours, at the same time that they furnish convenient places of meeting for all men who may be banded for an illicit purpose. I asked what the brahmins said to this. He answered that the brahmins themselves were many of them drunkards, and some of them Decoits, and that he thought what influence they retained was less for good or moral restraint, than evil. Yet he said that they had a good deal of influence still, while this had been quite lost by the Mussulman Imams[1] and Moulahs.[2] He spoke, however, favourably of the general character of the people, who are, he said, gentle, cheerful, and industrious, these great crimes being, though unhappily more common than in Europe, yet certainly not universal. He had learned from different circumstances, more of the internal economy of the humbler Hindoo families than many Europeans do, and had formed a favourable opinion of their domestic habits and happiness. As there is among the cottagers no seclusion of women, both sexes sit together round their evening lamps in very cheerful conversation, and employ themselves either in weaving, spinning, cookery, or in playing at a kind of dominos. He says it is untrue that the women in these parts, at least, are ignorant of sewing, spinning, or embroidery, inasmuch as, while the trade of Dacca flourished, the sprigs, &c. which we see on its muslins, were very often the work of female hands.[3] This is a strange and blended tissue of human life and human character! which it is most painful to hear of, since one cannot contemplate the evening enjoyments of a happy and virtuous family, such as is described, without anticipating the possibility of their cottage being made during the night, a scene of bloodshed, torture, and massacre. Yet, alas! can we forget that in all these respects, India is too like Ireland!

August 1.—At Surdah is one of the Company's silk manufactures, and the river on which it stands is also the usual route

---

[1] Prayer-leaders at mosques. [2] Muslim leader.
[3] In some parts of Bengal needlework was regarded as work for men.

from Dacca to the upper provinces. We here stood directly up the
Ganges in a north-west direction, favoured by a little breeze. The
crew on leaving the shore set up as usual, though I believe I never
before mentioned it, their cry of 'Allah hu Allah'. I cannot help
admiring in the Mussulmans the manner in which their religion
apparently mixes itself with every action of their lives, and though
it is but too true that all this has a tendency to degenerate into
mere form or cant, or even profanation of holy things, for the
constant use of God's name in the manner in which some of them
use it, scarcely differs from swearing, it might be well if Christians
learned from them to keep their faith and hope more continually
in their minds, and more frequently on their lips than the greater
number of them do. Above all, it seems to be an error, particularly in a heathen country, to act as if we were ashamed of our
religion, to watch the servants out of the room before we kneel
down to our prayers, or to dissemble in secular matters the hope
and trust which we really feel in Providence. By the way, it is
only during this journey that I have had occasion to observe how
strictly the Mussulmans conform to the maxim of St James, to
say, 'if the Lord will, we shall live and do this or that'. All the
Mohammedans whom I have heard speak of their own purposes,
or any future contingencies, have qualified it with 'Insh Allah'.

Abdullah asked me if the Gunga was one of the rivers of
Paradise? I told him it was a difficult question, but that the four
rivers of Irak were generally supposed to be those meant by
Moses. I instanced the Frat and Dikkel, but had forgotten the
modern names of the other two. He seemed sorry the Ganges had
no chance, but expressed some satisfaction that he himself had
seen them all when with Sir Gore Ousley.[1] While passing
Surdah, I could easily distinguish a large brick building, with a
long range of tiled warehouses attached, which I was told was a
silk manufactory. Had it been another day I should have regretted
passing it unvisited. The Italian method of curing and managing
silk is practised here, having been introduced about 50 years ago,
by workmen brought from Italy at the Company's expense.
I know not whether it is now kept up with any spirit.

[1] Abdullah had been a servant of Sir Gore Ouseley, who had been sent to Iran
in 1811 as British Ambassador.

Bengal

We arrived at Bogwangola[1] between four and five, and stopped there for the night. I found the place very interesting, and even beautiful. A thorough Hindoo village, without either Europeans or Mussulmans, and a great part of the houses mere sheds or booths for the accommodation of the 'gomastas', (agents or supercargos) who come here to the great corn fairs, which are held, I believe, annually. They are scattered very prettily over a large green common, fenced off from the river by a high grassy mound, which forms an excellent dry walk, bordered with mango-trees, bamboos, and the date-palm, as well as some fine banians. The common was covered with children and cattle, a considerable number of boats were on the beach, different musical instruments were strumming, thumping, squeeling, and rattling from some of the open sheds, and the whole place exhibited a cheerfulness, and, though it was not the time of the fair, an activity and bustle which was extremely interesting and pleasing. The houses were most of them very small, but neat, with their walls of mats, which when new, always look well. One, in particular, which was of a more solid construction than the rest, and built round a little court, had a slip of garden surrounding its interior, filled with flowering shrubs, and enclosed by a very neat bamboo railing. Others were open all round, and here two parties of the fakir musicians, whose strains I had heard, were playing, while in a house near one of them were some females, whose gaudy dress and forward manner seemed pretty clearly to mark their profession as the Nâch girls[2] of the place.

Bogwangola has been several times, within these few years, removed to different situations in consequence of the havoc made by the Ganges. It has, therefore, no ancient building, and neither pagoda nor mosque of any kind that I could discover. Indeed it has the appearance rather of an encampment than a town, but is not on that account the less pretty.

August 4.—I saw, with a degree of pleasure which I did not anticipate, but which arose no doubt from the length of time during which I had been accustomed to a perfectly flat surface, a

---

[1] Bhagwangola.   [2] Dancing girls.

range of blue elevations on my right-hand. At first I watched them with distrust, fearing that they were clouds. They kept their ground, however, and I ran on deck to ask about them, and was told, as I expected, that they were the Rajmahâl hills. It is, I think, Jenny Deans who complains that, after she lost sight of Ingleborough in her way through Yorkshire, Nottinghamshire, and Lincolnshire, 'the haill country seemed to have been trenched

1   Boats on the Ganges

and levelled'.[1] But what would she have said if she had traversed Bengal? At the place where we stopped for the night there were some fine trees, but the rest of the country, for a considerable space, was mere sand, on which the peasants were raising a few patches of cucumbers and pulse. One of these men, who was pursuing his work by moonlight, told me that there had been a very large village on this spot, with its gardens, mango-orchards, meadows, &c.; but that the dreadful inundation of last year swept away every thing, and covered the place with sand, as we now saw it. I walked up and down this scene of desolation for some time,

[1]   W. Scott, *The heart of Midlothian.*

but found nothing to mark that any habitation had ever stood here. The sand lay smooth, yet wavy as we see it on a coast exposed to heavy seas, and there were no marks of any thing living or having lived, except some scattered sculls and bones of animals, probably brought from a distance by the terrible stream which had blotted out and hidden the community of this place. Abdullah who joined me, after making some enquiries about our morrow's course, said that the place was very like the deserts, not of Persia, which are stony, but of the Arabian Irak and the country near Bussorah. He observed, naturally enough, that this was a sad place to look upon, and this as naturally brought on a conversation about God's judgements, Hilleh and the Birz ul Nimrouz, or Babylon, and Nunya, or Nineveh.... He was less fortunate, however, in his attempt to account for the inundations of Gunga, which he ascribed, so far as I could understand him at all, to the combined influence of the north and south poles on the mountain Meru![1] I endeavoured to explain the matter a little better, but could not convince him that the Ganges did not rise immediately under the north pole. This is orthodox Hindoo geography, and it is curious to find that the Mussulmans in India have so completely adopted it.

[1] A mountain considered to be at the centre of the Hindu paradise; identified by some with the North Pole, and by others with a mountain in the Himalayas at the source of the Ganges. See also *infra*, pp. 142, 218, 222.

Part II

BIHAR

August 7.—[The Rajmahal Hills] in height as well as beauty, far exceed what I had expected. They rise from the flat surface of Bengal as out of the sea; a large waterfall is seen from a very considerable distance tumbling down the mountain in several successive cascades, that nearest the plain of very considerable height.

The people of these mountains, and of all the hilly country between this place and Burdwan, are a race distinct from those of the plain in features, language, civilization, and religion. They have no castes, care nothing for the Hindoo deities, and are even said to have no idols. They are still more naked than the Hindoo peasants, and live chiefly by the chace, for which they are provided with bows and arrows, few of them having fire-arms. Their villages are very small and wretched, but they pay no taxes, and live under their own chiefs under British protection. A deadly feud existed, till within the last 40 years, between them and the cultivators of the neighbouring lowlands, they being untamed thieves and murderers, continually making forays, and the Mahommedan Zemindars killing them like mad-dogs, or tygers, whenever they got them within gun-shot. An excellent young man, of the name of Cleveland, judge and magistrate of Bogli-poor,[1] undertook to remedy this state of things. He rigorously forbade, and promptly punished, all violence from the Zemindars (who were often the aggressors) against the Puharree[2] (Mountaineers); he got some of these last to enter his service, and took pains to attach them to him, and to learn their language. He made shooting parties into the mountains, treating kindly all whom he could get to approach him, and established regular bazars at the

[1] Bhagalpur. [2] Pahari.

villages nearest to them, where he encouraged them to bring down for sale game, millet, wax, hides, and honey, all which their hills produce in great abundance. He gave them wheat and barley for seed, and encouraged their cultivation by the assurance that they should not be taxed, and that nobody but their own chiefs should be their Zemindars. And, to please them still further, and at the same time to keep them in effectual order, and to bring them more into contact with their civilized neighbours, he raised a corps of Sepoys from among them, which he stationed at Sicligully,[1] and which enabled him not only to protect the peaceable part of them, but to quell any disturbances which might arise, with a body of troops accustomed to mountain warfare. This good and wise man died in 1784, in the 29th year of his age. A monument was raised to his memory near Boglipoor, at the joint expense of the highland Chiefs and lowland Zemindars, which still remains in good repair, having been endowed by them with some lands for its maintenance. A garrison of these Mountaineers, which was then kept up at Sicligully, has been since discontinued; the corps being considerably reduced in numbers, and partly quartered at Boglipoor, partly during the late call for men, at Berhampoor. Archdeacon Corrie's principal business at Boglipoor was to learn whether any encouragement existed for forming a mission among these people. Their being free from the yoke of caste seems to make them less unlikely to receive the Gospel, than the bigotted inhabitants of the plains.

August 10.—I arrived at Boglipoor, or Bhaugulpoor, about 7 o'clock in the morning, and found, to my great joy, my friends the Corries still there, established very comfortably in the circuit house (a bungalow provided in each of the minor stations for the district judges when on their circuit), which had been lent them by the judge and magistrate Mr Chalmers.[2] I breakfasted with them, and went afterwards with Mr Chalmers to see the objects principally worth notice,—the gaol, a very neat and creditable building, with no less than six wards for the classification of the

[1] Sakrigali.

[2] W. A. Chalmers: appointed Judge and Magistrate of Bhagalpur in 1821; died 1826.

prisoners, Mr Cleveland's house and monument, and a school
established for the Puharrees by Lord Hastings. Mr Cleveland's
monument is in the form of a Hindoo mut, in a pretty situation on
a green hill. The land with which it was endowed, is rented by
government, and the cutcherry,[1] magistrate's-house, circuit-
house, &c. are built on it, the rent being duly appropriated to the
repair of the building. As being raised to the memory of a
Christian, this last is called by the natives 'Grige', (Church) and
they still meet once a year in considerable numbers, and have a
handsome 'Poojah', or religious spectacle in honour of his
memory.

2   Cleveland's monument

The school is adjoining to the lines, and occupies a large and
neat bungalow, one room in which is the lodging of the schoolmaster, a very handsome and intelligent half-caste youth; the
other, with a large verandah all round, was, when I saw it, filled
with Puharree Sepoys and their sons, who are all taught to read,
write, and cypher in the Kythee[2] character, which is that used by
the lower classes in this district for their common intercourse,
accounts, &c. and differs from the Devanagree[3] about as much as
the written character of Western Europe does from its printed.
The reason alleged for giving this character the preference is its
utility in common life, but this does not seem a good reason for

---

[1] Court-house.   [2] Kaithi.
[3] The script used for Sanskrit and Hindi.

teaching it only, or even for beginning with it. No increase of knowledge, or enlargement of mind, beyond the power of keeping their accounts and writing a shop-bill, can be expected from it, inasmuch as there is no book whatever printed in it, except Mr Rowe's spelling-book, and no single Hindoo work of any value or antiquity written in it. I urged this to the schoolmaster, who said that by and by, when they had made some progress in the Kythee he might teach them the Nagree, but they might, I am convinced, easily learn both together, or if one at a time, then the printed character, as simpler, is to be preferred. In the Kythee I heard several, both men and boys, read fluently, and I could understand their Hindoostanee very well. They are described as quick and intelligent, fond of learning, and valuing themselves on their acquirements. This school was originally set on foot by Cleveland, but till Lord Hastings' visit had been shamefully neglected by his successors in office. It was revived by Lord Hastings, and is now very carefully and judiciously attended to by the Adjutant, Captain Graham,[1] an intelligent Scots officer, on whom the whole management of the corps has, for the last five years, devolved, the commanding officer, Captain Montgomerie,[2] being in the last stage of a decline. The corps consisted originally of 1300 men, who for many years were armed with their country weapons, the bow and arrow. And it is an instance of Cleveland's sound judgement and discrimination, that he named for their first native commandant, in opposition to the remonstrances and intreaties of all the Zemindars of the place, a chief named Jowrah, who was the Rob Roy, or, perhaps more strictly speaking, the Roderic Dhu[3] of the Rajmahâls, the most popular of all others among his own countrymen, and the most dreaded by the lowlanders. The choice was fully justified by the event, Jowrah having remained through life a bold, active, and faithful servant of the Company in different enterprises against outlaws, both in the Ramghur hills and his own mountains. After some years the men were armed with muskets instead of bows, and are now in all respects on the same footing with other native regiments, and equally available for general service. It had become a mere rabble,

---

[1] John Graham (1787–1859).   [2] Archibald Montgomerie (1784–1826).
[3] W. Scott, *The lady of the lake.*

addicted to all sorts of vice and disorder till Lord Hastings placed them on their present footing. In the first instance, he proposed to arm two companies with rifles, but the men disliked the service exceedingly, having a great objection to wear green; they now therefore are fusileers, but trained to light infantry manœuvres, in which they are said to excel. Their numbers, however, are reduced from 1300 to 700, of whom 200 are not genuine mountaineers, but Hindoos from the plain,—a mixture which is not found advantageous to the former, and which must, from their superstitions, materially impede the efficiency of the unfettered and unprejudiced Puharree; these last are said to be admirably adapted for soldiers, and to be very fond of the profession. Having no caste, and eating any food indiscriminately, they would be available for foreign service at a shorter notice than any Hindoo could be; accustomed to mountains and jungles, they would be extremely valuable on the eastern and northern frontier, as well as on the Nerbuddah and in Berar, and in the possible event of any general insurrection in India, it might be of great political importance to have a force of native troops who prefer (as these do) the English to the Hindoos, and whose native country occupies a strong and central place in the British territory,—a sort of little Tyrol.

At the school I met the present native commandant, one of Mr Cleveland's surviving pupils, an old man, much reverenced by his countrymen, and who passes a great deal of his time there, being extremely proud of his people, and interested in their improvement. He has also the character of a smart and intelligent soldier. His influence has been very valuable in getting the school together again, much pains having been taken by a Portuguese or two in the neighbourhood to dissuade the Puharrees from attending, or sending their children. Even now, though many of the younger children of the mountain-chiefs are sent, the eldest sons are kept away, owing to a notion circulated among them by these people, that they would forfeit the reversion of their pensions by receiving any benefit from the Company of another kind. This is an utter mistake, which Mr Chalmers hopes to rectify, but it has already done some harm. Captain Graham is very popular among them, and by all which I hear most deservedly so, and when once or twice he has talked of leaving them for some other regiment, they have expressed exceeding distress and concern. Those whom I saw, were middle sized, or rather little men, but extremely well made, with remarkably broad chests, long arms and clean legs. They are fairer, I think, than the Bengalees, have broad faces, small eyes, and flattish, or rather turned up noses; but the Chinese or Malay character of their features, from whom they are said to be descended, is lost in a great degree on close inspection. I confess they reminded me of the Welch; the expression of their countenances is decidedly cheerful and intelligent, and I thought two or three of their women whom I saw, really pretty, with a sort of sturdy smartness about them which I have not seen in their lowland neighbours. These tribes have a regular administration of justice among themselves, by the ancient Hindoo institution of a ' Punchaet', or jury of five old men in every village, and as I mentioned before, they remain free from all taxes, and are under the government of their own chiefs, but in all other respects, they were great sufferers by Mr Cleveland's death; all his plans for teaching them the simple manufactures, as well as for furnishing them with seeds and implements of husbandry, fell with him. Even the school was dropped. The pensions which had been promised to the Hill Chiefs in consideration of their maintaining peace and the authority of the Company in their districts, though regularly paid by the Supreme Government, never reached their destination, being embezzled on various pretences. And the old encroachments of the Zemindars on their frontiers were allowed to be renewed with impunity. The only man who, during this interval, appears to have done his duty towards these people, was Lieutenant (afterwards Colonel) Shaw, who was appointed to the command of the Rangers in 1787, and whose memory is still highly respected by them. He published an account (which I have not seen) of their customs, in an early volume of the Asiatic Researches.[1]

Lord and Lady Hastings went on a short excursion into the hills in their return from the upper country, and were greatly interested by them and their highlands. Lord Hastings promised

---

[1] Thomas Shaw, 'On the Inhabitants of the Hills near Rajmahall', *Asiatic Researches*, iv, Calcutta, 1795, 45–107.

their chiefs to send a good stock of the most useful tools of husbandry (they have at present no implements of this kind but sharpened stakes) and a quantity of seed potatoes. He did not forget the promise, and Captain Graham heard him give orders for its performance after his return to Calcutta. But a Sovereign can seldom do all the good he desires; nothing in fact was done, and the chiefs have since more than once complained that they were forgotten. They are, however, better off now than at any time since the death of Cleveland, for Mr Chalmers, who is an active and honourable man, has seen justice done to them in the payment of their little stipends, which had frequently been embezzled on various pretences by the native agents, and Government are making a fresh survey of the debateable land, with a view to an equitable arrangement of the claims both of the Puharrees and the Zemindars, by which it is said the former will be great gainers. Mr Chalmers, and Captain Graham, with Colonel Franklin, well known as an excellent Oriental scholar and antiquarian,[1] who is inspecting field-officer of this district, think very favourably of the Puharrees. Notwithstanding their poverty, their living chiefly by the chace and always going armed, the general conduct both of chiefs and people has been orderly and loyal ever since their fathers swore allegiance. They are hospitable according to their small means, and have no sort of objection to eat with or after Europeans. They are a little too fond of spirits, a taste which Cleveland unfortunately encouraged, by sending them presents of the kind, and allowing them to drink when at his house. Though accustomed to make predatory inroads on their lowland and here-ditary enemies, among themselves they have always been honest, and what is an immense distinction indeed between them and the Hindoos, they hate and despise a lie more than most nations in the world. The soldiers who have committed any fault, own it readily, and either ask pardon or submit to their punishment in silence; in the Cutcherry, the evidence of a Puharree is always trusted more than that of half a dozen Hindoos, and there is hardly any instance on record of a chief violating his word. Though dirty in their persons in comparison with the Hindoos, they are very clean in

[1] William Franklin (1763–1839); author of *Inquiry concerning the site of the ancient Palibothra*, *The history of the reign of Shah Aulam*, and other works.

their cottages, and their villages are kept free from the vile smells which meet us in those of Bengal. The men dislike hard work, and are chiefly occupied in hunting, but the women are very industrious in cultivating the little patches of garden round their villages. They are also generally chaste, and it no doubt contributes to keep them so, that the premature and forced marriages of the Hindoos are unknown; that their unions take place at a suitable age, and that the lad has generally to wait on the lass during a pretty long courtship. They make very good and faithful household servants, but are not fond of the way of life, and do not agree well with their Hindoo fellow domestics. Both men and women are intelligent and lively, but rather passionate, and they differ from most of the Hindoos, in being fond of music, and having a good ear. Captain Graham has instructed some of their boys as fifers, and found them apt scholars. They are fond of pedigree and old stories, and their chiefs pique themselves on their families. No clanship, or feudal subjection, however, appears to exist. If a man is dissatisfied with the head of his village, there is nothing to prevent his removal to another. In short, Emily,[1] they are *Welch*, and one of these days I will take you into their hills, to claim kindred with them!

Mr Corrie has obtained a little vocabulary of their language, which, certainly, differs very remarkably from the Hindoostanee, and I am told from the Bengalee. The old commandant, who has been on service towards the Berar frontier, says he could converse perfectly with the Bheels and Gooand[2] tribes, so that they are apparently different branches of the same great family, which pervades all the mountainous centre of India, the 'Gaels' of the East, who have probably, at some remote period, been driven from all but these wildernesses, by the tribes professing the brahminical faith.

The following is Captain Graham's account of their religion. The Hill-people offer up frequent prayers to one Supreme Being, whom they call 'Budo Gosaee', which in their language means 'Supreme God'. Prayer to God is strictly enjoined morning and evening. They also offer up propitiatory sacrifices of buffaloes,

---

[1] The Bishop's wife, Amelia.
[2] Bhils and Gonds. For the Bhils, see *infra*, Part VII.

goats, fowls, and eggs to several inferior, and some evil deities.

'Malnad' is the tutelary genius of each village; 'Dewannee' the household god. 'Pow' is sacrificed to before undertaking a journey. They appear to believe in a future state of rewards and punishments chiefly carried on by means of transmigration, the souls of the good being sent back to earth in the bodies of great men, and those of the wicked in brutes and even trees.

The great God made every thing. Seven brothers were sent to possess the earth; they give themselves the credit of being descended from the eldest, and say that the sixth was the father of the Europeans. Each brother was presented, on setting out, with a portion of the particular kind of food which he and his descendants were to eat. But the eldest had a portion of every kind of food, and in a *dirty dish*. This legend they allege as their reason for observing no restriction of meats, and for eating with or after any body. They say they are strictly forbidden by God to beat, abuse, or injure their neighbours, and that a lie is the greatest of all crimes. Hogs' blood appears to answer with them all the purposes which holy-water does with some other nations. If a person is killed by a tyger, it is the duty of his relations to avenge his death by killing one of those animals in return, on which occasion they resort to many strange ceremonies. They are great believers in witchcraft; every ache which the old commandant feels in his bones, and every disappointment or calamity which befalls him or any of his friends, he imputes to this cause, and menaces or bribes some old woman or other. They have also many interpreters of dreams among them, whom they call 'Damauns', and believe to be possessed by a familiar spirit. When any of these die, they expose his body, without burial, in the jungle. They also suppose certain diseases to be inflicted by evil spirits, to whom they expose the bodies of such as die of them, those who die of small-pox are cast out into the woods, those who die of dropsy into the water.

They have no idols or images of any kind; a black stone found in the hills, is by some ceremonies consecrated and used as an altar. They have several festivals which are held in high reverence. The Chitturia is the greatest, but seldom celebrated on account of its expense. It lasts five days, during which buffaloes, hogs, fruits, fowls, grains, and spirits are offered up to the gods, and afterwards feasted on. This is the only festival in which females are permitted to join. During its continuance they salute nobody, all honour being then appropriated to the gods. Polygamy is not forbidden, but seldom practised. The bridegroom gives a feast on occasion of the marriage; the bride's father addresses a speech to him, exhorting him to use his daughter well; the bridegroom then marks her forehead with red paint, links his little finger in hers, and leads her to his house. The usual mode of making oath is to plant two arrows in the ground, the person swearing taking the blade of one and the feather of the other between his finger and thumb. On solemn occasions, however, salt is put on the blade of a sabre, and after the words of the oath are repeated, the blade being placed on the under lip of the person sworn, the salt is washed into his mouth by him who administers it.

Thus far I have learnt from Captain Graham; Mr Corrie tells me that further particulars of this interesting race are given in the Calcutta Annual Register for 1821;[1] what follows I learnt from different persons in the course of the day.

The Hill country is very beautiful, and naturally fertile, but in many parts of it there is a great scarcity of water, a want which the people urge as an excuse for their neglect of bathing. As so much rain falls, this might and would by a civilized people be remedied, but the Puharrees neither make tanks, nor have any instrument proper for digging wells. The thick jungle makes the hills unwholesome to Europeans during the rains, but at other times the climate is extremely agreeable, and in winter more than agreeably cold. Mr Chalmers one night had a jug of water completely frozen over to a considerable thickness in his tent, and close to his bed. The Puharrees are a healthy race, but the small-pox used to make dreadful ravages among them. Vaccination has now been generally introduced; they were very thankful for it, bringing their children from thirty and fifty miles off to Boglipoor to obtain it. Wild animals of all kinds are extremely abundant, from the

[1] W. Franklin, 'A Journey from Bhaugulpoor through the Raj Muhal Hills in the months of December and January 1820–1'; *Calcutta Annual Register*, 1821, Chapter v, 1–13.

jackall to the tyger, and from the deer to the elephant and rhinoceros. Their way of destroying the large animals is, generally, by poisoned arrows. The poison is a gum which they purchase from the Garrows,[1] a people who inhabit the mountains to the north of Silhet, at Peer-pointee[2] fair.

No attempt has yet been made to introduce them to the knowledge of Christianity. The school at Boglipoor has scarcely been in activity for more than 18 months, and being supported by Government, it cannot, in conformity with the policy which they pursue, be made a means of conversion. Mr Corrie is strongly disposed to recommend the establishment of a Missionary at Boglipoor; but I am myself inclined to prefer sending him immediately, (or as soon as he may have gained some knowledge of the Puharree language), into one of the mountain villages. I also would wish to employ some person to accompany the Missionary or Schoolmaster, who may instruct the natives in weaving or pottery; and to choose, in either of these capacities, some one who had himself a little knowledge of gardening. Civilization and instruction will thus go hand in hand,—or rather, the one will lead the way to the other, and they will think the better of a religion whose professors are seriously active in promoting their temporal interests. The Puharrees seem to have no prejudices hostile to Christianity, any other than those which men will always have against a system of religion which requires a greater degree of holiness than they find it convenient to practise. The discreet exertions of Missionaries among them will give no offence either to Hindoos or Mussulmans, and a beginning may thus be made to the introduction both of Christianity and civilization, through all the kindred tribes of Gundwana and the Western Bheels, who are, at this moment, in the same habits of rapine and savage anarchy which the Puharrees were in before the time of Cleveland.[3]

August 12.—We passed this morning an encampment of gypseys... The name by which they go in this country is

---

[1] The Garos, of the Assam hills.　　　[2] Pirpainti.

[3] Shortly after this the S.P.G. missionary Thomas Christian was stationed at Bhagalpur, and he started to work among the Paharis. He died however in 1827.

'Kunja'. The men, many of them, wore large pink turbans; three of the women, and the children, followed us begging. These did not conceal their faces, and indeed had no clothes at all, except a coarse kind of veil thrown back from the shoulders, and a wretched ragged cloth wrapped round their waists like a petticoat. They are decidedly a taller handsomer race than the Bengalee. One of the women was very pretty, and the forms of all three were such as a sculptor would have been glad to take as his model. Their arms were tattooed with many blue lines, and one of them had her forehead slightly marked in a similar manner. They had no bangles on their wrists and ankles, but the children, though perfectly naked, were not without these ornaments. As we could not stop our boat, I rolled up some pice in paper, and gave it to one of the dandees to throw ashore. Unfortunately the paper burst, and the little treasure fell into the river, while the wind freshening at the moment, it was quite out of my power to give more. The dandees expressed great concern; indeed they are, to their narrow means, really charitable; they club a small portion of each mess every day, to give to the beggars who come to the ghâts,[1] and if none appear, they always throw it to some dog or bird. A more touching instance of this nature was told me by a lady, which she herself witnessed of in a voyage last year. The Serang of the boat by an accident lost his son, a fine young man. Every evening afterwards he set apart a portion, as if the young man were yet alive, and gave it in charity, saying, 'I have not given it, my son has given it!'

Monghyr stands on a rocky promontory, with the broad river on both sides, forming two bays, beyond one of which the Rajmahâl hills are visible, and the other is bounded by the nearer range of Curruckpoor. The town is larger than I expected, and in better condition than most native towns. Though all the houses are small, there are many of them with an upper story, and the roofs, instead of the flat terrace or thatch, which are the only alternations in Bengal, are generally sloping with red tiles, of the same shape and appearance with those which we see in Italian pictures; they have also little earthenware ornaments on their

---

[1] Steps for descending to a river or pond.

gables, such as I have not seen on the other side of Rajmahâl. The shops are numerous, and I was surprised at the neatness of the kettles, tea-trays, guns, pistols, toasting-forks, cutlery and other things of the sort, which may be procured in this tiny Birmingham. I found afterwards that this place had been from very early antiquity celebrated for its smiths, who derived their art from the Hindoo Vulcan, who had been solemnly worshipped, and was supposed to have had a workshop here. The only thing which appears to be wanting to make their steel excellent, is a better manner of smelting, and a more liberal use of charcoal and the hammer. As it is, their guns are very apt to burst, and their knives to break, precisely the faults which, from want of capital, beset the works of inferior artists in England. The extent, however, to which these people carry on their manufactures, and the closeness with which they imitate English patterns, shew plainly how popular those patterns are become among the natives.

August 13.—Mr Templer,[1] the judge and magistrate, break-fasted with me this morning, and gave me such an account of Monghyr and its spiritual concerns, as made me decide on staying over Sunday. There are besides his own family, five or six others here of the upper and middling classes, and above thirty old English pensioners, many of them married and with families, without any spiritual aid except what is furnished by a Baptist missionary, who is established here. Of him Mr Templer spoke very favourably, but said that the members of the Church of England, though in a manner compelled to attend his ministry, would value extremely an opportunity of attending divine service, and receiving the sacrament in their own way, while the number of children of different ages, whose parents might be expected to bring them for Baptism, was far from inconsiderable. I, therefore, requested Mr Templer to give publicity to my arrival, and intention of performing divine service on the Sunday. I dined with him, and he afterwards drove me through what is really one of the prettiest countries that I have seen, very populous, but cultivated in a rude and slovenly manner. The rent of the best land is about two rupees for a customary bega, nearly

[1] J. W. Templer: appointed Register of Bhagalpur and Joint-Magistrate stationed at Monghyr 1823.

equal to an English acre, or to three Bengalee begas. They get three crops in succession every year from the same lands, beginning with Indian corn, then sowing rice, between which, when it is grown to a certain height, they dibble in pulse, which rises to maturity after the rice is reaped. The district is very fertile, and most articles of production cheap. The people are quiet and industrious, and the offences which come before the magistrate both in number and character far less, and less atrocious, than is the case either in Bengal or farther on in Hindostan. Theft, forgery, and house-breaking, being the besetting sins of the one, and violent affrays, murders, and high-way robberies, being as frequent among the other people, and all being of very rare occurrence in the Jungleterry district. The peasants are more prosperous than in either, which may of itself account for their decency of conduct. But Mr Templer was inclined to ascribe both these advantages in a great degree to the fact, that the Zemindarries in this neighbourhood are mostly very large, and possessed by the representatives of ancient families, who by the estimation in which they are held, have the more authority over the peasants, and as being wealthy have less temptation to oppress them, or to connive at the oppression of others. Though a Zemindar of this kind has no legal control over his people, he possesses greater effective control, than a great land-owner in England exercises over his tenants. Most of them still hold cut-cherries, where they attend almost daily to hear complaints and adjust differences, and though doubtless oppressions may some-times occur in these proceedings, yet many quarrels are stifled there, and many mischievous persons discountenanced, who might else give much trouble to the magistrate.

In the upper parts of Bahar, and in the neighbourhood of Benares, the Zemindarries are small, and much divided between members of the same family. In consequence the peasants are racked to the utmost, and still farther harassed by the law-suits of the joint or rival owners, each sending their agents among them to persuade them to attorn to him, and frequently forcibly ejecting them from their farms unless they advanced money, so that they have sometimes to pay a half-year's rent twice or three times over. Nor are the small freeholders, of whom there are, it appears, great

numbers all over Bahar, so fortunate in their privileges as might
have been expected. They are generally wretchedly poor; they
are always involved in litigations of some kind or other, and there
is a tribe of Harpies, of a blended character between an informer
and a hedge-attorney, who make it their business to find out
either that there is a flaw in their original title, or that they have
forfeited their tenure by some default of taxes or service. These
free, or copy-holders, have been decidedly sufferers under Lord
Cornwallis's settlement,[1] as have also been a very useful description of people, the 'Thannadars', or native agents of police, whose
'Jaghires', or rent-free lands, which were their ancient and legal
provision all over India, were forgotten, and therefore seized by
the Zemindars, while the people themselves became dependent on
the charity of the magistrate, and degraded altogether from the
place which they used formerly to hold in the village society.
The permanent settlement was regarded by some as a very hasty
and ill-considered business. Many undue advantages were given
by it to the Zemindars, at the same time that even so far as they
were concerned, it was extremely unequal, and in many instances
oppressive. Like our old English land-tax, in some districts it
was ridiculously low, in others, though the increase of cultivation
had since brought the lands more up to the mark, it was first
ruinously high, so that, in fact, quite as many of the ancient
Zemindarrie families had been ruined, as had been enriched, while
taking all the districts together, the Company had been losers to
the amount of many millions. I should have supposed that by its
permanency at least, it had been the chief cause of the prodigious
extension of cultivation, which every body allows has occurred in
Bengal and Bahar since they were placed under the immediate
government of the Company. But that increase, I was told, might
be accounted for by other causes, such as the maintenance of
public peace, the perfect exemption from invasion and the march
of hostile armies, and the knowledge that a man was tolerably
sure of reaping the immediate fruits of his labour, and that the
acquisition of wealth did not expose him to the malignant

[1] The Permanent Settlement of Bengal (1793), under which the *zamindars* of
the province were recognised as landowners liable to pay rent to the Government
at a rate fixed for ever.

attention of government. In Bahar at least, the Zemindars had not, even yet, any real confidence in the permanence of the rate, and in fact there had been in so many instances revisions, re-measurements, re-examinations, and surcharges, that some degree of doubt was not unnatural. In all these cases, indeed, fraud on the part of the original contractors had been alleged by Government, but as some of the Bahar landlords had observed, they did not hear of any abatement made by the Company in those instances where the advantage of the bargain had been notoriously on their side, while, they also observed, so long as, in the recent measure adopted by Mr Adam, the government possessed and exercised the power of taxing the raw produce of the soil to any amount they pleased in its way to market, it was of no great advantage to the landholder that the direct land-tax remained the same.

On the whole, what I heard confirmed my previous suspicion, that the famous measure of Mr Law[1] was taken on an imperfect acquaintance with the interests of India, and that in the first instance at least, a decennial valuation, executed in a liberal spirit, would have avoided many inconveniences without losing any great advantage. Mr Templer surprised me by what he said of the size of farms in this part of India. A wealthy 'ryot', or peasant, on one of the large Zemindarries, often holds as much as 200 English acres.

August 14.—I had this morning one christening, and Mr Corrie had several. The child I christened was a very fine boy of two years old, the son of an invalid serjeant, who came, attended by his wife, a very pretty young half-caste, and by two of his comrades and one of their wives as sponsors. All these were very well-behaved decent old men; they stayed talking with me sometime; they spoke well of India, but complained of the want of some occupation for their minds. A lending library, they said, would be a great comfort to their little society. I afterwards mentioned the subject to Mr Templer, and, I hope, put him in the proper way to get one from Government, as well as a school for these poor men's children, such of them as, by any accident, were prevented from going to the Military Orphan Asylum.

[1] Thomas Law (1759–1834); the architect of the Permanent Settlement in Bihar.

I understand that these old soldiers are in general men of very decent character, and though poor, brought up their families very decently. Some of them, however, are liable to sudden fits of drunkenness or infatuation, sometimes after many months of sobriety, during which nothing can keep them from brandy so long as they have either money, credit, or clothes. Monghyr is the station generally chosen by the more respectable characters, the reprobates preferring Moorshedabad. The Company give them the choice of residing either at Moorshedabad, Monghyr, Buxar, or Chunar, and they sometimes change repeatedly before they fix.

In consequence of the intention I had expressed to have service to-morrow, Mr Templer told me that the Baptists had given notice that their own meeting should not open, so that he said we should probably have all the Christian residents of the place and vicinity. The Baptist congregation in this neighbourhood was first collected by Mr Chamberlain,[1] an excellent man and most active missionary, but of very bitter sectarian principles, and entertaining an enmity to the Church of England almost beyond belief. He used to say that Martyn, Corrie, and Thomason, were greater enemies of God, and did more harm to his cause, than fifty stupid drunken 'Padre....' inasmuch as their virtues, and popular conduct and preaching, upheld a system which he regarded as damnable, and which else must soon fall to the ground. The present preacher, Mr Lesley,[2] is a very mild, modest person, of a far better spirit, and scarcely less diligent among the Heathen than Chamberlain was. He has, however, as yet, had small success, having been but a very short time in the country. Mr J. Lushington,[3] whom I found here, has been detained some days, owing to the dandees belonging to the horse-boat running away, a practice very common on this river, these people getting their wages in advance, and then making off with them. One of the party asked Mr Lushington whether there had been any quarrel between the

[1] John Chamberlain worked as a missionary at several places in north India from 1803 until his death in 1821.

[2] Andrew Leslie; d. 1870.

[3] J. S. Lushington, who was to be Heber's companion on much of his journey through north India, was on his way to take up his appointment as assistant to the Political Agent at Ajmer. He died in 1832.

dandees and his servants, or himself; on his answering in the negative, it was observed that one fertile cause of boatmen's desertion was the ill-conduct of Europeans, who often stimulated them to do things which, in their weak and clumsy boats, were really dangerous, and, against all law or right, beat them when they refused or hesitated. A general-officer was some time since heard to boast, that when his cook-boat lagged behind, he always fired at it with ball! I suppose he took care to fire high enough, but the bare fact of putting unarmed and helpless men in fear, in order to compel them to endeavour to do what was, perhaps, beyond their power, was sufficiently unfeeling and detestable. They are, I suppose, such people as these who say that it is impossible to inspire the Hindoos with any real attachment for their employers!

August 15.—During this stay at Monghyr, I was advised by many old Indians to supply myself with spears to arm my servants with in our march. Colonel Francklyn particularly told me that the precaution was both useful and necessary, and that such a shew of resistance often saved lives as well as property. Monghyr, I was told, furnished better and cheaper weapons of the kind than any I should meet with up the country: they are, indeed, cheap enough, since one of the best spears may be had complete for 20 anas. I have consequently purchased a stock, and my cabin looks like a museum of Eastern weapons, containing eight of the best sort for my own servants, and eight more for the Clashees[1] who are to be engaged up the country. These last only cost 14 anas each. This purchase gave me a fair opportunity of examining the fire-arms and other things which were brought for sale. My eye could certainly detect no fault in their construction, except that the wood of the stocks was slight, and the screws apparently weak and irregular. But their cheapness was extraordinary; a very pretty single barrelled fowling-piece may be had for 20 S. rupees, and pistols for 16 the brace.

August 17.—We had a fine breeze part of the day, and stood over to the other bank, which we found, as I had expected, really

---

[1] Tent-pitchers.

very pretty, a country of fine natural meadows, full of cattle, and interspersed with fields of barley, wheat, and Indian corn, and villages surrounded by noble trees, with the Curruckpoor hills forming a very interesting distance. If the palm-trees were away, (but who would wish them away?) the prospect would pretty closely resemble some of the best parts of England. In the afternoon we rounded the point of the hills, and again found ourselves in a flat and uninteresting, though fruitful country. The last beautiful spot was a village under a grove of tall fruit-trees, among which were some fine walnuts; some large boats were building on the turf beneath them, and the whole scene reminded me forcibly of a similar builder's yard, which I had met with at Partenak in the Crimea. Many groupes of men and boys sate angling, or with their spears watching an opportunity to strike the fish, giving much additional beauty and liveliness to the scene.

I have been much struck for some days by the great care with which the stock of fruit-trees in this country is kept up. I see every where young ones of even those kind which are longest in coming to maturity, more particularly mangoes, and the toddy or tara palm (the last of which I am told must be from thirty to forty years old before it pays any thing) planted and fenced in with care round most of the cottages, a circumstance which seems not only to prove the general security of property, but that the peasants have more assurance of their farms remaining in the occupation of themselves and their children, than of late years has been felt in England.

The village near which we brought to for a short time in the evening, belonged to brahmins exclusively, who were ploughing the ground near us, with their strings floating over their naked shoulders; the ground was sown with rice, barley, and vetches, the one to succeed the other. Abdullah asked them to what caste of brahmins they belonged, and on being told they were Pundits, enquired whether 'a mixture of seeds was not forbidden in the Puranas?' An old man answered with a good deal of warmth, that they were poor people and could not dispute, but he believed the doctrine to be a gloss of Bhuddha, striking his staff with much anger on the ground at the name of the heresiarch. The brahmin labourers are now resting after their toil, and their groupes are very picturesque. The ploughman, after unyoking his oxen, lifted up his simple plough, took out the coulter, a large knife shaped like a horn, wiped and gave it to a boy, then lifted up the beam and yoke on his own shoulders, and trudged away with it. These brahmins, I observe, all shave their heads except a tuft in the centre, a custom which not many Hindoos, I think, besides them observe.

Having a good wind we proceeded a little further before sunset; we passed a herd of cows swimming across a nullah about as wide as the Dee ten miles below Chester, the cowman supporting himself by the tail and hips of the strongest among them, and with a long staff guiding her in a proper direction across the stream. We soon after passed a similar convoy guided by a little boy, who, however, did not confine himself to one animal, but swam from one to another turning them with his staff and his voice as he saw proper. So nearly aquatic are the habits of these people, from the warmth of the climate, their simple food, their nakedness, and their daily habits of religious ablution. I saw a very smartly dressed and rather pretty young country-woman come down to the Ghât at Monghyr to wash. She went in with her mantle wrapped round her with much decency and even modesty, till the river was breast high, then ducked under water for so long a time that I began to despair of her re-appearance. This was at five o'clock in the morning, and she returned again at twelve to undergo the same process, both times walking home in her wet clothes without fear of catching cold. The ancient Greeks had, I am convinced, the same custom, since otherwise the idea of wet drapery would hardly have occurred to their statuaries, or, at least, would not have been so common.

August 18.—This morning, after leaving the nullah, we proceeded with a fine breeze, along the left-hand bank of the river, which is very fertile and populous, with a constant succession of villages, whose inhabitants were all washing themselves and getting on their best attire, it being the Hindoo festival of Junma Osmee.[1]

The day was a very brilliant one, and, though hot, rendered

---

[1] Janmasthami—in celebration of the birth of Krishna.

supportable by the breeze, while the whole scene was lively and cheerful,—all the shops having their flags hoisted,—little streamers being spread by most of the boats which we passed, and a larger banner and concourse of people being displayed at a little pagoda under the shade of some noble peepul and tamarind trees.

The river is all this time filled with boats of the most picturesque forms; the peasants on the bank have that knack of grouping themselves, the want of which I have heard complained of in the peasantry of England.

August 20.—We arrived at the south-east extremity of Patna about nine o'clock; it is a very great, and from the water at some little distance, a very striking city, being full of large buildings, with remains of old walls and towers, and bastions projecting into the river, with the advantage of a high rocky shore, and considerable irregularity, and elevation of the ground behind it. On a nearer approach, we find, indeed, many of the houses whose verandahs and terraces are striking objects at a distance, to be ruinous; but still in this respect, and in apparent prosperity, it as much exceeds Dacca as it falls short of it in the beauty and grandeur of its ruins.

I had an invitation from Sir Charles D'Oyley,[1] and stopped my boat literally at the gate of his house, which stands very pleasantly on a high bank above the river. . . . I found great amusement and interest in looking over Sir Charles's drawing-books; he is the best gentleman artist I ever met with. He says India is full of beautiful and picturesque country, if people would but stir a little way from the banks of the Ganges, and his own drawings and paintings certainly make good his assertion.

After dinner Lady D'Oyley took me round the only drive which is at this time of year practicable, being, though of smaller extent, much such a green as the race-ground at Barrackpoor. We passed a high building shaped something like a glass-house, with

---

[1] Then the Opium Agent in Bihar. He published several books of lithographs and engravings of Indian life and scenery.

a stair winding round its outside up to the top, like the old prints of the Tower of Babel. It was built as a granary for the district, in pursuance of a plan adopted about 35 years ago by Government, after a great famine, as a means of keeping down the price of grain, but abandoned on a supposed discovery of its inefficacy, since no means in their hands, nor any buildings which they could construct, without laying on fresh taxes, would have been sufficient to collect or contain more than one day's provision for the vast population of their territories. It is not only in a time of

3   The granary at Patna

famine, that in a country like India, the benefit of public granaries would be felt. These would of course be filled by the agents of the Company in those years and those seasons when grain was cheapest, and when the cultivator was likely to be ruined by the impossibility of obtaining a remunerating price. But the presence of an additional, a steady and a wealthy customer at such times in the market, to the amount of $\frac{1}{365}$ of the whole produce, or even less than that, would raise the price of grain 10 or even 20 per cent, and thus operate as a steady and constant bounty on agriculture, more popular by far, and as I conceive, more efficient than any Corn Law which could be devised. It appears to me, therefore, that a system of such granaries, even on a very moderate scale

throughout the Provinces, would not only essentially relieve
famine, if it came, but, in some degree, prevent its coming; that it
would improve the situation both of Ryot and Zemindar, and
make them more able to pay their dues to Government, while, as
there is no necessity or advantage (but rather the contrary) that
the corn thus hoarded should be given away, the expense to the
Company would not be very much more than the first cost and
subsequent repair of the buildings, and the wages of the needful
agents and labourers. I am well aware of the usual answer, that it
is better to leave these things to private competition and specu-
lation, that much of the grain thus collected would be spoiled, and
become unfit for use, &c. But the first assumes a fact which in

4   Houses and carriages

India, I believe, is not correct, that there is either sufficient
capital or enterprise to enable or induce individuals to store up
corn in the manner contemplated. As for the second, it would
obviously be in years of over production, an equal benefit to the
cultivator to have a part of his stock purchased and withdrawn
from present consumption, even though what was thus purchased
were actually burnt, while, though to keep the granaries full of
good grain, would of course be more expensive to Government
from the perishable nature of the commodity, yet it would be easy
so to calculate the selling price as to cover this charge, and avoid
the necessity of imposing fresh public burthens. On the whole,
therefore, I am inclined to believe that the measure was a wise

one, and well adapted to the state of India, though it is one, undoubtedly, which could only be carried into effect in peaceable times, and when there was a considerable surplus revenue. I know my dear wife has no objection to this sort of politico-economical discussion, and therefore send it without fearing to tire her. The building which has called it forth is said to have many imperfections, which made it very unfit for its destination. The idea itself, which is to pour the corn in at the top, and take it out through a small door at the bottom, I think a good one. But it is said to be ill-built, and by far too weak to support the weight of its intended contents, while by a refinement in absurdity, the door at the bottom is made to open inwards, and consequently when the granary was full, could never have been opened at all. It is now occasionally used as a powder magazine, but is at this moment quite empty, and only visited sometimes for the sake of its echo, which is very favourable to performances on the flute or bugle.

August 24.—Sir C. D'Oyley sent me in his carriage half-way to Dinapoor, where Mr Northmore's[1] carriage met me. The Archdeacon went in a 'Tonjon', a chair with a head like a gig, carried by bearers. The whole way lies between scattered bungalows, bazars, and other buildings, intermixed with gardens and mangoe groves; and three days without rain had made the direct road not only passable, but very reasonably good. As we approached Dinapoor, symptoms began to appear of a great English military station, and it was whimsical to see peeping out from beneath the palms and plantains, large blue boards with gilt letters 'Digah Farm, Havell, Victualler', &c. 'Morris, Tailor'. 'Davis, *Europe* Warehouse', &c. The cantonment itself is the largest and handsomest which I have seen, with a very fine quay, looking like a battery, to the river, and I think three extensive squares of barracks uniformly built, of one lofty ground-story well raised, stuccoed, and ornamented with arcaded windows, and pillars between each. There are also extensive and, I understood, very handsome barracks for the native troops which I did not see, those which I have described being for Europeans, of whom there

---

[1] T. W. Northmore: appointed chaplain of the Dinapur cantonment in 1822.

are generally here one King's regiment, one Company's, and a numerous corps of artillery. Every thing in fact is on a liberal scale, except what belongs to the Church, and the spiritual interests of the inhabitants and neighbourhood. The former I found merely a small and inconvenient room in the barracks, which seemed as if it had been designed for a hospital-ward; the reading-desk, surplice, books, &c. were all meaner and shabbier than are to be seen in the poorest village chapel in England or Wales; there were no punkahs, no wall-shades, or other means for lighting up the Church, no glass in the windows, no font, and till a paltry deal stand was brought for my use out of an adjoining warehouse, no communion table. Bishop Middleton objected to administer Confirmation in any but Churches regularly built, furnished and consecrated. But though I do not think that in India we need be so particular, I heartily wished, in the present case, to see things more as they should be, and as I had been accustomed to see them. Nor, in more essential points, was there much to console me for this neglect of external decencies. I had only fourteen candidates for Confirmation, some of them so young that I almost doubted the propriety of admitting them, and there were perhaps a dozen persons besides in the Church. It is very true that the King's regiment (the 44th) was absent, but the Company's European regiment, most of them young men, might have been expected to furnish, of itself, no inconsiderable number... There are, likewise, several indigo-planters in the neighbourhood, many of them with families, and many others who had themselves never been confirmed, to whom the Chaplain of the station had long since sent notice, but who had none of them given any answer to his letters; he, indeed, (whom I found extremely desirous of contributing to the improvement of the people under his care,) lamented in a very natural and unaffected manner the gross neglect of Sunday, the extraordinary inattention on the part of the lower classes to all religious concerns, and the indifference hitherto shewn by the Company's military officers now at Dinapoor to every thing like religious improvement. While the 44th was here, a very different and admirable example was set by Colonel Morrison and his officers, and the men themselves were most of them patterns of decent conduct and regular attendance in Church, not only in the morning but in the evening, at which time their attendance was perfectly voluntary.

There had been a school for the European children and those recruits who could not read, but this had fallen to decay, because nobody would subscribe, and the Chaplain alone could not support it. The Government sent six months ago, a lending library for the use of their European soldiers, and allowed eight rupees a month to the clerk for keeping it, but the brigade major, to whom the books were consigned, had never unpacked them, alleging (of which he was not the proper judge) 'that they were too few to be of any use', and 'that there was no place to put them in', as if a corner of the room now used as a Church would not have answered the purpose perfectly.

Of the European regiment, though it was 'in orders' that the men should attend Church every Sunday, very few ever came, and seldom any officer but the Adjutant, and the neighbouring planters seemed utterly without religion of any kind, never applying to the Clergyman except for marriage, burial, and the baptizing of their children. Mr Northmore, who gave me this account, complained that he was often sadly discouraged, and led to fear that some deficiency in himself was the cause of this neglect of his ministry, but that he was comforted to find his attendance both acceptable and useful to the sick men in the hospital, where, indeed, I hear his conduct is marked by very great diligence and humanity. For the lamentable state of things of which he complains, there are many reasons for which he can in nowise be accountable, and which, to prevent his being discouraged, I took care to point out to him. One of these I shall probably find but too prevalent throughout the Indian army, where the early age at which the officers leave England, the little control to which they are afterwards subjected, and the very few opportunities afforded to most of them of ever hearing a sermon, or joining in public prayer, might be expected to heathenize them even far more than we find is the case.

But at Dinapoor something may be also ascribed to the exceeding bad conduct of the late chaplain, which must have driven many from the church, whom it would be very difficult for the most popular preacher to entice back again. And the want of a decent church is the strongest cause of all. The present room barely affords accommodation for half the soldiers who might be expected to attend, without leaving any for the officers' families, or the neighbouring planters. These, therefore, though room is generally to be had, have an excuse to offer to their consciences for not attending; and it is really true, that for women and children of the upper class to sit jostling with soldiers in a small close room, without punkahs,[1] with a drive of perhaps three or four miles before and after service, is not a prospect which would make a man very fond of bringing his family to attend Divine service. A spacious and airy church would greatly remove these difficulties. Government did, I understand, promise one some time back; but the military officers, to whom the preparation of the estimate and plan were left, took no trouble in the business. On the whole, what I saw and heard, both at and after church, made me low and sad, to which perhaps the heat of the day, the most oppressive I have yet felt in India, greatly contributed.

I endeavoured to put Mr Northmore in the way of getting some of those aids from the military officers of the cantonment, to which, by the regulations of Government, he is entitled. And afterwards at dinner, where were present most of the officers now in garrison, I succeeded, I hope, in getting the re-establishment of the school, together with the assurance from the colonel of the European regiment, that he would urge his recruits to attend, and promote only those men to be non-commissioned officers who could read and write; a measure which would soon make reading and writing universal. The brigade-major was not present, but I said all I could to the colonel about the lending library, and a more regular attendance of the troops in church, and was glad to find what I said, extremely well taken. The library I think I have secured, since every body present seemed pleased with the idea, when the nature of its contents and the system of circulation were explained. The heat was something which a man who had not been out of Europe would scarcely conceive, and the party, out of etiquette on my account, were all in their cloth uniforms. I soon put them at their ease, however, in this particular, and

---

[1] Ceiling fans, manually operated.

I am most inclined to hope that the white jackets which were immediately sent for, put them in better humour both with me and my suggestions.

I was much pressed to stay over the next Sunday, or at least a few days longer; but it is only by going to-morrow that I can hope to reach Ghazeepoor, or even Buxar, by Sunday next; and all agreed, on telling them what I had to do, that I had no time to spare in order to reach Bombay before the hot winds.

Part III

BANARAS AND ALLAHABAD

August 31.—Ghazeepoor is celebrated throughout India for the wholesomeness of its air, and the beauty and extent of its rose-gardens. . . . The rose-fields, which occupy many hundred acres in the neighbourhood, are described as, at the proper season, extremely beautiful. They are cultivated for distillation, and for making 'attar'. Rose-water is both good and cheap here. The price of a seer, or weight of 2lbs. (a large quart), of the best, being 8 annas, or a shilling. The attar is obtained after the rose-water is made, by setting it out during the night and till sun-rise in the morning, in large open vessels exposed to the air, and then skimming off the essential oil which floats at the top. The rose-water which is thus skimmed bears a lower price than that which is warranted with its cream entire, but Mr Bayley[1] said there is very little perceptible difference. To produce one rupee's weight of attar, 200,000 well-grown roses are required. The price, even on the spot, is extravagant, a rupee's weight being sold in the bazar (where it is often adulterated with sandal-wood,) for 80 S.R. and at the English warehouse, where it is warranted genuine, at 100 S.R. or £10! Mr Melville,[2] who made some for himself one year, said he calculated that the rent of the land, and price of utensils, really cost him at the rate of five pounds for the above trifling quantity, without reckoning risk, labour of servants, &c.

The whole district of Ghazeepoor is fertile in corn, pasture,

[1] Charles Bayley: appointed Commercial Resident for Banaras and the surrounding districts in 1823; retired from the Company's service 1836.

[2] W. L. Melville: appointed Judge and Magistrate at Ghazipur in 1820; retired 1838.

and fruit-trees. The population is great, and the mosques, and Mussulmans in the shops and streets are so numerous, and there are so few pagodas of any importance visible, that I thought I had bidden adieu for the present to the followers of Brahma. Mr Melville, however assured me, to my surprise, that it was in the large towns only that the Mussulmans were numerous, and that, taking the whole province together, they were barely an eleventh part of the population, among the remainder of whom Hindooism existed in all its strength and bigotry. Suttees are more abundant here than even in the neighbourhood of Calcutta, but chiefly confined to the lower ranks. The last yearly return amounted to above forty, and there were several of which no account was given to the magistrate. It has been, indeed, a singular omission on the part of Government, that, though an ordinance has been passed, commanding all persons celebrating a suttee to send in notice of their intention to the nearest police officer, no punishment has been prescribed for neglect of this order, nor has it ever been embodied in the standing regulations, so as to make it law, or authorize a magistrate to commit to prison for contempt of it. If Government mean their orders respecting the publicity of suttees to be obeyed, they must give it the proper efficacy; while, if suttees are not under the inspection of the police, the most horrible murders may be committed under their name. This struck me very forcibly from two facts which were incidentally told me. It is not necessary, it seems, for the widow who offers herself, to burn actually with the body of her husband. His garments, his slippers, his walking-staff,—any thing which has at any time been in his possession, will do as well. Brahmin widows indeed, are, by the Shaster, not allowed this privilege, but must burn with the body or not at all. This, however, is unknown or disregarded in the district of Ghazeepoor, and most other regions of India. But the person of whom I was told was no brahmin; he was a labourer, who had left his family in a time of scarcity, and gone to live, (as was believed,) in the neighbourhood of Moorshedabad, whence he had once, in the course of several years, sent his wife a small sum of money from his savings, by a friend who was going up the country. Such remittances, to the honour of the labouring class in India are usual, and equally to their honour, when entrusted to any one to convey, are very seldom embezzled. Some years after, however, when the son of the absentee was grown up, he returned one day from a fair at a little distance, saying he had heard bad news, and that *a man unknown* had told him his father was dead. On this authority the widow determined to burn herself, and it was judged sufficient that an old garment of the supposed dead man should be burned with her. Now, it is very plain how easily, if the son wanted to get rid of his mother, he might have brought home such a story to induce her to burn, and it is also very plain, that whether she was willing or no, he might carry her to the stake, and (if the police are to take no cognizance of the matter) might burn her under pretence of a suttee. How little the interference of neighbours is to be apprehended in such cases, and how little a female death is cared for, may appear by another circumstance which occurred a short time ago at a small distance from the city of Ghazeepoor, when, in consequence of a dispute which had taken place between two small freeholders about some land, one of the contending parties, an old man of 70 and upwards, brought his wife of the same age, to the field in question, forced her with the assistance of their children and relations, into a little straw hut built for the purpose, and burned her and the hut together, in order that her death might bring a curse on the soil, and her spirit haunt it after death, so that his successful antagonist should never derive any advantage from it. On some horror and surprise being expressed by the gentleman who told me this case, one of the officers of his court, the same indeed who had reported it to him, not as a horrible occurrence, but as a proof how spiteful the parties had been against each other, said very coolly, 'why not?—she was a very old woman,—what use was she?' The old murderer was in prison, but my friend said he had no doubt that his interference in such a case *between man and wife* was regarded as singularly vexatious and oppressive; and he added, 'The truth is, so very little value do these people set on their own lives, that we cannot wonder at their caring little for the life of another. The cases of suicide which come before me, double those of suttees; men, and still more, women, throw themselves down wells, or drink poison, for apparently the slightest reasons, generally out of some quarrel, and in order that their blood may lie at their enemy's door, and unless the criminal in question had had an old woman at hand and in his power, he was likely enough to have burned himself.' Human sacrifices, as of children, are never heard of now in these provinces, but it still sometimes happens that a leper is burnt or buried alive, and as these murders are somewhat blended also with religious feeling, a leper being supposed to be accursed of the gods, the Sudder Dewannee, acting on the same principle, discourages, as I am told, all interference with the practice. The best way, indeed, to abolish it, would be to establish lazar-houses, where these poor wretches should be maintained and, if possible, cured, or at all events kept separate from the rest of the people, a policy, by which more than any thing else, this hideous disease has been extirpated in Europe.

All these stories have made a very painful impression on me. If I live to return to Calcutta, it is possible that by conversation with such of my friends as have influence, and by the help of what additional knowledge I may have acquired during this tour, I may obtain a remedy for some of them. And it is in order that this anxiety may not pass away, but that I may really do some little for the people among whom my lot is thrown, that I have put down more fully the facts which have come to my knowledge. I have on a former occasion noticed the opinions of most public men in India, on the important question of putting down suttees by authority. Whether this is attempted or not, it seems at least highly necessary that the regulations should be enforced which the Indian Government itself had declared desirable, and that those instances which are really murder, on Hindoo as well as Christian principles, should not escape unpunished. Of the natural disposition of the Hindoo, I still see abundant reason to think highly, and Mr Bayley and Mr Melville both agreed with me, that they are constitutionally kind-hearted, industrious, sober, and peaceable, at the same time that they shew themselves on proper occasions, a manly and courageous people. All that is bad about them appears to arise either from the defective motives which their religion supplies, or the wicked actions which it records of their gods, or encourages in their own practice. Yet it is strange to see, though this is pretty generally allowed, how slow men are to admit the advantage or necessity of propagating Christianity among them. Crimes unconnected with religion are not common in Ghazeepoor. There are affrays, but such as arise out of disputes between Mahommedan and Hindoo processions at the time of the Mohurrun,[1] in which blood is sometimes drawn. The police is numerous and effective, and the Thannadars, &c. though they had been here also, in the first instance, forgotten in the perpetual settlement, have been better provided for since than those of Bahar; but the tenants on the small and divided estates in these provinces, are worse off than those on the larger properties in Bahar. Estates here are seldom large, and the holdings very minute.

The language spoken by the common people is Hindoostanee, of a very corrupt kind. The good 'Oordoo' is chiefly confined to the army and courts of justice.[2] When a person under examination once answered in it with unusual fluency and propriety, Mr Melville's native chief officer said, with a sagacious nod, 'That fellow talks good Oordoo! He has been in prison before to-day!' All legal writings, records, &c. are in Persian, a rule which Mr Melville thinks good. Persian holding in India the place of Latin in Europe, in consequence of this regulation, all the higher officers of the court are educated persons. Persian is, as a language, so much superior in clearness and brevity to Hindoostanee, that business is greatly facilitated by employing it, and since even Oordoo itself is unintelligible to a great part of the Hindoos, there is no particular reason for preferring it to the more polished language. The honesty of the Hindoo law-officers is spoken very ill of; they seem to become worse the nearer they approach the seat of justice. The reason perhaps is not hard to discover; they are in situations where they may do a great deal of mischief; their regular salaries are wretchedly small, a part even of these arise from fees often oppressive and difficult to obtain, and they are so much exposed to getting a bad name even while they exact merely what is their due, that they become careless of reputation, and anxious

---

[1] Processions are held by Shia Muslims during the month of Muharram to commemorate the death of Husain, the Prophet Muhammed's grandson, at the battle of Karbala in A.D. 680 (see also *infra*, p. 174).

[2] Urdu developed originally in the court and army of the Mughal Emperors. See also *infra*, p. 157 and n.

by all underhand means to swell their profits. Much evil arises in India from the insufficient manner in which the subaltern native servants of Government are paid. In the case of the town duties, a toll-keeper, through whose hands the dues of half a district pass, receives as his own share three rupees a month! For this he has to keep a regular account, to stop every boat or hackery, to search them in order to prevent smuggling, and to bear the abuse and curses of all his neighbours. What better could be expected from such a man, but that he should cheat both sides, withholding from his employers a large portion of the sums which he receives, and extracting from the poor country-people, in the shape of presents, surcharges, expedition and connivance-money, a far greater sum than he is legally entitled to demand?

On 3 September Heber arrived at Sikraul, a cantonment on the outskirts of Banaras.

September 6.—I went this morning with Mr Frazer[1] to the Mission School in [Banaras], which is kept in a large house well adapted for the purpose, and made over to the Church Missionary Society, together with other tenements adjoining, by a rich Bengalee baboo, not long since dead in Benares, whom Mr Corrie had almost persuaded to become a Christian, but who at length appears to have settled in a sort of general admiration of the beauty of the Gospel, and a wish to improve the state of knowledge and morality among his countrymen.[2] In these opinions he seems to have been followed by his son, Calisunker Gossant, now living, and also a liberal benefactor to this and other establishments for national education in India.[3] The house is a native dwelling, containing on the ground-floor several small low rooms, in which are the junior classes, and, above, one large and lofty hall supported by pillars, where the Persian and English classes meet, besides a small room for a library. The boys on the establishment are about 140, under the care of an English schoolmaster, assisted by a Persian Moonshee, and two Hindoostanee

[1] William Frazer: appointed chaplain at Banaras 1820.

[2] This was Jai Narayan Ghosal, who had founded the school and in 1818 handed it over to the management of the C.M.S. He died in 1821.

[3] Kali Sankar Ghosal had in 1816 donated the land for the first C.M.S. school in Calcutta. He was a friend of Ram Mohan Roy.

writing-masters, the whole under the inspection of a catechist, Mr Adlington,[1] a clever young man, and a candidate for orders. The boys read Oordoo, Persian, and English before me extremely well, and answered questions both in English and Hindoostanee with great readiness. The English books they read were the New Testament, and a compendium of English history. They also displayed great proficiency in writing, (Nagree, Persian, and English) arithmetic, in which their multiplication table extended to 100×100, geography, and the use of the globes. To judge from their dress, they were mostly belonging to the middling class of life. Many, I think the majority, had the brahminical string. I asked the catechist and school-master if any of these boys or their parents objected to their reading the New Testament. They answered that they had never heard any objection made, nor had the least reason to believe that any was felt. The boys, they said, were very fond of the New Testament, and I can answer for their understanding it. I wish a majority of English school-boys might appear equally well-informed. The scene was a very interesting one; there were present the patron of the school, Calisunker Gossant, a shrewd and rather ostentatious, but a well-mannered baboo, his second son, a fine and well-educated young man, Mr Macleod[2] and Mr Prinsep,[3] the magistrates of the place, both very acute critics in Hindoostanee and Persian, some ladies, and a crowd of swords, spears, and silver-sticks on the stair-case, (whose bearers, by the way, seemed to take as much interest as any of us in what was going on.) One, however, of the most pleasing sights of all, was the calm but intense pleasure visible on Archdeacon Corrie's face, whose efforts and influence had first brought this establishment into activity, and who now, after an interval of several years, was witnessing its usefulness and prosperity.

In our way to and from the school I had an opportunity of seeing something of Benares, which is a very remarkable city,

[1] John Adlington: a Eurasian who served with the C.M.S. between 1817 and 1828. Heber ordained him in December 1825.

[2] Norman Macleod: appointed Judge and Magistrate of the City Court of Banaras 1821; died September 1825.

[3] This must have been James Prinsep (1799–1840), the numismatist and antiquarian, who at that time was the Assay Master of the Banaras Mint.

more entirely and characteristically Eastern than any which I have yet seen, and at the same time altogether different from any thing in Bengal. No Europeans live in the town, nor are the streets wide enough for a wheel-carriage. Mr Frazer's gig was stopped short almost in its entrance, and the rest of the way was passed in tonjons, through alleys so crowded, so narrow, and so winding, that even a tonjon sometimes passed with difficulty. The houses are mostly lofty, none I think less than two stories, most of three, and several of five or six, a sight which I now for the first time saw in India. The streets, like those of Chester, are considerably lower than the ground-floors of the houses, which have mostly arched rows in front, with little shops behind them. Above these, the houses are richly embellished with verandahs, galleries, projecting oriel windows, and very broad and over-hanging eaves, supported by carved brackets. The number of temples is very great, mostly small and stuck like shrines in the angles of the streets, and under the shadow of the lofty houses. Their forms, however, are not ungraceful, and they are many of them entirely covered over with beautiful and elaborate carvings of flowers, animals, and palm-branches, equalling in minuteness and richness the best specimens that I have seen of Gothic or Grecian atchitecture. The material of the buildings is a very good stone from Chunar, but the Hindoos here seem fond of painting them a deep red colour, and, indeed, of covering the more con-spicuous parts of their houses with paintings in gaudy colours of flower-pots, men, women, bulls, elephants, gods and goddesses, in all their many-formed, many-headed, many-handed, and many-weaponed varieties. The sacred bulls devoted to Siva,[1] of every age, tame and familiar as mastiffs, walk lazily up and down these narrow streets or are seen lying across them, and hardly to be kicked up (any blows, indeed, given them must be of the gentlest kind, or woe be to the profane wretch who braves the prejudices of this fanatic population) in order to make way for

---

[1] One of the gods of the Hindu triad comprising Brahma, the Creator; Vishnu, the Preserver; and Siva, the Destroyer. Siva is particularly associated with Banaras, where he is worshipped as Mahadeva, the Great God—representing all the functions of the triad. He is also worshipped as Lord of the cosmic dance; as the personi-fication of fertility; and as the great Ascetic. The bull is his vehicle. Cf. also *infra*, pp. 268, 276.

the tonjon. Monkeys sacred to Hunimaun, the divine ape who conquered Ceylon for Rama,[1] are in some parts of the town equally numerous, clinging to all the roofs and little projections of the temples, putting their impertinent heads and hands into every fruiterer's or confectioner's shop, and snatching the food from the children at their meals. Faqueer's[2] houses, as they are called, occur at every turn, adorned with idols, and sending out an unceasing tinkling and strumming of vinas, biyals, and other discordant instruments, while religious mendicants of every Hindoo sect, offering every conceivable deformity, which chalk, cow-dung, disease, matted locks, distorted limbs and disgusting and hideous attitudes of penance can shew, literally line the principal streets on both sides. The number of blind persons is very great (I was going to say of lepers also, but I am not sure whether the appearance on the skin may not have been filth and chalk) and here I saw repeated instances of that penance of which I had heard much in Europe, of men with their legs or arms voluntarily distorted by keeping them in one position, and their hands clenched till the nails grew out at the backs. Their pitiful exclamations as we passed, 'Agha Sahib', 'Topee Sahib', (the usual names in Hindostan for an European) 'khana ke waste kooch cheez do', 'give me something to eat', soon drew from me what few pice I had, but it was a drop of water in the ocean, and the importunities of the rest as we advanced into the city, were almost drowned in the hubbub which surrounded us. Such are the sights and sounds which greet a stranger on entering this 'the most Holy City' of Hindostan, 'the Lotus of the world, not founded on common earth, but on the point of Siva's trident', a place so blessed that whoever dies here, of whatever sect, even though he should be an eater of beef, *so he will but be charitable to the poor brahmins*, is sure of salvation. It is, in fact, this very holiness which makes it the common resort of beggars; since, besides the number of pilgrims, which is enormous from every part of India, as well as from Tibet and the Birman empire, a great multitude of rich individuals in the decline of life, and almost all the great

[1] In the *Ramayana*—see *infra*, pp. 159–61.

[2] Fakirs'—strictly speaking this term denotes a Muslim religious mendicant, but was often applied by the British in India to Hindus also, as here.

men who are from time to time disgraced or banished from home by the revolutions which are continually occurring in the Hindoo states, come hither to wash away their sins, or to fill up their vacant hours with the gaudy ceremonies of their religion, and really give away great sums in profuse and indiscriminate charity. Amrut Row, for a short period of his life Peishwa of the Maharattas,[1] and since enjoying a large pension from our Government in addition to a vast private fortune, was one of the chief of these almsgivers. On his name-day, that is in Hindostan, the day on which his patron god is worshipped, he annually gave a seer of rice and a rupee to every brahmin, and every blind or lame person who applied between sun-rise and sun-set. He had a large garden a short distance from the city with four gates, three of which were set open for the reception of the three different classes of applicants, and the fourth for the Peishwa and his servants to go backwards and forwards. On each person receiving his dole, he was shewn into the garden, where he was compelled to stay during the day lest he should apply twice, but he had shade, water, company, and idols enough to make a Hindoo (who seldom eats till sun-set) pass his time very pleasantly. The sums distributed on these occasions are said to have in some instances amounted to above 50,000 rupees. His annual charities altogether averaged, I was informed, probably three times that amount. He died the second night of my residence at Secrole; Mr Brooke said he was really a good and kind man, religious to the best of his knowledge, and munificent, not from ostentation but principle. There are yet, I understand, some living instances of splendid bounty among the Hindoos of Benares, indeed Calisunker is no bad specimen, and on the whole my opinion of the people improves, though it was never so unfavourable as that of many good men in Calcutta. 'God', I yet hope and believe, in the midst of the aweful and besotted darkness which surrounds me, and of which, as well as its miserable consequences, I am now more sensible than ever, 'God may have much people in this city!'

By the time the examination of the school was over, the sun was too high to admit of our penetrating further into these

[1] Amrit Rao, Baji Rao II's adoptive brother, who had been raised to the Peshwaship for a few months in 1802–3 by Jaswant Rao Holkar.

crowded streets. Close to the school, however, was a fine house belonging to two minors, the sons of a celebrated baboo, who had made a vast fortune as Dewan[1] to some Europeans high in office, as well as to some natives of rank resident in and near Benares, which we had time to see. It was a striking building, and had the advantage, very unusual in Benares, of having a vacant area of some size before the door, which gave us an opportunity of seeing its architecture. It is very irregular, built round a small court, two sides of which are taken up by the dwelling-house, the others by offices. The house is four lofty stories high, with a tower over the gate of one story more. The front has small windows of various forms, some of them projecting on brackets and beautifully carved, and a great part of the wall itself is covered with a carved pattern of sprigs, leaves, and flowers, like an old fashioned paper. The whole is of stone, but painted a deep red. The general effect is by no means unlike some of the palaces at Venice as represented in Canaletti's views. We entered a gateway similar to that of a college, with a groined arch of beautifully rich carving, like that on the roof of Christ Church great gateway, though much smaller. On each side is a deep richly carved recess, like a shrine, in which are idols with lamps before them, the house-hold gods of the family. The court is crowded with plantains and rose-trees, with a raised and ornamented well in its centre; on the left-hand a narrow and steep flight of stone steps, the meanest part of the fabric, without balustrades, and looking like the approach to an English granary, led to the first story. At their foot we were received by the two young heirs, stout little fellows of thirteen and twelve, escorted by their uncle, an immensely fat brahmin pundit, who is the spiritual director of the family, and a little shrewd-looking, smooth spoken, but vulgar and impudent man, who called himself their Moonshee. They led us up to the showrooms, which are neither large nor numerous; they are, however, very beautifully carved, and the principal of them which occupies the first-floor of the gateway, and is a square with a Gothic arcade round it, struck me as exceedingly comfortable. The centre, about 15 feet square, is raised and covered with a carpet, serving as a divan. The arcade round is flagged with a good deal

---

[1] In this context the term denotes an agent.

of carving and ornament, and is so contrived that on a very short notice, four streams of water, one in the centre of each side, descend from the roof like a permanent shower-bath, and fall into stone basins sunk beneath the floor, and covered with a sort of open fret-work, also of stone. These rooms were hung with a good many English prints of the common paltry description which was fashionable twenty years ago, of Sterne and poor Maria, (the boys supposed this to be a doctor feeling a lady's pulse) the sorrows of Werter, &c. together with a daub of the present Emperor of Delhi, and several portraits in oil of a much better kind, of the father of these boys, some of his powerful native friends and employers, and of a very beautiful woman of European complexion, but in an Eastern dress, of whom the boys knew nothing, or would say nothing more than that the picture was painted for their father by Lall-jee of Patna. I did not, indeed, repeat the question, because I know the reluctance with which all Eastern nations speak of their women, but it certainly had the appearance of a portrait, and as well as the old baboo's picture, would have been called a creditable painting in most gentlemen's houses in England.

I have indeed, during the journey, been surprised at the progress which painting appears to have made of late years in India. I was prepared to expect glowing colours, without drawing, perspective, or even shadow, resembling the illuminations in old Monkish chronicles, and in the oriental MSS. which are sometimes brought to England. But at Sir C. D'Oyley's, I saw several miniatures by this same Lall-jee, dead some years since, and by his son now alive, but of less renowned talent, which would have done credit to any European artist, being distinguished by great truth of colouring, as well as softness and delicacy. The portraits which I now saw, were certainly not so good, but they were evidently the works of a man well acquainted with the principles of his art, and very extraordinary productions, considering that Lall-jee had probably no opportunity of so much as seeing one Italian picture.[1]

Our little friends were very civil, and pressed us to stay for

[1] This 'Lall-jee' was one of a group of painters who worked in Patna during the nineteenth century—possibly the father of Hulas Lal (*c.* 1785–1875).

breakfast, but it was already late. We looked, however, before
we went, at the family pagoda, which stood close to the house, and
was, though small, as rich as carving, painting, and gilding could
make it. The principal shrine was that of Siva, whose emblem[1]
rose just seen amid the darkness of the inner sanctuary, crowned
with scarlet flowers, with lamps burning before it. In front, and
under the centre cupola, was the sacred bull richly painted and
gilt, in an attitude of adoration, and crowned likewise with scarlet
flowers, and over all hung a large silver bell, suspended from the
roof like a chandelier. I thought of the Glendoveer and Mount
Calasay,[2] but in the raree-show before me there was nothing
sublime or impressive. One of the boys in the Mission school,
whose quickness had attracted my notice, and who appeared so
well pleased with my praise that I found him still sticking close to
me, now came forward, shewed his brahminical string, and
volunteered as cicerone, telling us in tolerable English the history
of the gods and goddesses on the walls. The fat pundit seemed
pleased with his zeal, but it was well perhaps for the little urchin,
that the corpulent padre did not understand the language in which
some of the remarks were made. They opened my eyes more fully
to a danger which had before struck me as possible, that some of
the boys brought up in our schools might grow up accomplished
hypocrites, playing the part of Christians with us, and with their
own people of zealous followers of Brahma, or else that they
would settle down into a sort of compromise between the two
creeds, allowing that Christianity was the best for us, but that
idolatry was necessary and commendable in persons of their own
nation. I talked with Mr Frazer and Mr Morris[3] on this subject
in the course of the morning; they answered, that the same danger
had been foreseen by Mr Macleod; and that in consequence of his
representations they had left off teaching the boys the Creed and
the Ten Commandments, as not desiring to expose them too early
to a conflict with themselves, their parents, and neighbours, but

[1] The *lingam*: phallic symbol.

[2] This is a reference to Southey's poem *The curse of Kehama*, especially section
xix. The Glendoveer was an angelic being; Mount Calasay was the heavenly
mountain, the abode of Siva.

[3] Thomas Morris, the first C.M.S. missionary at Banaras, where he worked from
1820 to 1826.

choosing rather that the light should break on them by degrees, and when they were better able to bear it. They said, however, that they had every reason to think that all the bigger boys, and many of the lesser ones, brought up at these schools, learned to despise idolatry and the Hindoo faith less by any direct precept, for their teachers never name the subject to them, and in the Gospels, which are the only strictly religious books read, there are few if any allusions to it, than from the disputations of the Mussulman and Hindoo boys among themselves, from the comparison which they soon learn to make between the system of worship which they themselves follow and ours, and above all, from the enlargement of mind which general knowledge and the pure morality of the Gospel have a tendency to produce. Many, both boys and girls, have asked for Baptism, but it has been always thought right to advise them to wait till they had their parents' leave, or were old enough to judge for themselves; and many have, of their own accord, begun daily to use the Lord's Prayer, and to desist from shewing any honour to the image. Their parents seem extremely indifferent to their conduct in this respect. Prayer, or outward adoration, is not essential to caste. A man may believe what he pleases, nay, I understand, he may almost say what he pleases, without the danger of losing it, and so long as they are not baptized, neither eat nor drink in company with Christians or Pariars,[1] all is well in the opinion of the great majority, even in Benares. The Mussulmans are more jealous, but few of their children come to our schools, and with these there are so many points of union, that nothing taught there is at all calculated to offend them.

September 7.—This morning, accompanied by Mr Macleod, Mr Prinsep, and Mr Frazer, I again went into the city, which I found peopled as before with bulls and beggars; but what surprised me still more than yesterday, as I penetrated further into it, were the large, lofty, and handsome dwelling-houses, the beauty and apparent richness of the goods exposed in the bazars, and the evident hum of business which was going on in the midst of all this wretchedness and fanaticism. Benares is, in fact, a very

[1] Strictly speaking, a low caste of south India; but the term was often used loosely, as here, to denote outcastes.

industrious and wealthy as well as a very holy city. It is the great
mart where the shawls of the north, the diamonds of the south,
and the muslins of Dacca and the eastern provinces, centre, and it
has very considerable silk, cotton, and fine woollen manufactories
of its own; while English hardware, swords, shields, and spears
from Lucknow and Monghyr, and those European luxuries and
elegancies which are daily becoming more popular in India,
circulate from hence through Bundlecund, Gorruckpoor, Nepaul,
and other tracts which are removed from the main artery of the
Ganges. The population, according to a census made in 1803,
amounted to above 582,000,—an enormous amount, and which
one should think must have been exaggerated; but it is the nearest
means we have of judging, and it certainly becomes less improb-
able from the real great size of the town, and the excessively
crowded manner in which it is built. It is well drained, and stands
dry on a high rocky bank sloping to the river, to which circumstance, as well as to the frequent ablutions and great temperance
of the people, must be ascribed its freedom from infectious
diseases. Accordingly, notwithstanding its crowded population,
it is not an unhealthy city; yet the only square, or open part in
it, is the new market-place, constructed by the present Government, and about as large as the Peckwater Quadrangle in
Oxford.

Our first visit was to a celebrated temple, named the Vish-
vayesa,[1] consisting of a very small but beautiful specimen of
carved stone-work, and the place is one of the most holy in
Hindostan, though it only approximates to a yet more sacred
spot adjoining, which Aulum Gheer defiled,[2] and built a mosque
on it, so as to render it inaccessible to the worshippers of Brahma.
The temple-court, small as it is, is crowded like a farm-yard with
very fat and very tame bulls, which thrust their noses into every
body's hand and pocket for gram and sweetmeats, which their
fellow-votaries give them in great quantities. The cloisters are
no less full of naked devotees, as hideous as chalk and dung can
make them, and the continued hum of 'Ram! Ram! Ram! Ram!'

[1] A temple of Siva.
[2] In 1669 the Emperor Aurangzeb (Alamgir) razed the original temple to the
ground.

is enough to make a stranger giddy. The place is kept very clean, however,—indeed the priests seem to do little else than pour water over the images and the pavement, and I found them not merely willing, but anxious, to shew me every thing,—frequently repeating that they were Padres also, though it is true that they used this circumstance as an argument for my giving them a present. Near this temple is a well, with a small tower over it, and a steep flight of steps for descending to the water which is brought by a subterraneous channel from the Ganges, and, for some reason or other, is accounted more holy than even the Ganges itself. All pilgrims to Benares are enjoined to drink and wash here. . . .

In another temple near those of which I have been speaking, and which is dedicated to 'Unna Purna'[1]. . .a Brahmin was pointed out to me, who passes his whole day seated on a little pulpit about as high and large as a dressing-table, only leaving it for his necessary ablutions, and at night, though then he sleeps on the pavement beside it. His constant occupation is reading or lecturing on the Vedas.[2] The latter he does to as many as will hear him, from eight in the morning till four in the evening. He asks for nothing, but a small copper bason stands by his pulpit, into which any who feel disposed may drop the alms on which only he subsists. He is a little pale man, of an interesting countenance, which he does not disfigure by such ostentatious marks of piety as are usual here, and is said to be eloquent, as well as extremely learned in the Sanscrit.

One of the most interesting and singular objects in Benares is the ancient Observatory, founded before the Mussulman conquest and still very entire, though no longer made any use of. It is a stone building, containing some small courts, cloistered round for the accommodation of the astronomers and their students, and a large square tower, on which are seen a huge gnomon, perhaps 20 feet high, with the arc of a dial in proportion, a circle 15 feet in diameter, and a meridional line, all in stone. These are very far from being exact, but are interesting proofs of the zeal

---

[1] Annapurna, the goddess of plenty.
[2] The oldest of the Hindu scriptures, dating from the second millennium B.C. They include hymns and sacrificial formulae.

with which science has at one time been followed in these countries. There is a similar observatory at Delhi.[1]

From the observatory we descended by a long flight of steps to the water's edge, where a boat was waiting for us. I had thus an opportunity of seeing the whole city on its most favourable side. It is really a very large place, and rises from the river in an amphitheatrical form, thickly studded with domes and minarets, with many very fine ghâts descending to the water's edge, all crowded with bathers and worshippers. Shrines and temples of various sizes, even within the usual limits of the river's rise, almost line its banks.

There yet remained to be visited the mosque of Aurungzebe, and the Vidalaya or Hindoo College, which fortunately both of them lay pretty nearly in our direct way home. The former is a handsome building in a very advantageous situation, but chiefly remarkable for the view from its minarets, which are very lofty, and derive still greater elevation from the hill on which they stand. The day was not favourable, but we still saw a great distance. The Himalaya range may, as I was told, be sometimes seen, but nothing of the sort was now visible, nor any mountains at all in a horizon of great extent. The ground, however, of this part of Hindostan is not without inequalities, and though it is certainly for the most part one immense plain, it is such a plain as one sees in miniature in England or on the Continent of Europe, not such a mere dead level as Bengal. The bank on which Benares itself stands, is of some height, and there were several ridges of hills as at Chunar and other places within sight, which would fully rank on a level with Hawkstone.[2]

The whole country seems in cultivation, but less with rice than wheat. The villages are numerous and large, but the scattered dwellings few, and there is but little wood. Fuel is, consequently, extremely dear, and to this circumstance is imputed the number of bodies thrown into the river without burning. Suttees are less numerous in Benares than many parts of India, but self-

[1] In fact both these observatories, as Heber came to realise, were constructed by Raja Jai Singh between 1690 and 1720. He was also the founder of Jaipur.
[2] A ridge of hills near Hodnet.

immolation by drowning is very common. Many scores, every year, of pilgrims from all parts of India, come hither expressly to end their days and secure their salvation. They purchase two large kedgeree pots between which they tie themselves, and when empty these support their weight in the water. Thus equipped, they paddle into the stream, then fill the pots with the water which surrounds them, and thus sink into eternity. Government have sometimes attempted to prevent this practice, but with no other effect than driving the voluntary victims a little further down the river; nor indeed when a man has come several hundred miles to die, is it likely that a police-officer can prevent him. Instruction seems the only way in which these poor people can be improved, and that, I trust, they will by degrees obtain from us.

The Vidalaya is a large building divided into two courts galleried above and below, and full of teachers and scholars, divided into a number of classes, who learn reading, writing, arithmetic (in the Hindoo manner,) Persian, Hindoo law, and sacred literature, Sanscrit, astronomy according to the Ptolemaic system, and astrology![1] There are 200 scholars, some of whom of all sorts came to say their lessons to me, though, unhappily, I was myself able to profit by none, except the astronomy, and a little of the Persian. The astronomical lecturer produced a terrestrial globe, divided according to their system, and elevated to the meridian of Benares. Mount Meru he identified with the north pole, and under the southern pole he supposed the tortoise 'chukwa' to stand, on which the earth rests. The southern hemisphere he apprehended to be uninhabitable, but on its concave surface, in the interior of the globe, he placed Padalon.[2] He then shewed me how the sun went round the earth once in every day, and how, by a different but equally continuous motion, he also visited the signs of the zodiac. The whole system is precisely that of Ptolemy, and the contrast was very striking between the rubbish which these young men were learning in a Government establishment, and the rudiments of real knowledge

[1] This was the institution which Duncan had founded in 1791—see Introduction, p. 7.
[2] Patala—the underworld. Heber's spelling occurs in Southey's *Curse of Kehama*, from which it is evidently copied.

which those whom I had visited the day before had acquired, in the very same city, and under circumstances far less favourable. I was informed that it had been frequently proposed to introduce an English and mathematical class, and to teach the Newtonian and Copernican system of astronomy; but that the late superintendant of the establishment was strongly opposed to any innovation, partly on the plea that it would draw the boys off from their Sanscrit studies, and partly lest it should interfere with the religious prejudices of the professors. The first of these arguments is pretty much like what was urged at Oxford, (substituting Greek for Sanscrit,) against the new examinations,[1] by which, however, Greek has lost nothing. The second is plainly absurd, since the Ptolomaic system, which is now taught, is itself an innovation, and an improvement on the old faith of eight worlds and seven oceans, arranged like a nest of boxes.[2]

The truth is, that even the pundit who read me this lecture, smiled once or twice very slily, and said, '*our people* are taught so and so', as if he himself knew better. And Mr Prinsep afterwards told me that learned brahmins had sometimes said to him, that our system was the most rational, but that the other answered all their purposes. They could construct almanacs, and calculate eclipses tolerably by the one as well as the other, and the old one was quite good enough, in all conscience, to cast nativities with. Nor can we wonder at their adherence to old usage in these respects, when we consider that to change their system would give them some personal trouble, and when we recollect that the church of Rome has not even yet withdrawn the Anathema which she levelled at the heresy that the earth turned round, as taught by Copernicus and Galileo. There are in this college about 200 pupils, and 10 professors, all paid and maintained by Government.

During my progress through the holy places I had received garlands of flowers in considerable numbers, which I was told it was uncivil to throw away, particularly those which were hung round my neck. I now, in consequence, looked more like a *sacrifice*

[1] Since 1800 the examination system at Oxford had been reformed and its scope had been widened by the introduction of the honours schools of Literae Humaniores and Mathematics.

[2] Better envisaged as a series of concentric rings, of land and sea alternatively, with the Earth at the centre—like a flat dish.

than a priest, and on getting again into the gig was glad to rid myself of my ornaments. On talking with Mr Macleod on the civility and apparent cordiality with which I had been received by these heathen priests, he said that my coming had excited considerable curiosity, from the idea that I was the Patriarch of Constantinople! He had heard this from a learned Mussulman Moulavie,[1] Abdul-Khadur, who spoke of it as the current news that such a person was to arrive, and asked when he might be expected. The origin of the idea, when explained, was not an unnatural one. Of the Bishop of Calcutta, *eo nomine*, I had previously reason to believe nothing had been heard or known in Hindostan, or any where out of the immediate neighbourhood of the Presidency; but the news now was that the 'Sirdar Padre', or 'Mufti', of all the 'Sahib log' was coming to visit the different Churches. The only two persons they had heard of answering to this character were the Pope and the Patriarch. They were not ignorant of the religious difference between the English and the Roman Catholics, so that they could not suppose me to be the former. But they are not equally well informed as to our discrepancy from the second; and many of them believe, that though we abhor images, we still pay some reverence to pictures. The Moulavie himself thus explained his meaning, saying, (in consequence of Mr Macleod's expressing his surprise at his first question, 'Whether the Papi Roum were not coming?') that he did not mean old but new Rome, or Islambol,[2] and that he meant the head of those Christians, who, like his Honour, abhorred images, but not pictures. I know not whether he quite believed Mr Macleod's disclaimer of such worship, but he professed himself ignorant till that moment of the existence of a third sect among the Nazarani, and glad to find that the Sahibs differed, even less than he had supposed, from the true believers. None of the gentlemen most conversant with the natives apprehended that my arrival had created any suspicious or jealous feeling, or that my avowed errand, (to see that the inferior Padres did their duty,) was thought other than natural and commendable. It is, however, thought that the natives do not really like us, and that if a fair opportunity offered, the Mussulmans, more particularly, would

---

[1] One learned in Muslim law; a judge. [2] Istanbul.

gladly avail themselves of it to rise against us. But this is from political, not religious feeling; and it has been increased of late years by the conduct of Lord Hastings to the old Emperor of Delhi, a conduct which has been pursued by succeeding administrations, but which entirely differed from the outward respect and allegiance which the Company's officers had professed to pay him, from Lord Clive downwards. The elevation of the Nawâb of Oude to the kingly title, and Lord Hastings's refusal to pay him the same homage which *all* his predecessors had courted every opportunity of doing,[1] and which even the Maharattas did not neglect when the late Shah Aullum was their prisoner, have awakened questions and scruples among the fierce Mahommedans about obeying an unbelieving nation, which were quite forgotten while the English Company acted as the servant and 'Dewan' of the house of Timur.[2] The behaviour of Lord Hastings was very disadvantageously contrasted in Benares with that of Warren Hastings, who, in the height of his power and conquests, gained infinite popularity by riding publicly through the city, as usual with the high functionaries of the court of Delhi, behind the howdah of the hereditary prince, with a fan of peacock's feathers in his hand.[3] This, however, is a digression. I am satisfied from all I hear, that the natives of this neighbourhood have at present no idea that any interference with their religion is intended on the part of Government; that if any thing, they rather esteem us the more for shewing some signs of not being without a religion, and that any fancies of a different tendency which have arisen, on this subject, in Bengal or other parts of India, have been uniformly put into their heads by ill-designing persons among the Portuguese, half-caste, or European residents. Nevertheless, all my informants here, as well as in most other places where I have heard

[1] In fact after the East India Company's conquest of the Delhi area in 1803 successive Governors-General treated the Emperor as its pensionary rather than its suzerain. When Lord Hastings proposed to call on Akbar II he made it clear that he would wish to sit in his presence and would not present *nazars*—the customary gifts from a subordinate to a ruler. Hastings' encouragement to the Nawab of Oudh to assume the title of King (1819) was also regarded as a slight to the Imperial dignity.

[2] The Mughal Emperors were descended from Timur, the Turkish chieftain who had sacked Delhi in 1398.

[3] In 1784.

the question discussed, are of opinion that a direct interference on the part of Government with any of the religious customs of the country, (the suttees for example,) would be eagerly laid hold of and urged as the first step in a new system, by all who wish us ill, and that though it would probably not of itself occasion a rebellion, it would give additional popularity, and a more plausible pretext, to the first rebellion which such disaffected persons might find opportunity for attempting. Meanwhile I cannot learn that the missionaries and the schools which they establish, have excited much attention, or of an unfavourable nature. Their labours, after all, have been chiefly confined to the wives of the British soldiers, who had already lost caste by their marriage, or to such Mussulmans or Hindoos as of their own accord, and prompted by curiosity, or a better motive, have come to their schools or churches, or invited them to their houses. The number of these enquirers after truth is, I understand, even now not inconsiderable, and increasing daily. But I must say, that of actual converts, except soldiers' wives, I have met with very few, and these have been all, I think, made by the Archdeacon.

The custom of street-preaching, of which the Baptist and other dissenting missionaries in Bengal are very fond, has never been resorted to by those employed by the Church Missionary Society, and never shall be as long as I have any influence or authority over them. I plainly see it is not necessary, and I see no less plainly that though it may be safe among the timid Bengalees, it would be very likely to produce mischief here. All which the Missionaries do, is to teach schools, to read prayers, and preach in their Churches, and to visit the houses of such persons as wish for information on religious subjects. Poor Amrut Row, the charitable Ex-Peishwa (whose ashes I saw yet smoking on Ali Bhaee's Ghât as I passed it) was, I find, one of these enquirers. Mr Morris, the missionary, had received a message with his Highness's compliments, desiring him to call on him the middle of the week, as he 'was anxious to obtain a further knowledge of Christianity!' It is distressing to think that this message was deferred so long, and that, short as the interval which he had calculated on was, his own time was shorter still. Yet surely one may hope for such a man that his knowledge and faith may have been greater than the world supposed, and that, at all events, the feeling which made him, thus late in life, desirous to hear the truth, would not be lost on Him whose grace may be supposed to have first prompted it.

The city of Benares is certainly the richest, as well as probably the most populous in India; it is also the best governed in respect to its police, which is carried on by a sort of national guard, the Chuprassies,...chosen by the inhabitants themselves, and merely approved of by the magistrates. There are about 500 of these in the city, which is divided into 60 wards, with a gate to each, which is shut at night, and guarded by one of these people. In consequence, notwithstanding the vast population, the crowds of beggars and pilgrims of all countries, (of Maharatta pilgrims alone there are generally some 20,000 in the place, many of them armed, and of warlike and predatory habits) robberies and murders are very rare, while the guards being elected and paid by the respectable householders, have an interest in being civil, well-behaved, and attentive.

The army at Secrole is never called in except in cases of extremity, according to an excellent rule laid down and strictly observed by the government of Bengal, never to employ the military force except in affairs of real war, or where an active and numerous police is visibly incompetent to provide for the public safety. Only one instance of the military being called in has occurred at Benares during the last twenty-five years, which was on occasion of [a] quarrel...between the Mussulmans and Hindoos.[1] At that time Mr Bird[2] was magistrate, and he gave me a far more formidable idea of the tumult than I had previously formed. One half of the population was literally armed against the other, and the fury which actuated both was more like that of demoniacs than rational enemies. It began by the Mussulmans breaking down a famous pillar, named Siva's walking-staff,[3] held in high veneration by the Hindoos. These last in revenge burnt

[1] In 1809.

[2] This was William Wilberforce Bird. Heber met him at Allahabad (see *infra*, p. 159), where he was the Second Member of the Mufasil Special Commission. Bird was acting Governor-General for a few weeks in 1844, and died in 1857.

[3] The Lat Bhairon.

and broke down a mosque, and the retort of the first aggressors was to kill a cow, and pour her blood into the sacred well. In consequence every Hindoo able to bear arms, and many who had no other fitness for the employment than rage supplied, procured weapons, and attacked their enemies with frantic fury wherever they met them. Being the most numerous party, they put the Mussulmans in danger of actual extermination, and would certainly have at least burned every mosque in the place before twenty-four hours were over, if the Sepoys had not been called in. Of these last, the temper was extremely doubtful. By far the greater number of them were Hindoos, and perhaps one half brahmins; any one of them, if he had been his own master, would have rejoiced in an opportunity of shedding his life's blood in a quarrel with the Mussulmans, and of the mob who attacked them, the brahmins, yoguees, gossains,[1] and other religious mendicants formed the front rank, their bodies and faces covered with chalk and ashes, their long hair untied as devoted to death, shewing their strings, and yelling out to them all the bitterest curses of their religion, if they persisted in urging an unnatural war against their brethren and their gods. The Sepoys, however, were immoveable. Regarding their military oath as the most sacred of all obligations, they fired at a brahmin as readily as at any one else, and kept guard at the gate of a mosque as faithfully and fearlessly as if it had been the gate of one of their own temples. Their courage and steadiness preserved Benares from ruin.

One observation of some of the Hindoo Sepoys was remarkable. The pillar, the destruction of which led to all the tumult, had originally stood in one of the Hindoo temples which were destroyed by Aurungzebe, and mosques built over them. In the mosque, however, it still was suffered to exist, and pilgrimages were made to it by the Hindoos through the connivance of the Mussulmans, in consequence of their being allowed to receive half of all the offerings made there. It was a very beautiful shaft of one stone, forty feet high, and covered with exquisite carving. This carving gave offence to several zealous Mahommedans, but the quarrel which hastened its destruction arose as I have stated, from the unfortunate rencontre of the rival processions. Res-

[1] Priests or devotees of the Vaishnavite sect.

148

pecting the pillar a tradition had long prevailed among the Hindoos, that it was gradually sinking in the ground, that it had been twice the visible height it then shewed, and that when its summit was level with the earth, all nations were to be of one caste, and the religion of Brahma to have an end. Two brahmin Sepoys were keeping guard in the mosque, where the defaced and prostrate pillar lay, 'Ah,' said one of them, 'we have seen that which *we* never thought to see, Siva's shaft has its head even with the ground; we shall all be of one caste shortly, what will be our religion then?' 'I suppose the Christian', answered the other. 'I suppose so too', rejoined the first, 'for after all that has passed, I am sure we shall never turn Mussulmans.'

After the tumult was quelled, a very curious and impressive scene succeeded; the holy city had been profaned; the blood of a cow had been mixed with the purest water of Gunga, and salvation was to be obtained at Benares no longer. All the brahmins in the city, amounting to many thousands, went down in melancholy procession, with ashes on their heads, naked and fasting, to the principal ghâts leading to the river, and sate there with their hands folded, their heads hanging down, to all appearance inconsolable, and refusing to enter a house or to taste food. Two or three days of this abstinence, however, began to tire them, and a hint was given to the magistrates and other public men, that a visit of condolence and an expression of sympathy with these holy mourners would sufficiently comfort them, and give them an ostensible reason for returning to their usual employment. Accordingly all the British functionaries went to the principal ghât, expressed their sorrow for the distress in which they saw them, but reasoned with them on the absurdity of punishing themselves for an act in which they had no share, and which they had done their utmost to prevent or avenge. This prevailed, and after much bitter weeping, it was resolved that Ganges was Ganges still, that a succession of costly offerings from the laity of Benares might wipe out the stain which their religion had received, and that the advice of the judges was the best and most reasonable. Mr Bird, who was one of the ambassadors on this occasion, told me that the scene was very impressive and even aweful. The gaunt squalid figures of the devotees, their visible and apparently unaffected anguish and dismay, the screams and outcries of the women who surrounded them, and the great numbers thus assembled, altogether constituted a spectable of woe such as few cities but Benares could supply.

Yet even this was exceeded by a spectacle of a kind almost similar, which Benares offered on another occasion. Government had then, unadvisedly, imposed a house-tax of a very unpopular character, both from its amount and its novelty.[1] To this the natives objected, that they recognised in their British rulers the same rights which had been exercised by the Moguls,—that the land-tax was theirs, and that they could impose duties on commodities going to market, or for exportation: but that their houses were their own,—that they had never been intermeddled with in any but their landed property, and commodities used in traffic,— and that the same power which now imposed a heavy and unheard of tax on their dwellings, might do the same next year on their children and themselves. These considerations, though backed by strong representations from the magistrates, produced no effect in Calcutta; on which the whole population of Benares and its neighbourhood determined to sit 'dhurna' till their grievances were redressed. To sit 'dhurna', or mourning, is to remain motionless in that posture, without food, and exposed to the weather, till the person against whom it is employed consents to the request offered; and the Hindoos believe, that whoever dies under such a process becomes a tormenting spirit to haunt and afflict his inflexible antagonist. This is a practice not unfrequent in the intercourse of individuals, to enforce payment of a debt, or forgiveness of one. And among Hindoos it is very prevailing, not only from the apprehended dreadful consequences of the death of the petitioner, but because many are of opinion, that while a person sits dhurna at their door, they must not themselves presume to eat, or undertake any secular business. It is even said that some persons hire brahmins to sit dhurna for them, the thing being to be done by proxy, and the dhurna of a brahmin being naturally more aweful in its effects than that of a soodra could be. I do not know whether there is any example under their ancient princes of a considerable portion of the people taking this strange method of

[1] By Regulation XV of 1810.

remonstrance against oppression, but in this case it was done with great resolution, and surprising concert and unanimity. Some of the leading brahmins sent written handbills to the wards in Benares nearest the college, and to some of the adjoining villages, declaring very shortly the causes and necessity of the measures which they were about to adopt, calling on all lovers of their country and national creed to join in it, and commanding, under many bitter curses, every person who received it to forward it to his next neighbour. Accordingly it flew over the country, like the fiery cross in the 'Lady of the Lake', and three days after it was issued, and before Government were in the least apprised of the plan, above 300,000 persons, as it is said, deserted their houses, shut up their shops, suspended the labour of their farms, forbore to light fires, dress victuals, many of them even to eat, and sate down with folded arms and drooping heads, like so many sheep, on the plain which surrounds Benares.

The local government were exceedingly perplexed. There was the chance that very many of these strange beings would really perish, either from their obstinacy, or the diseases which they would contract in their present situation. There was a probability that famine would ensue from the interruption of agricultural labours at the most critical time of the year. There was a certainty that the revenue would suffer very materially from this total cessation of all traffick. And it might even be apprehended that their despair, and the excitement occasioned by such a display of physical force would lead them to far stronger demonstrations of discontent than that of sitting dhurna. On the other hand, the authorities of Benares neither were permitted, nor would it have been expedient, to yield to such a demand, so urged. They conducted themselves with great prudence and good temper. Many of the natives appeared to expect, and the brahmins perhaps hoped, that they would still further outrage the feelings of the people, by violently suppressing their assemblage. They did no such thing, but coolly reasoned with some of the ringleaders on the impossibility that Government should yield to remonstrances so enforced. They however told them expressly, in answer to their enquiries, that if they chose to sit dhurna, it was their own affair; and that so long as they only injured themselves, and were peaceable in their behaviour to others, government would not meddle with them. They did not omit, however, to bring a strong body of Europeans from Dinapoor and Ghazepoor, to the neighbouring cantonment, without appearing to watch the conduct of the natives, or putting it into their heads that they suspected them of violent intentions. At last the multitude began to grow very hungry, and a thunder-shower which fell made them wet, cold, and uncomfortable. Some of the party proposed a change of operations, and that a deputation of 10,000 should be sent to address the Governor-General personally. This was eagerly carried by a majority heartily tired of their situation, and the next question was, how these men should be maintained during their journey? when one leading brahmin proposed a tax on houses. A string was here struck which made the whole instrument jar. 'A tax on houses! If we are to pay a tax on houses after all, we might as well have remained on good terms with our Government, sitting under our vines and fig-trees, and neither hungry nor rheumatic.' A great number caught at the excuse for a rupture, and rose to go home, but the remainder determined that all should go to the Governor, every man at his own charge. The seeds of disunion were already sown, and the majority absented themselves from the muster which was held three days after. From ten to twenty thousand, however, really assembled with such provisions as they could collect, and began their march, still unmolested by the magistrates, whose whole conduct was wise and merciful; they well calculated that provisions would soon fall short, and travelling become wearisome, and merely watched their motions at some distance with a corps of cavalry. They knew that hunger would make them plunder, and that the hilly and jungly road from Benares to the neighbourhood of Burdwan, afforded few facilities for the subsistence of so great a multitude. Accordingly, in a few days they melted away to so small a number, that the remainder were ashamed to proceed. The supreme Government followed up their success most wisely by a repeal of the obnoxious tax, and thus ended a disturbance which, if it had been harshly or improperly managed, might have put all India in a flame.

Benares being in many respects the commercial, and in all, the ecclesiastical metropolis of India, I was not surprised to find persons from all parts of the Peninsula residing there. But I was astonished to hear of the number of Persians, Turks, Tartars, and even Europeans, who are to be met with. Among them is a Greek, a well-informed and well-mannered man, who has fixed himself here for many years, living on his means, whatever they are, and professing to study the Sanscrit. I heard a good deal of him afterwards in Allahabad, and was much struck by the singularity and mystery of his character and situation. He is a very good scholar in the ancient language of his country, and speaks good English, French, and Italian. His manners are those of a gentleman, and he lives like a person at his ease. He has little intercourse with the English, but is on very friendly terms with the principal Hindoo families. He was once an object of suspicion to Government, but after watching him for a long time they saw nothing in his conduct to confirm their suspicions, and during Lord Hastings's first Pindarree war, he voluntarily gave, on different occasions, information of much importance. So few Europeans, however, who can help it, reside in India, that it seems strange that any man should prefer it as a residence, without some stronger motive than a fondness for Sanscrit literature, more particularly since he does not appear to meditate any work on the subject. He was a partner in a Greek house in Calcutta, but is now said to have retired from business. There is also a Russian here, who by a natural affinity lives much with the Greek. He is, however, a trader, and has apparently moved in a much humbler rank of society than his friend.

Though Benares is the holy place of India, the brahmins there are less intolerant and prejudiced than in most other places. The eternal round of idle ceremonies in which they pass their time, is said to have produced, in many of them, a degree of weariness of their own system, and a disposition to enquire after others which does not exist in Calcutta. I was told that the Archdeacon, when here, was an object of great interest and respect with them, and had he resided longer it is probable that he would have had more converts than at Agra. It is also generally speaking, loyal, and well-affected to the Company's Government, though its inhabitants being in fact superior in rank, wealth, and education, to those of the average of Indian towns, talk more of public men and public matters.

I was curious to know what Governors of India had stood highest in their good opinion, and found that they usually spoke of Warren Hastings and Lord Wellesley as the two greatest men who had ever ruled this part of the world, but that they spoke with most *affection* of Mr Jonathan Duncan. 'Duncan sahib ka chota bhaee', 'Mr Duncan's younger brother' is still the usual term of praise applied to any public man who appears to be actuated by an unusual spirit of kindness and liberality towards their nation. Of the sultan-like and splendid character of Warren Hastings, many traits are preserved, and a nursery rhyme, which is often sung to children, seems to shew how much they were pleased with the Oriental, (not European) pomp which he knew how to employ on occasion.

> 'Hat'hee pur howdah, ghore pur jeen,
> Juldee bah'r jata Sahib *Warren Husteen!!*'[1]

Of Lord Hastings I have not found that they have retained any very favourable impression. Yet the extent of his conquests, and his pleasing manners during his short visit, must, I should think, have struck them.

Heber left Banaras on 9 September and resumed his voyage up the Ganges.

September 15.—We passed Mirzapoor, the size and apparent opulence of which surprised me, as it is a place of no ancient importance or renown, has grown up completely since the English power has been established here, and under our government is only an inferior civil station, with a few native troops. It is, however, a very great town, as large, I should think, as Patna,

---

[1] With howdah on elephant, saddle on horse,
Sahib Warren Hastings rode quickly forth.'
There is however another version of this rhyme:
Ghore par howda, hathi par zin,   Howdah on horse, saddle on elephant,
Jaldi bhaggaya Warren Hastin   Swiftly fled Warren Hastings.'
This commemorates the confusion in which Warren Hastings retired from Banaras to Chunar in 1781, at the time of the insurrection consequent on his arrest of Raja Chait Singh; see C. C. Davies, *Warren Hastings and Oudh*, 1939, 137–8.

with many handsome native houses, and a vast number of mosques and temples, numerous and elegant bungalows in its outskirts and on the opposite side of the river,—a great number of boats of all kinds moored under its ghâts, and is computed to contain between 2 and 300,000 people.

This is, indeed, a most rich and striking land. Here, in the space of little more than 200 miles, along the same river, I have passed six towns, none of them less populous than Chester,—two, (Patna and Mirzapoor,) more so than Birmingham; and one, Benares, more peopled than any city in Europe, except London and Paris! And this besides villages innumerable. I observed to Mr Corrie that I had expected to find agriculture in Hindostan in a flourishing state, but the great cities ruined, in consequence of the ruin of the Mussulman nobles. He answered, that certainly very many ancient families had gone to decay, but he did not think the gap had been ever perceptible in his time, in this part of India, since it had been more than filled up by a new order rising from the middling classes, whose wealth had, during his recollection, increased very greatly. Far indeed from those cities which we had already passed, decaying, most of them had much increased in the number of their houses, and in what is a sure sign of wealth in India, the number and neatness of their ghâts and temples, since he was last here. Nothing, he said, was plainer to him, from the multitude of little improvements of this kind, of small temples and Bungalows, partly in the European style, but obviously inhabited by natives, that wealth was becoming more abundant among the middling ranks, and that such of them as are rich are not afraid of appearing so. The great cities in the Dooab, he said, were indeed scenes of desolation. The whole country round Delhi and Agra, when he first saw it, was filled with the marble ruins of villas, mosques, and palaces, with the fragments of tanks and canals, and the vestiges of inclosures. But this ruin had occurred before the British arms had extended thus far, and while the country was under the tyranny and never-ending invasions of the Persians, Affghans, and Maharattas. Even here a great improvement had taken place before he left Agra, and he hoped to find a much greater on his return. He apprehended that on the whole, all India had gained under British rule, except, perhaps, Dacca and its neighbourhood, where the manufactures had been nearly ruined.

September 18.—The east wind blew pleasantly all the afternoon, bringing up a good many clouds, but no actual rain. It helped us across some very bad passes of the stream, where without its aid, we might have been detained many hours, or even days. A little after five o'clock we arrived at a village called Diha, where there is a large nullah, which when navigable affords the easiest and most direct passage to Allahabad. At present the water was too shallow, and we went by the main stream. Mohammed wanted to stop here, but as we had wind and day-light still, I urged him to proceed a little further and to moor on the eastern bank, along which I apprehended the great dâk-road to run, and designed to push on in my palanqueen to Allahabad that night. Unfortunately the wind soon grew fainter, and the stream being very strong, it was quite dark before we reached the eastern shore. I determined on going myself to ascertain if there was a village near, both as liking to explore, and under the idea that by seeing the Than-nadar, could any such be found, I should judge better for myself as to the possiblity or expediency of engaging bearers, either immediately or for the next morning. I accordingly set out, having a dandee with a lantern, Abdullah and one of the Tindals[1] with each a spear, a defence which the former assured me might not be superfluous, and would at all events *make me respected.* I had only my great stick as usual, but that is a tolerably large one, and well used, would in this country be no inconsiderable weapon. I had another fruitless ramble through very high corn, some of it literally above my head, and over a broad extent of fallow and pasture, but found no village. Some lights were visible, but they were extinguished as my party drew near, and it was not easy to discover whence they proceeded. I had the caution to mark the position of the stars before I set out, or we should have had much trouble to find our way back again. At length we stumbled on a herdsman's shed, where we found two men, whom the sight of our spears put, not without some cause, in great alarm, and from whom we could get little for some time but protestations that

---

[1] Petty officer.

they were very poor, and entreaties not to hurt them. They had put out their fire, they said, because it was a lonely place, and seeing our light, and hearing our voices, they were afraid; they spoke of the nearest village as a coss and a half distant, and displayed great reluctance to undertake to guide us there. There was no Thannah, they said, nearer than two coss. They spoke not Oordoo, but what Abdullah said was the true Hindoo.[1] Milk they called not 'doodh', but 'gaoruss', '*cow-dew*', from 'russ', '*ros*'. Rain they called '*russ*' simply. They told us of a good path through the Indian corn to the river, in following which we came to another shed of the same sort, where a man with his wife and children were cooking their supper. The man called to us for heaven's sake not to come near him, for he was a brahmin, and our approach would oblige him to fling away his mess. In answer to my desire that he would sell some milk, he said he could sell us none, but if I chose to take a small jug which stood on one side, I might. 'Nay', said I, 'I take nothing without paying.' 'I am a brahmin', he replied, 'and dare not sell milk, but I give it you voluntarily.' 'Well, brahmin,' I answered, 'take up the jug and bring it to the boat, and I will give you a present, not for the milk, but voluntarily, and because you are a good fellow.' He immediately started up with exceeding good-will, and went with us, talking all the way, but in a dialect which I comprehended but little. I only understood that he boasted of his own courage in not being afraid of us when we came up; most people would have been so, he said, but he had a brother who was a Sepoy, and he had been to see him with his regiment at Sultanpoor, and therefore he was not afraid when he saw a Sahib at the head of the party. He said he was one of the village watchmen, and that it was less degrading for a brahmin to be thus employed, than as a cultivator, which seems to be by no means an usual occupation for them in this part of India, though it is often seen in other districts.

September 19.—Allahabad stands in perhaps the most favourable situation which India affords for a great city, in a dry and healthy soil, on a triangle, at the junction of the two mighty streams, Gunga, and Jumna, with an easy communication with Bombay and Madras, and capable of being fortified so as to become almost

---

[1] i.e. Hindi, derived from Sanskrit. Urdu's affiliations were rather with Persian.

impregnable. But though occasionally the residence of royalty, though generally inhabited by one of the Shah-zadehs,[1] and still containing two or three fine ruins, it never appears to have been a great or magnificent city, and is now even more desolate and ruinous than Dacca, having obtained, among the natives, the name of 'Fakeer-abad', 'beggar-abode'. It may, however, revive to some greater prosperity, from the increase of the civil establishment attached to it. It is now the permanent station (the castrum Hybernum) of the Sudder Mofussil commission, a body of judges whose office is the same with regard to these provinces as that of the Sudder Dewannee Udawlut for the eastern parts of the empire. The necessity for such a special court had become very great. The remoteness of the Sudder Dewannee had made appeals to it almost impossible, and very great extortion and oppression had been committed by the native agents of the inferior and local courts, sometimes with the connivance, but more often through the ignorance and inexperience of the junior magistrates and judges. They, when these provinces were placed under British Governors, having been previously employed in Bengal and Bahar, naturally took their Bengalee followers with them, a race regarded by the Hindoostanees as no less foreigners than the English, and even more odious than Franks, from ancient prejudice, and from their national reputation of craft, covetousness, and cowardice. In fact, by one means or other, these Bengalees almost all acquired considerable landed property in a short time among them, and it has been the main business of the Sudder Mofussil Udawlut, to review the titles to all property acquired since the English Government entered the Dooab.[2] In many instances they have succeeded in recovering all or part of extensive possessions to their rightful heirs, and the degree of confidence in the justice of their rulers, with which they have inspired the natives, is said to be very great. They make circuits during all the travelling months of the year, generally pitching their tents near towns, and holding their courts under trees, an arrangement so agreeable to Indian prejudices, that one of these

[1] Princes of the Imperial dynasty.
[2] The land between the Jamuna and the Ganges, to the north-west of Allahabad, which Wellesley had forced Oudh to cede in 1801.

judges said it was, in his opinion, one main source of their usefulness, inasmuch as an Indian of the humbler class, is really always
under constraint and fear in a house, particularly if furnished in
the European manner, and can neither attend to what is told him,
nor tell his own story so well as in the open air, and amidst those
objects from which all his enjoyments are drawn. At Allahabad,
however, where their permanent abodes are, these judges have a
court-house, though a very humble one, thatched, and inconvenient.

[At Allahabad the Bishop saw part of] the Ramayuna festival,
which consists in a sort of dramatic representation during many
successive days, of Rama's history and adventures. The first
evening I went with Mr Bird to the *show*, for as such it is now
considered, and so entirely divested of every religious character
as to be attended even by Mussulmans without scruple. I found
Rama, his brother Luchmun, and his betrothed wife Seeta, represented by three children of about twelve years old, seated in
Durbar, under an awning in the principal street of the Sepoy
lines, with a great crowd round them, some fanning them, of
which poor things they had great need, some blowing horns and
beating gongs and drums, and the rest shouting till the air rang
again. The two heroes were very fine boys, and acted their parts
admirably. Each had a gilt bow in his left hand, and a sabre in his
right, their naked bodies were almost covered with gilt ornaments and tinsel, they had high tinsel crowns on their heads, their
foreheads and bodies spotted with charcoal, chalk, and vermilion,
and altogether perfectly resembled the statues of Hindoo deities,

> 'Except that of their eyes alone
> The twinkle shewed they were not stone.'

Poor little Seeta, wrapt up in a gorgeous veil of flimsy finery, and
tired to death, had dropped her head on her breast and seemed
happily insensible to all which was going on. The brahmin Sepoys
who bore the principal part in the play, made room, with great
solicitude, for us to see. I asked a good many questions, and
obtained very ready answers in much the same way, and with no
more appearance of reverence or devotion than one should receive

from an English mob at a puppet-show. 'I see Rama, Seeta, Luchnum, but where is Hunimân?' (the famous monkey general.) 'Hunimân', was the answer, 'is not yet come; but that man', pointing to a great stout soldier of singularly formidable exterior, 'is Hunimân, and he will soon arrive.' The man began laughing as if half ashamed of his destination, but now took up the conversation, telling me that 'next day was to be a far prettier play than I now saw, for Seeta was to be stolen away by Ravana and his attendant evil spirits, Rama and Luchmun were to go to the jungle in great sorrow to seek for her',

('Rama, your Rama! to greenwood must hie!')

That 'then (laughing again) I and my army shall come, and we shall fight bravely, bravely.' The evening following I was engaged, but the next day I repeated my visit; I was then too late for the best part of the show, which had consisted of a first and unsuccessful attack by Rama and his army on the fortress of the gigantic ravisher. That fortress, however, I saw,—an enclosure of bamboos, covered with paper and painted with doors and windows, within which was a frightful paper giant, fifteen feet high, with ten or twelve arms, each grasping either a sword, an arrow, a bow, a battle-axe, or a spear. At his feet sate poor little Seeta as motionless as before, guarded by two figures to represent demons. The brothers in a splendid palkee,[1] were conducting the retreat of their army; the divine Hunimân, as naked and almost as hairy as the animal whom he represented, was gamboling before them, with a long tail tied round his waist, a mask to represent the head of a baboon, and two great painted clubs in his hands. His army followed, a number of men with similar tails and masks, their bodies dyed with indigo, and also armed with clubs. I was never so forcibly struck with the identity of Rama and Bacchus. Here were before me Bacchus, his brother Ampelus, the Satyrs, (smeared with wine lees) and the great Pan commanding them. The fable, however, can hardly have originated in India, and probably has been imported both by the Greeks and Brahmins from Cashmere, or some other central country where the grape grows, unless we suppose that the grape has been merely an

[1] Palanquin.

accidental appendage to Bacchus's character, arising from the fact that the festival occurs during the vintage. There yet remained two or three days of pageant, before Seeta's release, purification, and re-marriage to her hero lover, but for this conclusion I did not remain in Allahabad.

[On 30 September the Bishop left Allahabad and started the over-land part of his journey:] having sent off some hours before our motley train, consisting of twenty-four camels, eight carts drawn by bullocks, twenty-four horse-servants, including those of the Archdeacon and Mr Lushington, ten poneys, forty bearers and coolies of different descriptions, twelve tent-pitchers, and a guard of twenty Sepoys under a native officer. The whimsical caravan filed off in state before me; my servants, all armed with spears, to which many of them had added, at their own cost, sabres of the longest growth, looked, on their little poneys, like something between cossacks and sheriff's javelin-men; my new Turkman horse,[1] still in the costume of his country, with his long, squirrel-like tail painted red, and his mane plaited in love-knots, looked as if he were going to eat fire, or perform some other part in a melodrama; while Mr Lushington's horses, two very pretty Arabs, with their tails docked, and their saddles English ('Ungrigi') fashion, might have attracted notice in Hyde-park, the Archdeacon's buggy and horse had every appearance of issuing from the back gate of a college in Cambridge on a Sunday morning; and lastly came some mounted gens d'armes, and a sword and buckler-man on foot, looking exactly like the advanced guard of a Tartar army. Rain, however, long prayed for, but which was now an inconvenience to us, prevented our starting all together, and it was late in the evening before we arrived at Cooseah, 16 miles from Allahabad, where we found two excellent tents, of three apartments each, pitched for our reception, and the tea-kettle boiling under the shade of some stately trees in a wild country of ruins and jungle, now gemmed and glowing with the scattered fires of our cofilah.[2]

This was the first night I ever passed under canvas, and,

---

[1] Which Heber had bought in Allahabad, and named Cabul.
[2] Caravan.

independent of its novelty, I found the comforts of my dwelling greatly exceed my expectation. The breeze blew in very fresh and pleasantly through the tent door, the ground, covered with short withered grass, was perfectly dry, though rain had so lately fallen, and my bed and musquito-curtains were arranged with as much comfort as in Calcutta. The only circumstance which struck me as likely to be annoying, even to a lady, was the publicity of the situation,—her bed within a few inches of an open door, a body of men-servants and soldiers sleeping all round that door, and a sentry pacing backwards and forwards before it. After all, however, this publicity is more apparent than real. The check of the tent prevents effectually any person from seeing what passes within who does not come purposely up to peep, and this the sentry would not allow.

At five o'clock on the morning of October 1st we again began our march, and proceeded about twelve miles, to the second customary station, called Cussiah, a grove of neem-trees, more extensive than that which we had left, and at a small distance from a large but ruinous village. We passed through a country much wilder, worse cultivated, and worse peopled than any which I had seen in India. What cultivation there was consisted of maize, growing very tall, but sadly burnt by the continued drought. This, however, was only in patches, and the greater part of the prospect consisted of small woods, scattered in a very picturesque manner over a champaign country, with few signs of habitations, and those most of them in ruins. I was strongly reminded of the country of the Tchemoi-morski Cossaks, to which the groupes of people in dresses nearly similar, and all armed, who passed us on the road, undoubtedly, in a great measure, contributed. I had been disposed to wonder at Colonel Francklin's counsel to buy spears for my servants, and at the escort which had been ordered me; but I soon found, that whether necessary or not, such precautions were at least customary. Every traveller whom we met, even the common people going to market, had either swords and shields, spears, or match-lock guns, and one man had a bow and quiver of arrows, in that circumstance, as well as in his dress and person, extremely resembling a Circassian warrior. The road was rugged; nothing, indeed, so far as I had yet seen, could appear more unfounded than the assurances which I have heard in Calcutta, that an open carriage is an eligible method of travelling in the Dooab, on any other ground than cheapness. I have been often told that the road as far as Meerut would answer perfectly for a gig. The fact is there are no roads at all, and the tracks which we follow are very often such as to require care even on horseback. . . .

Both men and women, whom we met on the road, I thought decidedly taller, fairer, and finer people than the Bengalees. Some of the Sepoys, indeed, of a regiment who passed us, were of complexions so little darker than those of Europe, that as they approached I really at first took them for Europeans. Every thing seems to assimilate gradually to the scenes and habits of the eastern and southern parts of Europe. The people no longer talk of their daily *rice*, but say 'it is time to eat *bread* to-day'. Instead of the softness and gentleness so apparent in those Indians whom we first saw, these men have a proud step, a stern eye, and a rough loud voice, such as might be expected from people living almost always in the open air, and in a country where, till its acquisition by the English, no man was sure that he might not at any moment be compelled to fight for his life or property. Much of this necessity is passed away, but something yet remains. The nation is still one of lawless and violent habits, containing many professed thieves, and many mercenary soldiers, who, in the present tranquillity of the country, are at any instant ready to become thieves, and the general sense of moral feeling is, in this particular, so low, that one ceases to wonder that banditti are from time to time heard of, and that every body finds it desirable to take his arms with him on a journey.

October 8.—In crossing a nuddee, which from a ford had become a ferry,[1] we saw some characteristic groupes and occurrences; the price of passage in the boat was only a few cowries, but a number of country-folk were assembled, who could not, or would not, pay, and were now sitting patiently by the brink, waiting till the torrent should subside, or, what was far less likely to happen, till the boat-men should take compassion on them. Many of these poor people came up to beg me to make the boat-

[1] There had been heavy rain recently.

men take them over, one woman pleading that her 'malik our bucher', (literally master, or lord, and young one) had run away from her, and she wanted to overtake them; another that she and her two grand-children were following her son, who was a havildar[1] in the regiment which we had passed just before; and some others, that they had been intercepted the previous day by this torrent, and had neither money nor food till they reached their homes. Four anas purchased a passage for the whole crowd, of perhaps 30 people, and they were really very thankful. I bestowed two anas more on the poor deserted woman, and a whimsical scene ensued. She at first took the money with eagerness, then as if she recollected herself, she blushed very deeply and seemed much confused, then bowed herself to my feet and kissed my hands, and at last said, in a very modest tone, 'it was not fit for so great a man as I was, to give her two anas, and she hoped that I and the "chota Sahib", (little lord) would give her a rupee each!' She was an extremely pretty little woman, but we were inexorable, partly I believe, in my own case at least, because we had only just rupees enough to take us to Cawnpoor, and to pay for our men's provisions; however I gave her two more anas, my sole remaining stock of small change.

When this was all done, the jemautdar of the neighbouring village came to ask for the usual certificate of his having rendered us assistance. I wrote it out for him on top of my palanqueen, having provided myself for such purposes with paper and Sir Thomas Acland's[2] inkstand, when a new scene followed. He was very grateful for the good word I gave him, but he had a brother, a fine young man, now in the service of the Peishwa Bajee Row, in the neighbouring town of Betourah, but who was anxious to get into the Company's service, 'would I have the goodness to give him a recommendation to the judge Sahib of Betourah?' 'I do not know the judge Sahib of Betourah.' 'But Huzoor (your worship) is Malik of the land, and your Firmaun[3] will be obeyed.' 'Suppose I could do your brother any good, I do not know him, how shall I recommend him?' 'Huzoor may believe me when I tell

---

[1] Non-commissioned officer.

[2] Sir Thomas Dyke Acland (1787–1871), M.P., an active supporter of religious enterprises, and a friend of Heber's.

[3] Order.

him that my brother is one of the best men in the world!' 'But I am only a traveller, and have no power.' 'Huzoor is pleased to say so—but'——in short I could hardly get him away from the palanqueen side, particularly as I did not chuse to set off till I had seen the poor people embark, for whose passage I had paid. We then parted, the jemautdar still declaring that he would follow me to Cawnpoor, and bring his brother with him.

The natives of India seem to attach very great importance to a written recommendation by an European, or person in a public station, in which, as in many other points, they strongly resemble the Russians. The whole scene which I have described, mutatis mutandis, (crucifixes for brahminical strings, &c.) might have occurred at a ferry on the Don or the Dnieper. The mixture of simplicity and cunning, the importunity, the patience and the flattery, seem to belong almost equally to the peasantry of both countries, or more accurately speaking, perhaps, to the state of society in which they are placed.

The Bishop arrived at Kanpur (Cawnpore) on 9 October. After a nine days' stay he left the town and started on his journey through the Kingdom of Oudh.

Part IV

OUDH

October 20.—The journey this morning was of seven very long coss, through bad roads, with a deep river, and several gullies made by the recent rain. Our station was a large walled village, with gates, and bazar in a much handsomer style than usual, but the walls bearing marks of decay, and many of the houses roofless, though the shops were neat, and the appearance of the people comfortable and thriving. All was quiet when we arrived; but the servants who had gone on before with the breakfast tents, had found the place in a state of siege. A large sum of money, said to be 30,000 rupees, on its way to the treasury at Lucknow, had attracted a number of the neighbouring peasantry, who were assembled outside the walls with their weapons, waiting for the departure of the treasure, while sentries were posted by the escort on all the old towers, and the gates were fast closed. One of our servants applied for a passage in vain; the warders were civil, but peremptory, pointing to the lurking enemy, and asking how they should endanger the treasure of 'the refuge of the world'.[1] At last, on more of our sepoys coming up, and finding that we were strong enough to protect them, they gladly opened their gates, and the armed peasantry dispersed themselves. Our camp was fixed beyond the town, near a large pool of water, amid some tall trees, and having at a little distance a grove surrounded by a high wall with a gothic gateway, the garden, as we were told, of a former minister of Oude, named Nawâll Sing, who had built the village, and from whom it derived its name.

Adjoining the pool we saw a crowd of people assembled round a fallen elephant; apprehending that it was one of our own I urged my horse to the spot. On asking, however, whose it was,

---

[1] A title of the King of Oudh.

a bystander said it belonged to 'the asylum of the world', and had fallen down from weakness, which was not surprising, since instead of an allowance of twenty-five rupees a month, necessary for the keep of an elephant, I was told that these poor creatures, all but those in the immediate stables of his majesty, had for some time back, owing to the dilapidated state of the finances, and the roguery of the commissariate, received only five! They had now given the wretched animal a cordial, and were endeavouring to raise it on its legs, but in vain. It groaned pitifully, but lay quite helpless, and was in fact a mountain of skin and bone. Another elephant of very large size, and in somewhat better plight, was brought to assist, and I was much struck with the almost human expression of surprise, alarm, and perplexity in his countenance, when he approached his fallen companion. They fastened a chain round his neck and the body of the sick beast, and urged him in all ways, by encouragement and blows, to drag him up, even thrusting spears into his flanks. He pulled stoutly for a minute, but on the first groan his companion gave he stopped short, turned fiercely round with a loud roar, and with his trunk and fore feet began to attempt to loosen the chain from his neck. In fact, his resistance and refusal to sanction their proceedings were so decisive, that an immediate cry arose of 'le-jao', take him away, in which I very cordially joined. I asked them if they could get nothing which the fallen animal was likely to eat, urging that weak as he was, even if they did get him to rise, he would certainly fall again. They seemed sensible of this, and two of them ran for a great bundle of greens and a pot of water; the greens he ate readily enough, but refused the water, which they accounted for by saying he supposed it was physic. He was said to be very old, which the size of his tusks confirmed. Among the groupe thus assembled were some of the tallest and finest men I have ever seen here, or indeed in Europe. All the crowd were civil and communicative, and I could not help thinking that the peasants of Oude, in every thing but honesty, bore a high rank among those of their own class throughout the world.

October 21.—We set out at half-past three o'clock, and for some time lost our way, there being no other road than such tracks as are seen across ploughed fields in England, the whole country being cultivated, though not enclosed, and much inter-sected by small rivers and nullahs. The King's suwarrs[1] were, I found, for shew only, since they knew nothing about the road, and as for defence I should have been very sorry to be obliged to rely on them. I was pleased, however, and surprised, after all which I had heard of Oude, to find the country so completely under the plough, since were the oppression so great as is some-times stated, I cannot think that we should witness so consider-able a population, or so much industry. Yet that considerable anarchy and mis-rule exist, the events of yesterday afforded a sufficient reason for supposing.

The bulk of the population is still evidently Hindoo. All the villages have pagodas, while many are without mosques; by far the greater part of the people who pass us on the road, have the marks of caste on their foreheads, and it being now a Hindoo festival, the drumming, braying, and clattering of their noisy music was heard from every little collection of houses which we passed through. At length, and sooner than we expected, we saw a considerable 'Suwarree', or retinue, of elephants and horses approaching us, and were met by Captain Salmon[2] and the King of Oude's officer, the latter followed by a train of elephants splendidly equipped with silver howdahs, and sufficient to accommodate more than three times the number of our party. A good many suwarrs, in red and yellow, followed Captain Salmon, and a most irregular and picturesque body of infantry, with swords and shields, long matchlock guns, and other guns of every sort and size, spears like spits, composed, sheath and all, of iron, and some silvered over, large triangular green banners, and every thing most unlike the appearance of European war, made up the cortége of Meer Hussun Khân. The whole formed a stage procession of the most interesting and shewy kind, in which there was no regularity and little real magnificence, for the dresses of the men and trappings of the elephants were all the worse for wear, and the silver howdahs did not bear a close

[1] Cavalry soldiers, who had been provided as an escort for Heber.
[2] W. B. Salmon (1787–1843), the commandant of the escort of the Resident at Lucknow.

examination, but where flowing and picturesque dresses, glowing colours, numbers, and the majestic size of the noble animals which formed the most prominent part of the groupe, produced an effect more pleasing in the eye of a poet or an artist, than the sprucest parade of a an English review.

While I was changing elephants, a decent looking man stepped up to me, and begged to know my name and titles at full length, in order, as he said, 'to make a report of them to the asylum of the world'. I found, on enquiry, that he was the writer of the court circular, a much more minute task, and one considered of far more importance here than in Europe. Every thing which occurs in the family of the King himself, the resident, the chief officers of state, or any stranger of rank who may arrive, is carefully noted and sent round in writing. And I was told that the exact hour at which I rose, the sort of breakfast I ate, the visits I paid or received, and the manner in which I passed my morning, would all be retailed by the King's chobdars, for the information of their master, whose own most indifferent actions, however, are with equal fairness written down for Mr Ricketts's[1] inspection. . . .

We now proceeded, three elephants abreast, that on which Mr Lushington and I rode, in the centre. Meer Hussun Khân on the right, and Captain Salmon on the left, with the motley multitude before and the spare elephants behind. The Corries had fallen back, being unable to keep up with us. We thus advanced into Lucknow, through a very considerable population, and crowded mean houses of clay, with the filthiest lanes between them that I ever went through, and so narrow that we were often obliged to reduce our front, and even a single elephant did not always pass very easily. A swarm of beggars occupied every angle and the steps of every door, and all, or nearly all the remaining population were, to my surprise, as much loaded with arms as the inhabitants of the country, a circumstance which told ill for the police of the town, but added considerably to its picturesque effect. Grave men in palanqueens, counting their beads and looking like Moullahs, had all two or three sword and buckler lacquies attending on them. People of more consequence,

---

[1] Mordaunt Ricketts, who had been appointed Resident at Lucknow in 1822 and retired in 1830.

on their elephants, had each a suwarree of shield, spear, and gun, little inferior to that by which we were surrounded, and even the lounging people of the lower ranks in the streets and shop-doors, had their shields over their shoulders, and their swords carried sheathed in one hand.

I recollected Sir W. Scott's picture of the streets of London in 'the Fortunes of Nigel', but I should apprehend that Lucknow offered at this moment a more warlike exterior than our own metropolis ever did during its most embroiled and troublesome periods. As we advanced, the town began to improve in point of buildings, though the streets remained equally narrow and dirty. We passed some pretty mosques and some large houses, built like the native houses in Calcutta, and the bazars seemed well filled, so far as I could distinguish from the height at which I sat, and the general narrowness of the area. At last we suddenly entered a very handsome street indeed, wider than the High-street at Oxford, but having some distant resemblance to it in the colour of its buildings, and the general form and Gothic style of the greater part of them. We saw but little of it, however, as we immediately turned up through some folding-gates into a sort of close, with good-looking houses and small gardens round it, and a barrack and guard-house at its entrance. One of these houses I was told belonged to the Resident, another was his banqueting-house, containing apartments for his guests, and a third very pretty upper-roomed house in a little garden was pointed out as that which the King had assigned to receive me and my party. Here, therefore, our companions took their leave, and Mr Lushington and I found ourselves in a very prettily arranged and well-furnished dwelling, with excellent stables and accommodations for our numerous followers. It was the house usually assigned to the King's physician, now absent, and was extremely well suited to my purpose, both as being near the Residency, and sufficiently detached from it to allow me to have some part of my mornings to myself. The Corries arrived in about half-an-hour, and shortly afterwards we were summoned to breakfast at the Residency, where we found so large a party as completely to give the idea of a watering-place. After breakfast I was told the prime-minister[1] was

---

[1] The Agha Mir.

come to call on me, and Mr Ricketts introduced us to each other in form. He is a dark, harsh, hawk-nosed man, with an expression of mouth which seems to imply habitual self-command struggling with a naturally rough temper. He is, I understand, exceedingly unpopular. He was originally khânsaman to the present King,[1] when heir-apparent and in disgrace with his father, Saadut Ali.[2] His house is the most splendid in Lucknow, and his suwarree exceeds that of the King, who is said to be so attached to him as to have given himself entirely into his hands. His manners, though not his appearance, are those of a gentleman; he is said to be man of undoubted courage, and to be a pleasant person to do business with, except that too much confidence must not be placed in him. He was very civil to me, and very tolerant of my bad Hindoo-stanee, but I saw that he was nursing some ill-humour towards Mr Ricketts, and found at length that offence had been taken because Lord Amherst had not himself written to the King to introduce me, as had, he said, been the constant custom with other Governors General whenever any person of a certain rank in the country visited Lucknow. We explained to him that my regular progress was through those stations where there were chaplains, and that, therefore, it was probable that Lord Amherst did not know that I intended to visit Lucknow, and he seemed satisfied. Possibly Lord Amherst was not aware that such an etiquette was usual, and in my own case it was certainly ignorance which pre-vented my asking for such credentials. However the minister seemed satisfied, his dark countenance cleared up, and he said that the introduction of their friend the Resident was quite enough for them and that the King hoped to make Lucknow not unpleasant to me. The remaining conversation was about the cities and countries which I had visited, how I liked the first sight of Lucknow, and concluded with the minister's inviting me, on the part of the King, to breakfast with him the Monday following.

This is the usual way of being presented at this court, and the reason given for not naming an earlier day, was that the King had a bad feverish cold. I found, indeed, half Lucknow laid up with the same influenza, though of a slighter degree, with that which had prevailed so universally in Calcutta during the rains. In fact,

[1] Ghazi-ud-din Haidar: reigned 1814–27.   [2] Reigned 1798–1814.

I know not how, the sight of the town, its various villainous smells, and its close population, gave me the idea of a very unhealthy place, though I found that the old residents disclaimed the imputation.

There are one or two very English-looking country-houses near Lucknow, all, I believe, the property of the king, and it may be said that from the Residency all the way down the principal street, and afterward through the park of Dil-Koushar,[1] and the neighbouring drives, Lucknow has more resemblance to some of the smaller European capitals (Dresden for instance) than any thing which I have seen in India. The King's troops, besides the irregular gentry of whom I saw a specimen on entering the city, are dressed in the same way that the British Sepoys used to be twenty years ago, and as they are represented in Kerr Porter's 'Storming of Seringapatam'. They are armed with musquets and bayonets under British officers, and not ill-disciplined, but their numbers are not more than are required for the usual purposes of parade and mounting sentries. His horse-guards are fine tall men, and well-mounted, but are in discipline and military appearance a little, and but a little, better than those which attend the Nawâb of Dacca. The British subsidiary force,[2] which is at the disposal of the Resident, is, by a strange choice, placed in a cantonment five miles from the town, separated by the broad and rapid stream of the Goomty, where there is indeed a fine old bridge, but one which might in a few minutes be rendered impassable by any force without a regular siege, so that in case of a commotion in the city, either King or Resident would have to rely entirely on the single company which is always on guard at the Residency, but which would be as nothing when opposed to such an armed population as that of Lucknow. That they have never yet been exposed to this danger seems a sufficient proof of the quiet disposition of the people, as well as of the opinion which they entertain of the supposed stability of the Company's empire; yet the English,

[1] The King of Oudh's summer palace.

[2] East India Company troops stationed in Lucknow; ostensibly to protect the King against his enemies but also to underpin the Company's influence over him. Similar forces had been introduced into several other princely states by that time.

both at Lucknow and Cawnpoor, often spoke of the anarchical
condition, the frequent affrays, the hatred of the European and
Christian name, the robberies and murders by which this city is
distinguished, and I was cautioned expressly by more people
than one, never to go into the populous parts of the city except on
an elephant, and attended by some of the Resident's or the King's
chuprassees. It so happened that the morning before this counsel
was given, Mr Lushington and I had gone on horseback through
almost the whole place, along streets and alleys as narrow and
far dirtier than those of Benares, and in a labyrinth of buildings
which obliged us to ask our way at almost every turn. So far from
having chuprassees, we had as it happened but one saees between
us, and he as much a stranger as ourselves, yet we found invari-
able civility and good nature, people backing their carts and
elephants to make room for us, and displaying on the whole a far
greater spirit of hospitality and accommodation than two
foreigners would have met with in London. One old man only,
when my horse shewed considerable reluctance to pass an
elephant, said, shaking his head in a sort of expostulating tone,
'this is not a good road for sahibs'. Some of the instances,
indeed, which were related of Europeans being insulted and
assaulted in the streets and neighbourhood of Lucknow, were
clearly traced to insolent or overbearing conduct on the part of
the complainants themselves, and though of course there are bad
and worthless people every where, though where every body is
armed, and there is no efficient police, street-brawls will be less
infrequent than in cities more fortunately circumstanced, and
though by night narrow streets ill-watched and unlighted must
be dangerous, I am not disposed to think that the people of
Oude are habitually ferocious or blood-thirsty, or that they are
influenced by any peculiar animosity against the English or the
Christian name. It is certain, however, that they have not a good
character, and that in no part of the country should valuable
property be trusted in their way without proper precaution. I had
heard of some travellers having been menaced by the villagers on
the Oude bank of the Ganges a short time before, and when, on
leaving Lucknow, I ordered my mate-bearer, who had staid with
me after the tents had set off, to follow, as I could do without him,

he pleaded (though he had a spear) that he was afraid to go alone. Abdullah laughed at this, but afterwards went very gravely to examine into the state of the pistols, and was careful at night to bring them to my bed-head, observing that 'in this country a man does not trust his own father'. This, however, is a digression. I return to Lucknow, and its public buildings.

The minister's house is a very large pile of building, in a bad part of the town, and both in architecture and situation a good deal resembling the house of the Mullich family in Calcutta.[1] There are many stately khâns, and some handsome mosques and pagodas scattered in different corners of these wretched alleys, but the most striking buildings in Lucknow are, the tombs of the late Nawâb Saadut Ali, and the mother of the present king, the gate of Constantinople ('Roumi Durwazu',) and the 'Imambara', or cathedral. The Imambara consists of two courts, rising with a steep ascent one above the other. It contains, besides a splendid mosque, a college for instruction in Mussulman law, apartments for the religious establishment maintained here, and a noble gallery, in the midst of which, under a brilliant tabernacle of silver, cut glass, and precious stones, lie buried the remains of its founder Asuphud Dowla.[2] The whole is in a very noble style of eastern Gothic, and when taken in conjunction with the Roumi Durwazu which adjoins it, (of which I add a sketch from memory,) I have never seen an architectural view which pleased me more from its richness and variety, as well as the proportions and general good taste of its principal features.

The details a good deal resemble those of Eaton,[3] but the extent is much greater and the parts larger. On the whole it is, perhaps, most like the Kremlin, but both in splendour and taste my old favourite falls very short of it. Close to this fine group, is a large and handsome, but dull and neglected looking pile, which is the palace or prison appropriated to the unfortunate widows and concubines of deceased sovereigns. Some ladies are still there, as it is said, who belonged to Asuphud Dowlah. Those of Vizier Ali[4]

---

[1] See *supra*, p. 64.

[2] Asaf-ud-daula: reigned 1775–97. The Nawabs of Oudh were Shias, and the Imambara was also a place for performance of the passion play in commemoration of Husain. It also housed a model of his tomb (see *supra*, p. 129).

[3] Eaton Hall, Cheshire.   [4] Wazir Ali, 1797–8 (see *supra*, p. 81, n.1).

and Saadut Ali are, naturally, many of them alive, though they must mostly be in years. An Indian King, who allows his elephants to be starved, is, I fear, not very likely to attend much to the feeding of his old women, and the allowance which these poor creatures receive is said to be always so miserably in arrear, that they have occasionally been reduced to extreme distress. Once they fairly broke loose from their prison, sallied in a body into the adjoining bazar, and carried off all they could lay hands on, exclaiming that they had already pawned or sold all their

5   The Lucknow Imambara

trinkets, and almost all their clothes, that they were perishing with hunger, and that the King must pay for what they took, as well as bear the disgrace of reducing his father's wives to shew themselves to the people. The measure was a bold one, but, probably, did them good as to their subsequent treatment, for the King is allowed by every body to be a kind-hearted, well-meaning man, and the general sympathy and horror excited were very great.

None of the royal palaces (there are I think three in Lucknow beside this gloomy one) are either very large or striking. That in which the King received us to breakfast, and which is the one which he usually occupies, is close to the Residency; a cluster of mean courts with some morsels of shewy architecture intermingled, like the offices of a college. We went there in long procession, the Resident in his state palanqueen, made open like the nuptial one which we saw in Chowringhee, I in a tonjon, the rest of the party in all manner of conveyances. The Resident had a very numerous suwarree of armed men, silver-sticks, &c. and my servants were so anxious that I should make a good appearance on the occasion, that they begged permission to put on their new blue coats, though the day was so hot it was painful to see them thus loaded. There was the usual show of horse and foot-guards in the approaches to the palace, and the street was lined with the same picturesque crowd of irregular gendarmerie, which I had seen on entering the town. We were set down at the foot of a strangely mean stone staircase, resembling rather that leading to a bathroom than any thing else, on the summit of which the King received us, first embracing the Resident, then me. He next offered an arm to each of us, and led us into a long and handsome, but rather narrow, gallery, with good portraits of his father and Lord Hastings over the two chimney-pieces, and some very splendid glass lustres hanging from the ceiling. The furniture was altogether English, and there was a long table in the middle of the room, set out with breakfast, and some fine French and English china. He sate down in a gilt arm-chair in the centre of one side, motioning to us to be seated on either hand. The Prime Minister sate down opposite, and the rest of the table was filled by the party from the Residency, and about an equal number of natives, among whom were one of the King's grandsons, the Commander-in-chief, and other public officers. The King began by putting a large hot roll on the Resident's plate, and another on mine, then sent similar rolls to the young Nawâb his grandson, who sate on the other side of me, to the Prime Minister, and one or two others. Coffee, tea, butter, eggs, and fish, were then carried round by the servants, and things proceeded much as at a public breakfast in England. The King had some mess of his own in a beautiful covered French cup, but the other Mussulmans eat as the Europeans did. There was a pillaw, which the King recommended to me, and which, therefore, I was bound to taste, though with much secret reluctance, as remembering the greasy dainties of the Nawâb of Dacca. I was surprised, however, to find that this was really an excellent thing, with neither ghee nor garlic, and with no fault except, perhaps, that it was too dry, and too exclusively fowl, rice, and spices. Mr Ricketts told me afterwards, that the high-bred Mussulmans of this part of India affect to dislike exceedingly, as vulgar, the greasy and fragrant dishes of the Bengalees and Hindoos, and that the merit of their cookery is to be dry, stimulant, and aromatic.

During the meal, which was not very long, for nobody ate much, the conversation was made up chiefly of questions from the King as to the countries which I had visited, the length of time which I had been in India, and the objects of my present journey; as also how I liked what I had seen of Lucknow, with the rest of what Falconbridge calls the 'ABC book' of a traveller, when such a 'piked man of countries' is at the breakfast table of a great man.[1] I took care to thank him for his kindness in sending the guard and the Aûmeen[2] to meet me, as also for the loan of the elephant and chariot. I understood pretty well all which he said, though he does not speak very distinctly, but I seldom ventured to answer him without the aid of Mr Ricketts's interpretation, being aware of the danger of giving offence, or using vulgar or 'unlucky' words. He said his servants had told him I spoke Hindoostanee remarkably well; I answered that I could speak it to people in the camp or on the river, but I was not used to speak it in such a presence. He said, very politely, I had only to go on according to the progress I had already made, and the next time I came to see him he would not allow me an interpreter. The fact is, however, that I have gained very little in Hindoostanee lately, considerably less than before I was constantly with the Archdeacon and Mr Lushington. It is much easier to get them to interpret than myself to labour at an explanation, and, in marching, I have little or no time to read. Hindoostanee, not Persian, is here the court language; I suppose this has arisen from the King's desertion of his old allegiance to the house of Timur, since which it has been a natural policy to frame the etiquette of his court on a different model from that of Delhi.[3]

After breakfast the King rose and walked, supported as before by Mr Ricketts and me, into a small adjoining drawing-room,

[1] W. Shakespeare, *King John*, Act I.
[2] *Amin*—trusted official.   [3] See *supra*, p. 145 and n.1.

where his crown stood on a sofa-table. It is a very elegant one, of what heralds call the 'Oriental' form, a velvet cap surrounded with pointed rays of diamonds, and a white heron's plume in front. I was no judge of the merit of the diamonds, but was able honestly to say, I had never, except on the Emperor of Russia's crown, seen a more brilliant show. He asked me if there was any difference between his crown and that of the King of England. I told him what the difference was, and said his Majesty's was more like that of the Emperor of Constantinople, 'Padshahi Roum'. The conversation ended by his giving me a copy of his own works, and a book of some sort to the Archdeacon. We then took leave, and ended the morning by making a tour of the palaces, the new Imambara, the Menagerie, and the tombs of the King's father and mother. We went as before in our tonjons; and Mr Ricketts, on going out of the palace-gate, sent me a purse of thirty rupees in quarters, saying it was usual, on such occasions, to throw silver among the beggars. He had scarcely done this when our chairs were actually swept away from each other by a crowd of miserable objects of all kinds, who had waited our coming out, and had already learned my name. I at once saw that in such a scramble the strong and young would get every thing, and therefore bid the chobdars and other people round me to keep them off, and bring near the blind, lame, leprous, and very old. They executed this work zealously and well.... I had, however, mortification to find that some of the weakest and most helpless of those who were admitted to the side of my chair, were hustled on their return to the crowd, to snatch from them the alms which they had received; and one poor old woman, to whom I gave half a rupee on account of her great age and infirmities, was, after I had passed, thrown down, trampled on, and her hands, arms, and breast dreadfully pinched and bruised, to compel her to unlock her grasp of the money. The Resident's people rescued her, or she probably would have been killed. I observed, by the way, that my chobdar and the rest of my escort, seemed to think that it was strange to give more to a woman than to most of the men; and I had noticed on many occasions, that all through India any thing is thought good enough for the weaker sex, and that the roughest words, the poorest garments, the scantiest alms, the most degrading labour, and the hardest blows, are generally their portion. The same chuprassee who, in clearing the way before a great man, speaks civilly enough to those of his own sex, cuffs and kicks any unfortunate female who crosses his path without warning or forbearance. Yet to young children they are all gentleness and indulgence. What riddles men are! and how strangely do they differ in different countries! An idle boy in a crowd would infallibly, in England, get his head broken, but what an outcry would be raised if an unoffending woman were beaten by one of the satellites of authority! Perhaps both parties might learn something from each other; at least I have always thought it very hard to see beadles, in England, lashing away children on all public occasions, as if curiosity were a crime at an age in which it is, of all others, most natural.

This custom of throwing away money at presentations and other 'high times', is said to be the cause of the number of beggars in Lucknow. They are, indeed, very numerous, but on no other occasion did I see a crowd of them, and in any large city, the certainty that money was to be scrambled for, would bring together a multitude, perhaps as great as that I saw to-day.

The King of Oude is rather a tall man, and being long-backed and sitting on a somewhat higher cushion than his neighbours, looks particularly so at his own table. He has evidently been very handsome, and has still good features and a pleasing countenance, though he looks considerably older than he is, or than he as yet chooses his painter to represent him. His curling hair and whiskers are quite grey, and his complexion has grown, I understand, much darker within these few years, being now indeed, perhaps, the darkest in his court. On Mr Home's[1] canvass, however, his locks are still 'like the raven', and his 'bonny brow is brent'. The same immutability of youth, indeed, I have noticed in other royal portraits. The King of Oude, however, is evidently fond of dress, and is said to be a critic in that of others as well as his own; and his palaces, his new Imambara, his throne-room, jewels, and all the many other fine things which we visited this day, though extremely costly, and marked by a cultivated taste, and an eye

[1] Robert Home, for some years chief painter to the King of Oudh; see *infra*, p. 182.

familiarized with European models, are less solid and massive in their properties, and impress the mind with far less magnificence than the proud Roumi Durwazu and the other works of his more frugal and fortunate father and uncle. His manners are very gentlemanly and elegant, though the European ladies who visit his court complain that he seldom pays them any attention. . . .

By a recent order of Government all presents of shawls, silks, ornaments, or diamonds, whether made to ladies or gentlemen, are taken from them on leaving the palace, by the Resident's chobdar, and sold on the account of Government. Nothing is kept but the silken cords which the King throws round the necks of his visitors at parting, and books, which, as nobody buys them, remain the unmolested property of the presentee.

Still presents are given and received, when such a public mark of respect is thought proper, but in a manner well understood by both parties. If a person of rank is introduced to the King, a tray of shawls is offered, accepted, and put by in store at the Residency. When the great man takes leave, on departing from Lucknow, he offers a similar nuzzur,[1] which the Company supplies, and which is always of rather superior value to that which the King has given. Thus the King gets his own shawls and something more returned to him in due course of circulation, and except that every such interchange of presents costs the Company about five hundred rupees, the whole is reduced to little more than a bow, and the occasion of a fee to his Majesty's chobdars and hurkarus. I was asked if I chose to go through this mock interchange of presents. But I had no authority to draw from the Company's funds the presents which I was to return, nor any desire to encroach on the discretion which is, in such case, exercised by the Resident. I answered, therefore, that, as a Clergyman, I could not be supposed to derive honour from the present of fine clothes and costly ornaments, and that I was anxious for nothing so much as the possession of his Majesty's works; this I found was well taken.

I had the usual compliment paid me of an offer to have a fight of animals under my window at breakfast, which I declined. It is a sight that religious persons among the Mussulmans themselves condemn as inhuman, and I did not want to be reckoned less

[1] Present.

merciful to animals than their own Moullahs. Nor was the King, who is himself pretty well tired of such sights, displeased, I found, that his elephants and rams had a holiday.

The King, to finish my court-days all at once, returned my visit on the Thursday following at the Residency, and was received by the Resident and myself at the head of the stairs, in all points as he received us, and was conducted between us, as before, to the middle of the long breakfast-table, and after breakfast I presented him with a copy of the Bible in Arabic, and the Prayer-Book in Hindoostanee, which I had got bound in red velvet, and wrapt up in brocade for the purpose. The morning went off so much like that which had preceded it, that I remember nothing of importance, except that during breakfast he asked me to sit for my portrait to his painter, and that after breakfast he offered me an escort of twenty suwarrs through his territory, of which, in conformity with the principle on which I acted, of declining all needless parade, I accepted only ten, stating that I found those his Majesty had sent me before quite sufficient.

I lastly met him again, under circumstances perfectly similar, at the Residency on the day of Mr Ricketts's marriage, at which he had expressed a wish to be present. At this breakfast he was more communicative than he had been, talked about steam-engines, and a new way of propelling ships by a spiral wheel at the bottom of the vessel, which an English engineer in his pay had invented; mentioned different circumstances respecting the earthquake at Shiraz[1] which had been reported to him, but were not named in the Calcutta newspapers, and explained the degree of acquaintance which he shewed with English books, by saying he made his aides-de-camp read them to him into Hindoostanee. He was full of a new scheme of authorship or editorship in the form of a Hindoostanee and Arabic Dictionary, which he was pleased to find was likely to be well received at the College of Fort William.[2] Captain Lockitt, indeed, said that it would in all probability be a very useful book, for he had men about him quite competent to do it respectably. He asked so much about my publications, that Mr

[1] In Iran.
[2] This institution was by Heber's time primarily a school of languages for the East India Company's servants; see also Introduction, p. 5.

Ricketts told me I was bound to offer to send them to him as soon as I returned to Calcutta, and, on my assenting, made a very pretty speech on my behalf. The King said he should receive them with great pleasure, and had no doubt he should get their meaning explained to him. I cannot tell how this may be, but am now bound to make the trial. The marriage ceremony went off very well. The King, his grandson, the minister, &c. remained in the room as spectators, and after it, Mr Ricketts presented him with a splendid velvet and gold saddle-cloth, and housings. Thus ended, after another embrace, and a promise of returning 'one of these days', my intercourse with one of the very few crowned heads I have ever come into contact with. I have been the more particular in describing what passed, because I know my wife will not be uninterested in it, and because this is in fact the most polished and splendid court at present in India. Poor Delhi has quite fallen into decay.

I sate for my portrait for Mr Home four times.[1] He has made several portraits of the King, redolent of youth, and radiant with diamonds, and a portrait of Sir E. Paget, which he could not help making a resemblance. He is a very good artist indeed, for a King of Oude to have got hold of. He is a quiet gentlemanly old man, brother of the celebrated surgeon in London, and came out to practise as a portrait painter at Madras, during Lord Cornwallis's first administration, was invited from thence to Lucknow by Saadut Ali a little before his death, and has since been retained by the King at a fixed salary, to which he adds a little by private practice. His son is a Captain in the Company's service, but is now attached to the King of Oude as equerry, and European aide-de-camp. Mr Home would have been a distinguished painter had he remained in Europe, for he has a great deal of taste, and his drawing is very good and rapid; but it has been, of course, a great disadvantage to him to have only his own works to study, and he, probably, finds it necessary to paint in glowing colours to satisfy his royal master.

Of the King's character, and the circumstances which have

[1] Archdeacon Corrie wrote to a friend 'the King was so taken with the Bishop, that he begged to have his picture; which was accordingly taken immediately'—*Memoirs of Corrie*, 370.

plunged this country into its present anarchy, I will now detail the outlines of what I have been able to learn. He was, by a very common misfortune attendant on heirs apparent,[1] disliked by his father, Saadut Ali, who had kept him back from all public affairs, and thrown him entirely into the hands of servants. To the first of these circumstances may be ascribed his fondness for literary and philosophical pursuits, to the second the ascendancy which his khânsaman minister has gained over him. Saadut Ali, himself a man of talent and acquirements, fond of business and well qualified for it, but in his latter days unhappily addicted to drunkenness, left him a country with six millions of people, a fertile soil, a most compact frontier, a clear revenue of two millions sterling, and upwards of two millions in ready money in the treasury, with a well regulated system of finance, a peasantry tolerably well contented, no army to maintain except for police and parade, and every thing likely to produce an auspicious reign. Different circumstances, however, soon blighted these golden promises. The principal of these was, perhaps, the young Nawâb's aversion to public business. His education had been merely Asiatic, for Saadut Ali, though he himself spoke English like a native, and very frequently wore the English uniform, had kept his son from all European intercourse and instruction. He was fond, however, as I have observed, of study, and in all points of Oriental philology and philosophy, is really reckoned a learned man, besides having a strong taste for mechanics and chemistry. But these are not the proper or most necessary pursuits of a King, and, in this instance, have rather tended to divert his mind from the duties of his situation, than to serve as graceful ornaments to an active and vigorous intellect. When I add to this, that at one period the chace occupied a considerable part of his time, it will be seen how many points of resemblance occur between him and our own James the First. Like James he is said to be naturally just and kind-hearted, and with all who have access to him he is extremely popular. No single act of violence or oppression has ever been ascribed to him or supposed to have been perpetrated with his knowledge, and his errors have been a want of method and economy in his expences, a want of accessibility to his subjects, a

[1] Heber no doubt had the Hanoverian dynasty particularly in mind.

blind confidence in favourites, and, as will be seen, an unfortunate, though not very unnatural, attachment to different points of etiquette and prerogative.

His father's minister, at the time of his death, was Hukeem Mendee,[1] a man of very considerable talents, great hereditary opulence and influence, and to the full as honest and respectable in his public and private conduct as an Eastern Vizier can usually be expected to be. The new sovereign was said not to be very fond of him, but there seemed not the least intention of removing him till his power was undermined, most unfortunately for all parties, by the British themselves.

The then Resident at Lucknow[2] was said to interfere too much in the private affairs of the King and in the internal and regular administration of the country. The minister would not allow it, and the King was so much irritated by this real, or supposed interference, that he sent, by some of his European servants, private intelligence to Lord Hastings...Lord Hastings readily took up the affair; but in the meantime some of the King's servants, among whom was his khânsaman, worked upon their master's timidity, by representing the danger of coming to an open quarrel with the Resident, the probability that the English would not credit the complaints brought against their own countryman, and urged him to a compromise before it was too late. In consequence the King retracted the complaint, and ascribed it to the incorrect information and bad advice of the Hukeem Mendee, who was in consequence deprived of many of his principal employments, which were transferred to the present minister,[3] with the general consent of all parties, and with the concurrence of the Hukeem himself, as a man personally acceptable to the Sovereign, of pliant and pleasing manners, and not likely to aim at, or obtain more power than it was thought fit to entrust to him. Soon after, however, the new influence succeeded in getting the Hukeem Mendee deprived of one profitable post after another, in stripping him of many of the Zemindarries in his hands, and at length in having him thrown into prison, whence he was only released by the interposition of the British Government. He now lives in great splendour at Futtehghur....

[1] Hakim Mehdi Ali Khan.   [2] Major Baillie.   [3] i.e. the Agha Mir.

Oudh

Hukeem Mendee was too powerful a man to be summarily got rid of, but more violent means were taken with others. One man of high rank was murdered in open day in the city; others were driven out of the country, and every death and every banishment was a fresh occasion of adding a new place, or a new Zemindarrie to the minister's hoard.

While he grew rich, the King grew more and more in debt. No check whatever was given either to the receipt or issue of public money. The favourite had succeeded in getting both the secretaryship and treasurership in his own hands; and all that was known was, that the Minister built a magnificent house, and the King lavished great sums in all manner of trinkets, while the troops and public functionaries were without pay, and the peasantry driven to despair by continual fresh exactions. Of the two millions which his father had left, the King had lent one to Lord Hastings to carry on the Nepâl war. For this he was to receive interest, but unfortunately for him, he accepted, instead of all payment, a grant of fresh territory under the Himalaya mountains, which is entirely unproductive, being either savage wilderness, or occupied by a race of mountaineers, who pay no taxes without being compelled, and whom he has not the means of compelling. After a second loan Lord Hastings encouraged the Vizier to assume the title of King. But the worst consequence of both these loans was, that by laying the British Government under a great obligation to the King, they compelled Lord Hastings to suspend all further urging of the different measures of reform in the administration of justice and the collection of the revenue, which had been begun in Saadut Ali's time, for the benefit of the people of Oude, and which the Hukeem Mendee, while he remained in power, had been gradually introducing, by the suggestion of the British Resident, and after the models afforded in our provinces. The chief of these was the substitution of a regular system of Zemindarrie collectors for the taxes, instead of a number of 'fermiers publics', who take them from year to year by a sort of auction, collecting them afterwards in kind or in any way which suits them best, and who, by a strange injustice, are themselves the assessors, and, in many instances, the only accessible court of appeal, as well as the principal persons who derive a profit from the amount collected. This wretched system, it must be owned, is very common throughout the native governments; but, when a sovereign is himself a man of talents and energy, or when his Minister has any regard for his own reputation, it has many checks which, in the present case, did not operate. In consequence, three or four times more than the sums really due were often extorted by these locusts, who went down and encamped in different parts of the country, and, under various pretences, so devoured and worried the people that they were glad to get rid of them on any terms. Nay, sometimes, when one Aûmeen had made his bargain with the land-owners and tenants, and received the greater part of the payment in advance, a second would make his appearance with more recent powers, (having out-bid his predecessors), and begin assessing and collecting anew, telling the plundered villagers that they had done wrong to pay before it was due, and that they must look to the first man for repayment of what they had been defrauded of. ' All this has been done ', was said to me, ' and the King will neither see it nor hear it.' It was not likely, however, to be done long without resistance. The stronger Zemindars built mud-forts, the poor Ryuts planted bamboos and thorny jungle round their villages; every man that had not a sword sold his garment to procure one, and they bade the King's officers keep their distance. The next step, however, of Government, was to call in the aid of British troops to quell these insurgents. This the King of Oude had, by the letter and spirit of existing treaties, a right to do. His father and uncle had purchased this right by the cession of nearly one-third of their whole territories,—by the admission of two or three garrisons of subsidiary troops into their remaining provinces, and by the disbanding of by far the greater part of their own army, on the express condition that the English should undertake to defend them against all external and internal enemies.[1] Still Saadut Ali had used this right very sparingly. He was not fond of admitting, far less requesting, any more foreign interference than he could help. And his own guards, consisting of 2000 regular infantry, 1000 horse, 300 artillery, and the irregulars whom I have noticed,

---

[1] By the treaty made with Wellesley in 1801, whereby the lower Doab and Rohilkhand were ceded to the East India Company.

were enough for all usual occasions, and were in excellent order and discipline. Now, however, all was changed. The soldiers themselves were so ill paid that it was difficult to keep them together; the artillery, a beautiful little corps, first mutinied and then disbanded themselves to the last man, and the King had really no option between either altering his system, or governing without taxes, or calling in British aid. That aid was demanded and given; and during the greater part of Lord Hastings' time this wretched country was pillaged under sanction of the British name, and under the terror of Sepoy bayonets, till at length the remonstrances of the British officers employed on this service became so urgent, and the scandal so notorious and so great, not to omit that the number of the disaffected increased daily, and that the more parties were sent out in support of the Aûmeens, the more were called for, while every peasant who lost lands or property in the progress of the system, became a Decoit and made inroads into the Company's provinces, that a different course was imperiously forced on Government. Accordingly, the Resident was instructed to urge anew on the King the adoption of a regular system of leasing the crown dues for a certain number of years, like that adopted in the Company's territories, and leasing them to the Zemindars themselves, not to these greedy Aûmeens. He was directed also to require proof, before granting the aid of troops, that the sums said to be withheld were really due. To the first of these proposals the King answered, that he would introduce the system gradually and with such modifications as suited his country. He even named a district in which he would begin it; but, though two years have now elapsed, nothing has yet been done. The second was met by sending a number of documents to the Resident, of whose history and authenticity he could know nothing, but which the officers sent with the detachment declared they believed to be often perfect forgeries. Mr Ricketts, therefore, about a year ago, declined granting any more military aid, unless the King would, first, immediately carry into effect his promised reform; secondly, unless he would allow an English commissioner, versed in such matters, to accompany each detachment, and determine on the spot the justice of the Aûmeen's claim; thirdly, unless he would himself, after the example of his royal ancestors, hold frequent and public Durbar, to receive petitions from his subjects, and attend to these specific complaints; and fourthly, unless, to prevent the constant incursion of robbers from his Majesty's into the Company's territories, he would allow the Judge and Magistrates of the adjoining districts to pursue and seize decoits within his frontier.

To these proposals his answers have been very ingenious and plausible. To the first he says that such great changes cannot be the work of a day; that, when half his subjects are in arms against him, is not precisely the time to obtain a fair assessment or a permanent settlement of the land; but if the British will first, as he calls on them in the terms of their treaty to do, put down his rebellious Zemindars, destroy their mud-forts, and disarm their people, he will pledge himself to adopt, in course of time, and with due deliberation, such a system as will give satisfaction. To the second he answers with some reason, that the introduction of English judges and revenue officers, for such the proposed commissioners would be, into his country, would make his own officers cyphers, and his own power contemptible, and that he would sooner bid adieu to his crown at once, and turn Faqueer. To the third, that he has not understood it to be the custom of either the King of England or the Governor-General, to hold such an open Durbar as they recommend, nor will those who have seen a Lucknow mob anticipate any beneficial effects from such excessive accessibility. But to prove his regard for his people, he has instructed his prime minister to hold a Durbar for these precise purposes twice a week, who is charged to report all cases of importance to his own ear. The fourth he answers by saying, that it is very hard to accuse him of harbouring robbers, while we refuse him all aid in putting down the very Zemindars whose fortresses and fastnesses are the common nests of robbery and rebellion; that if we help him to subdue his rebels, he will keep his robbers in order himself: but that it would be a cruel mockery to continue to call him a king, if any neighbouring magistrate might enter his dominions at pleasure. He urges that 'all his difficulties have arisen from his entire confidence in the friendship of the Company. That this induced him and his ancestors to disband an excellent army, till they scarce left sentries enough for the palace; and thus they have become unable, without help, to enforce payment of their ancient revenues. That this induced him to lend to the British Government all the money which would have else enabled him to ease the people of their burthens, and to meet without inconvenience whatever loss of income a new assessment may, for some time, render inevitable. That he never has refused, and never will refuse, to give the best consideration in his power to any measures of reform which may be, in a friendly manner, proposed to him; but he refers those who represent him as a tyrant, or who speak of his country as depopulated, to every traveller who has marched along its principal roads, and has observed the extent of cultivation through which they are carried.' He concludes by saying, that 'he is aware, that notwithstanding the tone of equality and independence which in their treaties and official correspondence the Company have allowed him to maintain, he is in fact in their power; but if he is to reign at all, for which he knows that he has no guarantee but British good faith, he intreats that his requests for the performance of a positive treaty may not be met by stipulations which would render that treaty vain, that he may be defended from the only enemies he has, or is likely to have, his rebellious Zemindars, and protected in the exercise of functions which are essential parts of that sovereignty which has been so solemnly and repeatedly guaranteed to him.' The statement, of which these are the purport, I thought very curious; they certainly shew strongly the perplexities and mischief arising from the subsidiary system which seems for so many years to have been our favourite policy in India, and to which it must be owned a considerable part of our political greatness is owing.

I can bear witness certainly to the truth of the King's statement, that his territories are really in a far better state of cultivation than I had expected to find them. From Lucknow to Sandee, where I am now writing, the country is as populous and well cultivated as most of the Company's provinces. The truth perhaps is that for more than a year back, since the aid of British troops has been withheld, affairs have been in some respects growing better. The Zemindars have in a few instances carried their point, the Aûmeens have been either driven away entirely, or been forced to a moderate compromise, and the chief actual sufferers at the present moment are the King, who gets little or nothing even of his undoubted dues, and the traveller, who unless he has such a guard as I have, had better sleep in a safe skin on the other side of the Ganges. It should be observed, however, that I have as yet seen no sign of those mud-forts, stockades, and fortresses, on which the Zemindars and peasantry are said to rely for safety; that the common people north of Lucknow are, I think, not so universally loaded with arms as those to the southward, and that though I have heard a good deal all the way of the distressed state of the country, as well as its anarchy and lawlessness, except in the single instance I have mentioned, where the treasure was attacked, I have *seen* no signs of either, or had any reason to suppose that the King's writ does not pass current, or that our Aûmeen would have the least difficulty in enforcing it in our favour, even without the small payment which I give, and which is evidently accepted as a gratuity. I cannot but suspect, therefore, that the misfortunes and anarchy of Oude are somewhat over-rated, though it is certain that so fine a land will take a long time in ruining, and that very many years of oppression will be required to depopulate a country which produces on the same soil, and with no aid but irrigation, crops of wheat and pulse every year.

It seemed strange to me why, since so much of the present calamities of the country were ascribed to the misconduct of the minister, his removal was not demanded in the first instance, after which all subsequent measures of reform might be looked forward to as attainable. But it was apprehended that the King would rather abdicate than be dictated to in this particular, and that it was thought better to urge an effectual change of system, than the mere removal of an individual who might be replaced by somebody not at all better. I asked also if the people thus oppressed desired, as I had been assured they did, to be placed under English Government? Captain Lockitt said that he had heard the same thing; but on his way this year to Lucknow, and conversing, as his admirable knowledge of Hindoostanee enables him to do, familiarly with the suwarrs who accompanied him, and who spoke out, like all the rest of their countrymen, on the weakness of the King and the wickedness of the Government, he fairly put the question to them, when the jemautdar, joining his hands, said with great fervency, 'miserable as we are, of all miseries keep us from that!' 'Why so?' said Captain Lockitt, 'are not our people far better governed?' 'Yes', was the answer, 'but the name of Oude and the honour of our nation would be at an end.' There are, indeed, many reasons why high-born and ambitious men must be exceedingly averse to our rule; but the preceding expression of one in humble rank savours of more national feeling and personal frankness than is always met with in India. He was a soldier, however, and a Mussulman who spoke thus. A Hindoo Ryut might have answered differently, and it is possible that both accounts may be true, though this only can I vouch for as authentic. It ought to be borne in mind, that the oppression and anarchy to which Oude is a prey, are chiefly felt and witnessed in the villages. In the towns the King's authority passes unquestioned, and I have not heard that the dustoury levied is irregular or excessive. An insurrection in Lucknow would be a dreadful thing, and most ministers will be careful how they excite it.

The population of Lucknow is guessed at three hundred thousand. But Mussulmans regard every attempt to number the people as a mark of great impiety, and a sure presage of famine or pestilence; so that nothing can be known with accuracy. It is, I really think, large enough and sufficiently crowded to contain that number. There are two bridges over the Goomty, one a very noble old Gothic edifice of stone, of, I believe, eleven arches; the other a platform laid on boats, and merely connecting the King's park with his palace. Saadut Ali had brought over an iron bridge from England, and a place was prepared for its erection; but on his death the present sovereign declined prosecuting the work on the ground that it was unlucky; so that in all probability it will lie where it is, till the rust reduces it to powder.

There are, in Lucknow, a considerable number of Christians of one kind or other. Besides the numerous dependants of the Residency, the King has a great many Europeans and half-castes in his employ. There are also many tradesmen of both these descriptions, and a strange medley of adventurers of all nations and sects, who ramble hither in the hope, generally a fruitless one, of obtaining employment.

Oudh

Heber left Lucknow on 1st November, and travelled twenty miles along the Shahjahanpur road on that day.

In the way, at Futtehgunge, I passed the tents pitched for the large party which were to return towards Cawnpoor next day, and I was much pleased and gratified by the Soubahdar[1] and the greater number of the Sepoys of my old escort running into the middle of the road to bid me another farewell, and again express their regret that they were not going on with me 'to the world's end'. They who talk of the ingratitude of the Indian character, should, I think, pay a little more attention to cases of this sort. These men neither got nor expected any thing by this little expression of good-will. If I had offered them money, they would have been bound, by the rules of the service and their own dignity, not to take it. Sufficient civility and respect would have been paid if any of them who happened to be near the road had touched their caps, and I really can suppose them actuated by no motive but good will. It had not been excited, so far as I know, by any particular desert on my part; but I had always spoken to them civilly, had paid some attention to their comforts in securing them tents, firewood, and camels for their knapsacks, and had ordered them a dinner, after their own fashion, on their arrival at Lucknow, at the expense of, I believe, not more than four rupees! Surely if good-will is to be bought by these sort of attentions, it is a pity that any body should neglect them!

The suwarrs furnished by the King for this journey were a very different description of men from those who previously accompanied me. They were evidently picked for the purpose, being tall, strong young fellows, on exceedingly good horses, and as well armed as could be wished for the nature of their service.

[Heber fell ill with what he thought was 'Lucknow influenza': but on 6 November, having arrived at Bilgram,] I found myself well enough in the evening to walk round the place, attended by the goomashta,[2] whom I found a very sensible man, willing to give information, and well acquainted with most points which relate to the agriculture, rent, and taxes of this part of India. He said,

---

[1] Commanding officer.
[2] In this context, the master of the Bishop's camels.

what I could easily believe from all which I saw, that the soil of Oude was one of the finest in the world; that every thing flourished here which grew either in Bengal or Persia; that they had at once rice, sugar, cotton, and palm-trees, as well as wheat, maize, barley, beans, and oats: that the air was good, the water good, and the grass particularly nourishing to cattle: but he said, 'the laws are not good, the judges are wicked, the Zemindars are worse, the Aûmeens worst of all, and the Ryuts are robbed of every thing, and the King will neither see nor hear'. I asked him the rent per begah of the land. He said generally four rupees, but sometimes six; and sometimes the peasant had all taken from him. I observed that it was strange that, under such usage, they continued to cultivate the land so well as they seemed to do. 'What can they do?' he answered, 'they must eat; and when they have put the seed in the ground they must wait till it comes up, and then take what they can get of it.' I still, however, suspect exaggeration in all these stories.

We passed a neat garden of turnips and some potatoes looking very promising; these last, he said, were at first exceedingly disliked by the people, but now were becoming great favourites, particularly with the Mussulmans, who find them very useful as absorbents in their greasy messes.

As I was slowly returning to my tents, a handsome young Mussulman came up, and seeing an European in plain clothes, with only three unarmed people, began talking civilly in point of language, but in a very free and easy sort of manner; he was smartly dressed, with a gold-laced skull-cap, an embroidered muslin shirt and drawers, ear-rings, collar, and ring, which professed to be of garnets with a few diamonds, and a shewy shawl wrapped round his body, but none of his clothes clean or well put on, and had that sort of jaunty air about him, which as it is more unusual, is even more offensive in an Eastern than a Western buck. He was followed by seven or eight very dirty ill-dressed fellows with swords, shields, and matchlocks, and had himself a sword, with a tarnished silver hilt, and a large pistol which he carried in his hand and kept playing with while he was speaking. He was evidently more than half drunk, and had the manner of a

foolish boy who wants to play the great man, but is not sure how
he will be received, and undecided whether he is to pick a quarrel
or no. He salamed, and asked me what I was about, and where
I had been, which I answered civilly but shortly; he then enquired
whence I came and where I was going. I asked him why he
wanted to know? to which he answered, that he was a man of
consequence in the neighbourhood, and it was his business to
make enquiries; but added more civilly, that seeing a Sahib, he
came to offer salutation. I said I was obliged to him, and asked his
name, which he told me, but which I forget, except that he professed to be a Syud,[1] enquiring at the same time what my name
was. 'Lord Padre Sahib' did not explain the matter at all; he
resumed, however, his enquiries about my route next day, and
where I intended to halt. I had forgotten the name, and on
turning towards the goomashta, he, very eagerly and with an
expressive look, said 'Sandee', which I knew was not the place,
but as he seemed to wish to see no more of the gentleman, I did
not interfere. He then again launched out into an account of his
own influence in the neighbourhood, 'East, West, North, and
South', he added, as I seemed a good man, he would come in the
morning with his friends to protect me. I thanked him, but said
he need not trouble himself, since besides my own servants, I had
already 50 Sepoys, and 10 of the King's suwarrs. While I said this
a very whimsical change took place in his countenance. His head
was before thrown back in a protecting way, and his eyes were half
shut. These he now opened very wide, and raised his head to a
perpendicular posture so suddenly, that, since I had, during the
conversation, drawn up pretty closely to him, in order to prevent,
if necessary, any further evolutions with his pistol, our noses and
breasts were almost brought into contact. He hastily drew back,
called me 'Huzoor',[2] instead of 'Ap', and again renewed his
offer, not of protection, but of service. I cut the matter short,
however, by taking a civil leave of this young descendant of
Fatima and the Imâms. When he was gone I asked the goomashta
if he knew any thing of him. He shook his head, saying that there
were many such hurramzadus[3] about the country, who were too

---

[1] One claiming to be descended from the Prophet Muhammad.
[2] A term of respect.　　　　　　　　　　[3] Rascal (lit., bastard).

proud to enter into the Company's army, and who could not find employ in the little army of the King, and were, consequently, idle, drunken, and ready for any mischief. I asked if he were a Zemindar; he said he did not believe that he was either Zemindar or Tusseeldar, or that, whatever his family might be, he had any other profession or character than that of suwarr, and a candidate for employment in some of the mercenary armies of India. He concluded with hoping we should see no more of him, which, indeed, I thought most likely. I was a little tired with my walk, but slept all the better for it, and waked at half-past three on Sunday the 7th, with no traces of sickness.

Some little adventures had occurred during this journey, in the detail of my escort, which I forgot to mention in their places. A sepoy had deserted with his musquet and clothes, which I chiefly notice, because it was regarded as utterly hopeless and idle to pursue, or even to describe him in my report of the circumstance to the officer of the next station, and still more, because his desertion was spoken of by all the camp with surprise, and as if it were the voluntary abandonment of a comfortable situation. Two other Sepoys had been ill for several days in much the same way with myself; I had treated them in a similar manner; and they were now doing well, but being brahmins of high caste I had much difficulty in conquering their scruples and doubts about the physic which I gave them. They both said that they would rather die than taste wine. They scrupled at my using a spoon to measure their caster-oil, and insisted that the water in which their medicines were mixed, should be poured by themselves only. They were very grateful however, particularly for the care I took of them when I was myself ill, and said repeatedly that the sight of me in good health would be better to them than all medicines. They seemed now free from disease, but recovered their strength more slowly than I did, and I was glad to find that the soubahdar said he was authorized, under such circumstances, to engage a hackery[1] at the Company's expence, to carry them till they were fit to march. He mentioned this in consequence of my offering them a lift on a camel, which they were afraid of trying.

[1] Light carriage.

Another sepoy, a very fine young fellow, called on me this evening to beg permission to go to see a brother who was with some companies cantoned at a little frontier post, eight coss to our left hand, the name of which I forget. He said that as he was to go into Rajapootana, he did not know when he should meet him again; and added that he could easily travel the eight coss that night, and would rejoin me at Shahjehanpoor. I told him not to hurry himself to do so, but to take the straight northern road to Bareilly, by which means he might fall in with me before I reached that city, and that I would give him a pass for four days. He was much delighted; and I mention the circumstance chiefly to shew the falsehood of the common notion, that these poor people will take no trouble for the sake of their kindred.

Part V

ROHILKHAND AND
KUMAON

On 10 *November Heber crossed the Oudh border and reached Shahjahanpur, in the British territory of Rohilkhand.*

Shahjehanpoor is a large place, with some stately old mosques, and a castle. These are most ruinous, but the houses are in good plight. The bazars show marks of activity and opulence, and I could not help observing that there really is a greater appearance of ease, security, and neatness among the middling and lower classes of the Company's subjects, than among those of the King of Oude. I found my tent pitched just beyond the town, not far from the gates of the Compound of Mr Campbell,[1] the Collector of the district, whose guest I was to be. I break-fasted and dined with him, and met most of the gentlemen of the station.

I found no professional duties to perform; but endeavoured, during the day, to persuade these gentlemen to remedy, in some little degree, in their secluded situation, the want of a chaplain (of which they complain, but which I see no chance of supplying at present), by meeting at some convenient place on Sundays, and taking it by turns to read a selection, which I pointed out, from the Church Prayers, the Psalms, and Lessons of the day, and a printed Sermon. I urged on them the example of Mr Ricketts at Lucknow, and hope I produced some effect; at any rate I am glad I made the trial, and I think I gave no offence by doing so.

The conquest of Rohilcund by the English,[2] and the death of its chief in battle, its consequent cession to the Nawâb of Oude,

---

[1] Archibald Campbell: appointed Collector of Shahjahanpur 1820; retired 1835.
[2] In 1774.

and the horrible manner in which Sujah ud Dowlah oppressed and misgoverned it, form one of the worst chapters of English history in India. We have since made the Rohillas some amends by taking them away from Oude,[1] and governing them ourselves; but, by all which I could learn from the society this day concerning the present state of the province of Bareilly, the people appear by no means to have forgotten or forgiven their first injuries. The Mussulman chiefs, who are numerous, are very angry at being without employment under Government, or hope of rising in the State or Army, and are continually breaking out into acts of insubordination and violence, which are little known in the other provinces of the Company's empire, but are favoured here by the neighbourhood of Oude, and the existence of a large forest along the whole eastern, southern, and northern frontiers. In this forest a rebel chief is by many supposed to have lurked the last seven years, for whose apprehension Government have vainly offered no less a sum than 10,000 rupees. Many robberies are, certainly, still perpetrated in his name; but the opinion of the magistrates at Shahjehanpoor is, that the man is really dead, and that his name only, like that of Captain Rock, remains as the rallying point of mutiny. The military officers of our dinner party had often been in this forest, which they describe as extensive, and in some places very picturesque, with some few tracts of high land, whence, even in this neighbourhood, the snowy range of Himalaya is visible.

The Rohilla insurgents are usually very faithful to each other, and, as in Oude there is neither police nor pursuit, it very seldom happens, if they once escape, that they can be laid hold of afterwards. One of the most notorious of them, who had long eluded justice, came into the hands of Government not long since under very singular circumstances. He had passed over into Oude, and bought a Zemindarry there, which was last year seized on, under circumstances of excessive injustice, by the servants of the favourite, who, at the same time, carried off one of his wives. The Zemindar, equally high-spirited and desperate with Hamilton of Bothwellhaugh under similar circumstances, rode immediately to Lucknow, scaled, by the assistance of his servants, the wall of the

---

[1] In 1801.

minister's private garden, and waited there well-armed, but alone, till his enemy should make his appearance. The minister did not himself appear, but his two youngest sons came out to walk with their ayahs.[1] The Rohilla knew them, pounced on them like a tyger, and holding them between his knees, told the terrified women to go and call their master. The palace was soon in an uproar, but he sate still, with his back against the wall, the infants under his knees, and a pistol in each hand, calling out 'draw near, and they are both dead!' The minister wept and tore his flesh, promising him every thing if he would let them go; to which he answered, 'the restoration of my wife, my own safety, and the guarantee of the British Resident for both!' The woman was immediately brought out, and the minister went like one frantic to the Residency, begging for God's sake either Mr Ricketts or Major Raper to go with him. The latter went, and the Rohilla, after a horrible pause, in which he seemed still to be weighing the sweetness of revenge against the promises held out to him, rose, took his wife by the hand, and led her away. He was not, however, satisfied with the security of his continuance in Oude, but soon after surrendered himself to the British, saying, that he knew he must look forward to a confinement of some time, but he preferred their severities to the tender mercies of the minister, who, in spite of his promise, had, he was convinced, already laid snares for him. He is now a prisoner in the castle of Allahabad, but it is generally believed that he has made his peace, and that his confinement will not be a long one, though his offences before were serious enough, and though it would be a strange reason for pardoning him, that he had been about to kill the two children of the prime minister of an allied power.

The soil and climate of Rohilcund are very fine; the former produces every thing which is to be found in Oude, and the commodities are reckoned better, because, being under a better system of government and lighter taxes, the peasants bestow more pains on them. Their sugar, rice, and cotton are the most high-priced in India, and I was surprised to see not only the toddy and date-palms, but plantains common, while walnuts, strawberries, grapes, apples, and pears likewise thrive here.

[1] Nurses.

There are five companies of Sepoys at Shahjehanpoor, and several similar detachments scattered up and down the country. They seem, indeed, to have their hands tolerably full of work, and to lead nearly the same lives which soldiers similarly situated do in Ireland. They have, however, not the misery of enforcing revenue laws, and the greater number of cases either arise from civil suits respecting property, the decrees of which it is not the manner of the Rohillas to attend to very scrupulously, or from an inveterate habit of 'lifting' cows and sheep, which the beggarly Zemindars and idle long-legged 'gillies' of one village are always apt to feel a pride in exercising against those of the next. 'Take care of that long-tailed horse of yours', was the first caution which I received. 'Keep him carefully at night under the sentry's eye, or you will never carry him over the ferry of Anopshehr.'[1] I, therefore, gave an especial caution to the people about Cabul. The other horse having his tail cut, they are not so likely to meddle with.

November 11.—A strange recipe was suggested for the benefit of Cabul's health, whose beauty attracts general notice, as well as his docility and fondness for me. It was a boiled sheep's head once in fourteen days! and the object was to make him strong and help his digestion. I asked Abdullah if he had ever heard of such a 'messala', or mess, before? He answered, it was sometimes recommended, and he had tried it himself to his sorrow, since the horse never lived to have the dose repeated.

The same adviser wanted me to take off a joint of Cabul's tail, under the hair, so as not to injure his appearance. 'It was known', he said, 'that by how much the tail was made shorter, so much the taller the horse grew.' I said 'I could not believe that God gave any animal a limb too much, or one which tended to its disadvantage, and that as He had made my horse, so he should remain.' This speech, such as it was, seemed to chime in wonderfully with the feelings of most of my hearers, and one old man said, that 'during all the 22 years that the English had held the country, he had not heard so grave and godly a saying from any of

[1] On the Ganges, east of Delhi.

them before'. I thought of Sancho Panza and his wise apothegms, but I regretted that, without doing more harm than good, I could not, with my present knowledge of Hindoostanee, tell them any thing which was really worth their hearing. Yet, if my life is spared, I trust the time may come.

A miserable little sickly man, wrapped in a ragged blanket, asked charity, saying, he was going with his wife and two children the pilgrimage to Mecca! What a journey for such a person! I advised him to return home, and serve God in his own land, adding, that He was every where, and might be worshipped in India as well as by the side of a black stone in Hejaz. He smiled in a melancholy way, as if he were partly of the same opinion, but said he had a vow. At home, indeed, he perhaps, to judge from his appearance, left nothing but beggary. I do not think that this pilgrimage is very popular with the Indian Mussulmans. This is only the fourth person whom I have met with who appeared to have made it, or to be engaged in it; and yet the title of Hajee, which such persons assume, would, apparently, point them out to notice.

November 13.—From Futtehgunge to Furreedpoor is seven coss, through a country equally well cultivated, and rather prettier, as being more woody, than that which I saw yesterday. Still, however, it is as flat as a carpet. The road is very good, and here I will allow a gig might travel well, and be a convenience, but it would have made a poor figure in the plashy country on the other side of Lucknow, and have not been very serviceable in any part of the King of Oude's territories. We encamped in a smaller grove of mangoe-trees than the four or five last had been, but the trees themselves were very noble. The chief cultivation round us was cotton. The morning was positively cold, and the whole scene, with the exercise of the march, the picturesque groupes of men and animals round me,—the bracing air, the singing of birds, the light mist hanging on the trees, and the glistening dew, had something at once so Oriental and so English, I have seldom found any thing better adapted to raise a man's animal spirits, and put him in good temper with himself and all the world. How I wish those I love were with me! How much my wife would enjoy this sort of life,—its exercise, its cleanliness, and purity; its constant occupation, and at the same time its comparative freedom from form, care, and vexation! At the same time a man who is curious in his eating, had better not come here. Lamb and kid, (and we get no other flesh,) most people would soon tire of. The only fowls which are attainable are as tough and lean as can be desired; and the milk and butter are generally seasoned with the never-failing condiments of Hindostan, smoke and soot. The milk would be very good if the people would only milk the cow into one of our vessels instead of their own; but this they generally refuse to do, and refuse with much greater pertinacity than those who live near the river. These, however, are matters to which it is not difficult to become reconciled, and all the more serious points of warmth, shade, cleanliness, air, and water, are at this season no where enjoyed better than in the spacious and well-contrived tents, the ample means of transport, the fine climate, and fertile regions of Northern Hindostan. Another time, by God's blessing, I will not be alone in this Eden; yet I confess there are very few people whom I greatly wish to have as associates in such a journey. It is only a wife, or a friend so intimate as to be quite another self, whom one is really anxious to be with one while travelling through a new country.

On 14 *November Heber arrived at Bareilly, where he stayed for four days.*

I had been for some time in much doubt as to the expediency, after the many delays which I had experienced in my journey, of proceeding to Almorah, but what I heard during these few days at Bareilly determined me in the affirmative. Though an important station, it has never been visited by any Clergyman; and I was very anxious not only to give a Sunday to its secluded flock, but to ascertain what facilities existed for obtaining for them the occasional visits, at least, of a minister of religion, and for eventually spreading the Gospel among these mountaineers, and beyond them into Thibet and Tartary. The former of these objects I have good hopes of being able to accomplish; a residence in these cold and bracing regions may, in many cases, do as much good to Chaplains and Missionaries, exhausted by the heat of the plains, as a voyage to Europe would do; and good men may be well employed here, who are unequal to exertion in other parts of our eastern empire. To the second there are many obstacles, not likely, as yet, to be overcome; and in encountering which considerable prudence and moderation will be necessary. But there are facilities and encouragements also, which I did not expect to find; and if God spare me life and opportunities, I yet hope to see Christianity revived, through this channel, in countries where, under a corrupted form indeed, it is said to have once flourished widely through the labours of the Nestorians.[1]

[On 18 November, about sixteen miles beyond Bareilly, Heber had] a first view of the range of the Himalaya, indistinctly seen through the haze, but not so indistinctly as to conceal the general form of the mountains. The nearer hills are blue, and in outline and tints resemble pretty closely, at this distance, those which close in the vale of Clwyd. Above these rose, what might, in the present unfavourable atmosphere, have been taken for clouds, had not their seat been so stationary and their outline so harsh and pyramidical, the patriarchs of the continent, perhaps the surviving ruins of a former world, white and glistening as alabaster, and even at this distance of, probably, 150 miles, towering above the nearer and secondary range, as much as these last, (though said to be 7600 feet high,) are above the plain on which we were standing. I felt intense delight and awe in looking on them, but the pleasure lasted not many minutes, the clouds closed in again, as on the fairy castle of St John, and left us but the former grey cold horizon, girding in the green plain of Rohilcund, and broken only by scattered tufts of peepul and mangoe-trees.

November 19.—This morning we went seven coss to Sheeshghur, over a worse cultivated country than the last day's stage, and one which had, evidently, suffered much from want of rain.

---

[1] Nestorian Christianity expanded eastwards from Persia, reaching China in A.D. 635; and until the fourteenth century Nestorian communities existed throughout Central Asia. They believed that there were two separate persons in the incarnate Christ, human and divine.

The heavy and happy fall which had given plenty to Oude and the Dooab did not extend here, and except in a few places, where irrigation had been used, the rice and Indian corn had generally failed, and the wheat and barley were looking very ill. Where there are rivers or streams, irrigation is practised industriously and successfully, but there are few wells, and they do not seem, as in the Dooab and Oude, to draw water from them by oxen for their fields. The rain which falls is, in most seasons, said to be sufficient.

On leaving our encampment we forded the river Bhagool, and afterwards, once or twice, fell in, during our march, with its windings. At last, soon after the sun rose, and just as we had reached a small rising ground, the mist rolled away and shewed us again the Himalaya, distinct and dark, with the glorious icy mountains, towering in a clear blue sky, above the nearer range. There were four of these, the names of three of which Mr Boulderson[1] knew, Bhadrinâth, Kedar Nâth, and the peak above the source of the Ganges,[2] the Meru of Hindoo fable. The fourth, to the extreme right, he did not know, and I could not find it in Arrowsmith's map.[3] Bhadrinâth, he told me, is reckoned the highest. From hence, however, it is not the most conspicuous of the four. That we saw the snowy peaks at all, considering their distance, and that mountains twice as high as Snowdon intervened, is wonderful. I need hardly say that I wished for my wife to share the sight with me. But I thought of Tandah and the Terrai, and felt, on recollection, that I should have probably been in considerable uneasiness, if she and the children had been to pass the intervening inhospitable country.

Sheeshghur is a poor village, on a trifling elevation which is conspicuous in this level country. It has a ruinous fort on its summit, and altogether, with the great surrounding flat and the blue hills behind it, put me in mind of some views of Rhydlan. The Clwydian chain, indeed, is not crowned by such noble pinnacles as Bhadrinâth and Gangotree, but I could not help feeling now, and I felt it still more when I began to attempt to

[1] S. M. Boulderson, the Collector of Bareilly, who had waited for the Bishop to guide him through the forests of the Terai at the foot of the mountains.

[2] Gangotri.

[3] Aaron Arrowsmith (1750–1823) produced several maps of India.

commit the prospect to paper, that the awe and wonder which I experienced were of a very complex character, and greatly detached from the simple act of vision. The eye is, by itself, and without some objects to form a comparison, unable to judge of such heights at such a distance. Carneth Llewellyn and Snowdon, at certain times in the year, make, really, as good a picture as the mountains now before me, and the reason that I am so much more impressed with the present view, is partly the mysterious idea of aweful and inaccessible remoteness attached to the Indian Caucasus, the centre of earth,

'Its Altar, and its Cradle, and its Throne';

and still more the knowledge derived from books, that the objects now before me are really among the greatest earthly works of the Almighty Creator's hands,—the highest spots below the moon— and out-topping, by many hundred feet, the summits of Cotopasi and Chimborazo.[1]

November 20.—The country is by no means ill-cultivated thus far, but as we approach the forest[2] it gradually grows marshy and unwholesome, and the whole horizon, at some little distance, was wrapped in a thick white mist which Mr Boulderson called 'Essence of Owl', the native name for the malaria fever. The villages which we passed were singularly wretched, though there is no want of materials for building, and the rate of land is very low. It seems, however, as if the annual ague and fever took away all energy from the inhabitants, and prevented their adopting those simple means of dry and well-raised dwellings, and sufficient clothing, which would go far to secure their health and life. They are a very ugly and miserable race of human beings, with large heads and particularly prominent ears, flat noses, tumid bellies, slender limbs, and sallow complexions, and have scarcely any garments but a blanket of black wool. Most of them have match-locks, swords, and shields, however; and Mr Boulderson pointed out two villages near which we passed, which had last year a deadly feud, ending in a sort of pitched battle, in which nine men were killed, and several wounded. It was necessary to dispatch

[1] Andean peaks. [2] In the Terai.

a corps of sepoys to the spot to settle the quarrel, by bringing a few of the ringleaders on both sides to justice. So expert are men, even when most wretched, in finding out ways and means of mutually increasing their misery!

The only satisfaction to be derived from a journey through such a country, is to look steadily at the mountains beyond it, which increase as we advance in apparent magnitude and beauty. The snowy peaks, indeed, are less and less distinguishable; but the nearer range rises into a dignity and grandeur which I by no means was prepared for, and is now clearly seen to be itself divided into several successive ridges, with all the wildest and most romantic forms of ravine, forest, crag, and precipice.

At the foot of the lowest hills a long black level line extends, so black and level that it might seem to have been drawn with ink and a ruler. This is the forest from which we are still removed several coss, though the country already begins to partake of its insalubrity. It is remarkable that this insalubrity is said to have greatly increased in the last fifteen years. Before that time Ruderpoor, where now the soldiers and servants of the police Thanna die off so fast that they can scarcely keep up the establishment, was a large and wealthy place, inhabited all the year through without danger or disease. Nay, Tandah itself, ten years back, was the favourite and safe resort of sportsmen from Bareilly and Moradabad, who often pitched their tents there, without injury, for ten days together. The forest was, in fact, under a gradual process of reclaimer; the cowmen and woodmen were pushing their incursions farther every year, and the plain where we were now travelling, though always liable to fever and ague, was as populous and habitable as many other parts of India where no complaints were heard. The unfavourable change is imputed by the natives themselves to depopulation; and they are no doubt philosophically right, since there seems to be a preservative in the habitation, cultivation, nay, perhaps in the fires, the breath, and society of men, which neutralizes malaria, even in countries naturally most subject to it. The instance of Rome and its adjacent territory is exactly a similar one, and I recollect being told that in proportion to the number of empty houses in a street, the malaria always raged in it. The depopulation of these countries arose from the invasion of Meer Khân,[1] in 1805. He then laid waste all these Pergunnahs, and the population, once so checked, has never recovered itself. There was, indeed, in former times, a cause which no longer exists, which tended materially to keep up the stock of inhabitants in the Terrai, inasmuch as, from the nature and circumstances of their country, they were free from many of the oppressions to which the other peasants of Rohilcund were liable, paying very light taxes, and living almost as they pleased under the patriarchal government of their own Rajas. Their taxes are still light enough, but the hand of the law is, under the present government, felt here as in other parts of the province; and as the inhabitants of the more wholesome district have fewer motives than formerly to fly from their homes to these marshes, so the inhabitants of the marshes themselves have less powerful reasons for clinging to their uncomfortable birth-place, and the tide of emigration is turned into a contrary direction.

The natives have a singular notion that it is not the air but the water of these countries which produces 'Owl'. The water is certainly not clear or well-tasted, either at Sheeshghur or Kulleanpoor, and Mr Boulderson has brought a stock of Bareilly water for our own drinking. I cannot, however, see any thing about it which is likely to do so much mischief, and the notion is an unfortunate one, inasmuch as it leads them to neglect all precautions against the other and more formidable causes of disease. I have tents sufficient to shelter all the people who accompany me, and I had offered, at Sheeshghur, if the sepoys found themselves crowded, to receive the Soubahdar and some of the non-commissioned officers, at night under my own tent. Yet it was with great difficulty that I could persuade either them or the camel-drivers to forsake their favourite system of sleeping with their heads wrapped up, but with the greater part of their clothes off, in the open air, round their fires. They were exceedingly unwilling to pitch their tents at all, saying, it did not signify,

[1] Amir Khan, leader of a band of Pathans who ravaged much of northern India before 1817, when he was persuaded to disarm and recognised as Nawab of Tonk.

that the fog did no harm, and the water was the cause of all the mischief.[1]

A local raja, Gurman Singh, came to visit the Bishop.

He mentioned, in the course of conversation, that there was a tyger in an adjoining tope,[2] which had done a good deal of mischief, that he should have gone after it himself had he not been ill, and had he not thought that it would be a fine diversion for Mr Boulderson and me. I told him I was no sportsman, but Mr Boulderson's eyes sparkled at the name of tyger, and he expressed great anxiety to beat up his quarters in the afternoon. Under such circumstances, I did not like to deprive him of his sport, as he would not leave me by myself, and went, though with no intention of being more than a spectator. Mr Boulderson, however, advised me to load my pistols for the sake of defence, and lent me a very fine double-barrelled gun for the same purpose. We set out a little after three on our elephants, with a servant behind each howdah carrying a large chatta, which, however, was almost needless. The Raja, in spite of his fever, made his appearance too, saying that he could not bear to be left behind. A number of people, on foot and horse-back, attended from our own camp and the neighbouring villages, and the same sort of interest and delight was evidently excited which might be produced in England by a great coursing party. The Raja was on a little female elephant, hardly bigger than the Durham ox, and almost as shaggy as a poodle. She was a native of the neighbouring wood, where they are generally, though not always, of a smaller size than those of Bengal and Chittagong. He sat in a low howdah, with two or three guns ranged beside him, ready for action. Mr Boulderson had also a formidable apparatus of musquets and fowling-pieces, projecting over his mohout's head. We rode about two miles, across a plain covered with long jungly grass, which very much put me in mind of the country near the Cuban. Quails and wild fowl rose in great numbers, and beautiful antelopes were seen scudding away in all directions. With them our party had no quarrel; their flesh is good for little, and they

[1] This period was of course long before it was discovered that malaria is a mosquito-born disease.
[2] A grove.

are in general favourites both with native and English sportsmen, who feel disinclined to meddle with a creature so graceful and so harmless.

At last we came to a deeper and more marshy ground, which lay a little before the tope pointed out to us; and while Mr Boulderson was doubting whether we should pass through it, or skirt it, some country people came running to say that the tyger had been tracked there that morning. We therefore went in, keeping line as if we had been beating for a hare, through grass so high that it reached up to the howdah of my elephant, though a tall one, and almost hid the Raja entirely. We had not gone far before a very large animal of the deer kind sprung up just before me, larger than a stag, of a dusky brown colour, with spreading, but not palmated horns. Mr Boulderson said it was a 'mohr', a species of elk; that this was a young one, but that they sometimes grew to an immense size, so that he had stood upright between the tips of their horns. He could have shot it, but did not like to fire at present, and said it was, after all, a pity to meddle with such harmless animals. The mohr accordingly ran off unmolested, rising with splendid bounds up to the very top of the high jungle, so that his whole body and limbs were seen from time to time above it. A little further, another rose, which Mr Boulderson said was the female; of her I had but an imperfect view. The sight of these curious animals had already, however, well repaid my coming out, and from the animation and eagerness of every body round me, the anxiety with which my companions looked for every waving of the jungle-grass, and the continued calling and shouting of the horse and foot behind us, it was impossible not to catch the contagion of interest and enterprize.

At last the elephants all drew up their trunks into the air, began to roar, and to stamp violently with their fore feet, the Raja's little elephant turned short round, and in spite of all her mohout could say or do, took up her post, to the Raja's great annoyance, close in the rear of Mr Boulderson. The other three, (for one of my baggage elephants had come out too, the mohout, though unarmed, not caring to miss the show,) went on slowly but boldly, with their trunks raised, their ears expanded, and their sagacious little eyes bent intently forward. 'We are close upon him', said Mr Boulderson, 'fire where you see the long grass shake, if he rises before you.'—Just at that moment my elephant stamped again violently. 'There, there', cried the mohout, 'I saw his head!' A short roar, or rather loud growl, followed, and I saw immediately before my elephant's head the motion of some large animal stealing away through the grass. I fired as directed, and, a moment after, seeing the motion still more plainly, fired the second barrel. Another short growl followed, the motion was immediately quickened, and was soon lost in the more distant jungle. Mr Boulderson said, 'I should not wonder if you hit him that last time; at any rate we shall drive him out of the cover, and then I will take care of him.' In fact, at that moment, the crowd of horse and foot spectators at the jungle side began to run off in all directions. We went on to the place, but found it was a false alarm, and, in fact, we had seen all we were to see of him, and went twice more through the jungle in vain. A large extent of high grass stretched out in one direction, and this we had now not sufficient day-light to explore. In fact, that the animal so near me was a tyger at all, I have no evidence but its growl, Mr Boulderson's belief, the assertion of the mohout, and what is perhaps more valuable than all the rest, the alarm expressed by the elephants. I could not help feeling some apprehension that my firing had robbed Mr Boulderson of his shot, but he assured me that I was quite in rule; that in such sport no courtesies could be observed, and that the animal in fact rose before me, but that he should himself have fired without scruple if he had seen the rustle of the grass in time. Thus ended my first, and probably my last essay, in the 'field-sports' of India, in which I am much mistaken, notwithstanding what Mr Boulderson said, if I harmed any living creature.

November 21.—Our road to-day was, though intersected by two or three water courses, rather less rugged than the day before. The country, however, is dismal enough, leaving every where the marks of having been cultivated at no distant period, but now almost all overgrown with a rank vegetation of a dusky, poisonous-looking plant, something like nightshade, and all jungle-grass, often considerably higher than the head of a man on horseback, through which we pushed our way like Gulliver in the Patagonian corn-field. At last we emerged on a somewhat higher and drier ground, where were some of the largest peepul-trees I ever saw, but still offering a wild and dismal shade choked up below with the vile underwood which I have mentioned, and a narrow and boggy path winding through it. On the other side we found ourselves among ill-cultivated rice-fields, beyond which was a magnificent range of mangoe-topes, and some tombs and temples peeping out from among them. On my expressing some surprise to see these appearances of wealth and splendour at Ruderpoor, Mr Boulderson observed that I should soon change my opinion.

We found, in fact, on drawing nearer, all the usual marks of a diminished and sickly population, a pestilential climate, and an over-luxuriant soil. The tombs and temples were all ruins, the houses of the present inhabitants, some two or three score of wretched huts, such as even the gypseys of the open country would hardly shelter in; the people sate huddled together at their doors, wrapped in their black blankets, and cowering round little fires, with pale faces and emaciated limbs, while the groves which looked so beautiful at a distance, instead of offering, as mangoe-topes do in well-peopled and cultivated spots, a fine open shade with a dry turf and fresh breeze beneath it, were all choked up with jungle and nightshade like the peepul-trees we had lately passed amongst.

We found the village magistrate ill of fever and ague, too ill indeed to come out to meet us. The second in authority, who brought his apology and nuzzur, said, however, that no new fevers were likely to be contracted now, the cold season having set in, and the people having begun to go out to burn the jungles. After breakfast I read prayers with Mr Boulderson and Abdullah; and when the day grew warm the head man of the village ventured out to call on me, and beg for some medicine. He was a decent-looking man, very neatly and cleanly dressed, but looking grievously ill, and I felt very sorry that I had so little skill to help him. His fever had been on him some time, and he had hot and cold fits every alternate day, but both increased at each return in violence and duration. I made him sit down, which he was very unwilling to do, though quite unfit to stand, and he told me his case very clearly and intelligently. His hot fit was then on him, his pulse high, and his tongue white, with a little mixture of yellow. No saffron could be yellower than his skin. I would have given him an emetic but was afraid, and judged beside that his complaint had been too long on him to receive benefit from it. I therefore gave him some calomel pills, bidding him take two as soon as he got home, and one or two every day the fever returned, giving him, for the intermitting days, a bottle of decoction of gentian, having scarcely any bark by me. Nothing could be more grateful than he seemed; and I am sure that, if faith in a remedy is likely to contribute to its efficacy, that requisite at least was not wanting in him. Mr Boulderson afterwards told me that gentian was an usual and valuable medicine in the malaria fever.

November 22.—We came to a tract where the fires had already been active, where little huts and herds of diminutive cattle were seen peeping out under the trees, and we overtook the rear-guard of our caravan, who told us we were near Bamoury. The population which we saw were Khasya, or inhabitants of Kemaoon, who yearly come down, after the unwholesome time is over, to graze their cattle and cultivate the best and driest spots of the forest with barley and wheat, which they reap and carry back with them before April is far advanced, when they return to reap the similar, but somewhat later crops, which they had sown before they left their own country. At the same time they obtain an opportunity of disposing of their honey and other commodities of the hills, and buying different little luxuries with which the plains only, and the more civilized parts of Hindostan can supply them. Many of them were close by the way-side, very dark and meagre people, but strongly and neatly made, and not so diminutive as the inhabitants of such mountains generally are. They were all wrapped up in the long black blankets of their marshland neighbours, but very few of them had arms. Mr Boulderson said they merely carried them against tygers, for there was scarcely a more peaceable or honest race in the world.

We now passed a rapid and gravelly brook of beautiful water, overhung by shady trees, with Khasya tents all round it, by which the main body of our caravan had halted to repose and drink. We pushed on, however, and soon began to rise up a gentle ascent, into the gorge of a delightful valley, with woody mountains on either side, and a considerable river running through it, dashing over a rocky bottom with great noise and violence.

November 23.—This morning I mounted Mr Traill's[1] poney, a stout shaggy little white animal, whose birth-place might have been in Wales, instead of the Himalaya.... After a good deal of trouble in getting the mules and coolies started, we proceeded on our journey as it began to dawn, a night march being not very safe amid these mountains, and the beauty of the scenery being of itself a sufficient motive to see all which was to be seen. The road was, certainly, sufficiently steep and rugged, and, particularly when intersected by torrents, I do not think it was passable by horses accustomed only to the plain. I was myself surprised to see how dexterously our poneys picked their way over large rolling pebbles and broken fragments of rock, how firmly they planted their feet, and with how little distress they conquered some of the steepest ascents I ever climbed. The country as we advanced became exceedingly beautiful and romantic. It reminded me most of Norway, but had the advantage of round-topped trees, instead of the unvaried spear-like outline of the pine. It would have been like some parts of Wales, had not the hills and precipices been much higher, and the vallies, or rather dells, narrower and more savage. We could seldom, from the range on which the road ran, see to the bottom of any of them, and only heard the roar and rush of the river which we had left, and which the torrents which foamed across our path were hastening to join.

We saw several interesting plants and animals; Mr Boulderson shot two black and purple pheasants, and a jungle hen; we saw some beautiful little white monkeys, called by the people 'Gounee', gamboling on the trees; and heard, which, perhaps, pleased me most of all, the notes of an English thrush. The bird, however, though Mr Boulderson said it is of the thrush kind, is

[1] G. W. Traill: appointed Commissioner for Kumaon and Garhwal in 1817; retired from the service 1836.

black. For a short distance the vegetation did not differ materially from that of the plains. The first peculiarities I saw were some nettles of very great size, and some magnificent creepers which hung their wild cordage, as thick as a ship's cable and covered with broad bright leaves, from tree to tree over our heads. After about an hour and a half's ascent, Mr Boulderson pointed out to me some dog-rose trees, and a number of raspberry bushes, with here and there a small but not very thriving ever-green oak. We soon after saw a good many cherry-trees, of the common wild English sort, in full blossom, and as we turned down a steep descent to Beemthâl, we passed under some pear-trees with the fruit already set, and a wild thicket, I will not call it jungle, of raspberry and bilberry bushes on either side of our path. We had sufficient proof during our ride, that the country, wild as it is, is not uninhabited. We met two or three companies of Khasiya peasantry going down to their annual cultivation in the forest. . . .

Their industry seems very great. In every part where the declivity was less steep, so as to admit a plough or a spade, we found little plots of ground, sometimes only four feet wide, and ten or twelve long, in careful and neat cultivation. Some of these were ranged in little terraces, one above the other, supported by walls of loose stones; and these evidences of industry and population were the more striking, because we literally did not pass a single habitation; and even at Beemthâl, besides the Company's guard-room and warehouses, only one miserable hut was visible. Beemthâl is, however, a very beautiful place. It is a little mountain-valley, surrounded on three sides by woody hills, and on the fourth by a tract of green meadow, with a fine lake of clear water. A small and very rude pagoda of grey stone, with a coarse slate roof, under some fine peepul-trees, looked like a little church; and the whole scene, except that the hills were higher, so strongly reminded me of Wales, that I felt my heart beat as I entered it.

November 24.—Mr Boulderson left me this morning, and I believe we parted with mutual regret; his pursuits and amusements were certainly very different from mine, but I found in him a fine temper and an active mind, full of information respecting the country, animals, and people among whom he had passed several years; and on the whole I do not think I have acquired so much of this kind of knowledge in so short a time from any person whom I have met with in India. I myself remained at Beemthâl this day, partly to rest my people after their two severe marches, partly to see another lake or 'Thâl' at a short distance, which was said to be finer than that before me.

I set off as soon as Mr Boulderson had left me, about six o'clock in the morning, on the white poney, with a Khasiyah guide, Mr Traill's saees, and two sepoys, who had for some time shewn on all occasions a great zeal to accompany me. One of these is the man who got leave to see his brother. The other is a brahmin, a very decent, middle-aged man, one of the number who was sick in Oude. He is fond of telling me stories of his campaigns, which he says have many of them been among mountains in Malwah and Bundelcund. He owns, however, that the mountains here are larger than any which he has yet visited; even respecting these I found him not ill-informed, both as to the holy places situated among them, Bhadrinâth, Gungootree, &c. the situation of the source of the Ganges, which he correctly stated, in answer to a question which I put to try him, to be on this side of the snowy mountains, and the scenes where battles were fought during the Gorkhali war. The other soldier had not much to say, but was exceedingly civil and willing to oblige, and had a pair of the longest and most nimble legs, and the strongest arms I have seen.

The Khasiyah nation pretend to be all Rajpoots of the highest caste, and very scrupulous in their eating and drinking. They will not even sell one of their little mountain-cows to a stranger, unless he will swear that he neither will kill it himself, nor transfer it to any body else in order to be killed: and as these cows give very little milk, and as their abhorrence of feathers leads the cottagers to keep no poultry, a stranger passing through their country, who cannot kill his own game, or who has not such a friend as Mr Boulderson to do it for him, stands a bad chance of obtaining any supplies, except very coarse black bread and water, with perhaps a little honey. They are a modest, gentle, respectful people, honest in their dealings, and as remarkable for their love of truth as the Puharrees of Rajmahal and Boglipoor. As their language is different from that of Hindostan, I was anxious to know whether it resembled that of these other mountaineers, but found that a party who, on one occasion, accompanied Mr Traill to Bengal were unintelligible to the southern Puharree. Indeed their real or pretended Rajpoot descent would, of itself, prove them to be a different race. Those who went with Mr Traill, I learned from Mr Boulderson, who was also of the party, took no notice whatever of the Rajmahal hills, even when passing over them. Mr Boulderson said, 'are you not pleased to see mountains again?' 'What mountains?' was their reply. 'These mountains to be sure', returned he. 'They are not mountains, they are playthings', was their answer. In comparison with their own they might, indeed, say so without affectation.

November 25.—This morning we began to pack by four o'clock, but owing to the restiveness of the mules and the clumsiness of the people, divers accidents occurred, the most serious of which was the bursting of one of the petarrahs.[1] At length we got off, and after coasting the lake for one mile, went for about thirteen more by a most steep and rugged road, over the neck of mount Gaughur, through a succession of glens, forests, and views of the most sublime and beautiful description. I never saw such prospects before, and had formed no adequate idea of such. My attention was completely strained, and my eyes filled with tears, every thing around was so wild and magnificent that man appeared as nothing, and I felt myself as if climbing the steps of the altar of God's great temple. The trees, as we advanced, were in a large proportion fir and cedar, but many were ilex, and to my surprise I still saw even in these Alpine tracts, many venerable peepultrees, on which the white monkeys were playing their gambols. A monkey is also found in these hills as large as a large dog, if my guides are to be believed. Tygers used to be very common and mischievous, but since the English have frequented the country, are scarce, and in comparison, very shy. There are also many wolves and bears, and some chamois, two of which passed near us. My sepoys wanted me to shoot one, and offered, with my leave, to do so themselves, if I did not like the walk which would

[1] Wicker baskets.

be necessary. But my people would not have eaten them. I myself was well supplied with provisions, and I did not wish to destroy an innocent animal merely for the sake of looking at it a little closer; I therefore told them it was not my custom to kill any thing which was not mischievous, and asked if they would stand by me if we saw a tyger or a bear. They promised eagerly not to fail me, and I do not think they would have broken their words. After winding up

> ' A wild romantic chasm that slanted
> Down the steep hill, athwart a cedar cover,
> A savage place, as holy and enchanted
> As e'er beneath the waning moon was haunted
> By woman wailing for her demon lover,'

we arrived at the gorge of the pass, in an indent between the two principal summits of mount Gaughur, near 8,600 feet above the sea. And now the snowy mountains, which had been so long eclipsed, opened on us in full magnificence.... Nundidevi was immediately opposite; Kedar Nâth was not visible from our present situation, and Meru only seen as a very distant single peak. The eastern mountains, however, for which I have obtained no name, rose into great consequence, and were very glorious objects as we wound down the hill on the other side. The guides could only tell me that 'they were a great way off, and bordered on the Chinese empire'. They are, I suppose, in Thibet.

November 26.—This morning we proceeded along a narrow valley to a broken bridge over the torrent, so like, in scenery and circumstances, to that called Alarm Brug., in Dovre in Norway, that I could have almost fancied myself there. We forded the stream without difficulty, though over a very rugged bed; but, during the rains, one of the chuprassees told me, a rope, which I saw hanging loosely across the ruined arch, was to transport the postman or any other passenger. He was seated in a basket hung by a loop on this rope, and drawn over, backwards and forwards, by two smaller ones fastened to the basket on each side. This is an ingenious though simple method of conveyance, which is practised also by the catchers of sea-fowl on many parts of the coast of Norway; it was the only way formerly in use of passing torrents or chasms in these countries; and the stone bridges which the English have erected are very ill able to resist the floods of the rainy season, which rush down these steep descents with great violence and rapidity.

The long-legged sepoy, who is I find a brahmin as well as his comrade, is certainly an excellent walker; when I stopped, as I made a point of doing from time to time, for my party and my horse to take breath, he always said he was not tired; and he fairly beat the Kemaoon chuprassees, though natives of the country. Both he and the elder man profess to like their journey exceedingly, and the latter was greatly delighted this morning, when on climbing a second mountain we had a more extensive and panoramic view of the icy range than we had seen before, and the guides pointed out Meru! 'That, my Lord, (he cried out) is the greatest of all mountains! out of that Gunga flows!' The younger who is not a man of many words, merely muttered Ram! Ram! Ram!

I had expected, from this hill, to see something like a table-land or elevated plain, but found instead, nothing but one range of mountains after the other, quite as rugged, and, generally speaking, more bare than those which we had left, till the horizon was terminated by a vast range of ice and snow, extending its battalion of white shining spears from east to west, as far as the eye could follow it; the principal points rising like towers in the glittering rampart, but all connected by a chain of humbler glaciers. On one of the middle range of mountains before us, a little lower than the rest, some white buildings appeared, and a few trees, with a long zig-zag road winding up the face of the hill. This, I was told, was the city and fortress of Almorah.

During the afternoon, and soon after I had finished my early dinner, a very fine cheerful old man with staff and wallet, walked up and took his place by one of the fires. He announced himself as a pilgrim to Bhadrinâth, and said he had previously visited a holy place in Lahore, whose name I could not make out, and was last returned from Juggernâth and Calcutta, whence he had intended to visit the Burman territories, but was prevented by the war. He was a native of Oude, but hoped, he said, before he fixed himself again at home to see Bombay and Poonah. I asked him what made him undertake such long journeys? He said he had had a good and affectionate son, a havildar in the Company's service, who always sent him money, and had once or twice come to see him. Two years back he died, and left him sixteen gold mohurs,[1] but since that time, he said, he could settle to nothing, and at length he had determined to go to all the most holy spots he had heard of, and travel over the world till his melancholy legacy was exhausted. I told him I would pay the gomashta for his dinner that day, on which he thanked me, and said 'so many great men had shewn him the same kindness, that he was not yet in want, and had never been obliged to ask for any thing'. He was very curious to know who I was, with so many guards and servants in such a place; and the name of 'Lord Padre' was, as usual, a great puzzle to him. He gave a very copious account of his travels, the greater part of which I understood pretty well, and he was much pleased by the interest which I took in his adventures. He remarked that Hindostan was the finest country and the most plentiful which he had seen. Next to that he spoke well of Sinde, where he said things were still cheaper, but the water not so good. Lahore, Bengal, and Orissa, none of them were favourites, nor did he speak well of Kemaoon. It might for all he knew, he said, be healthy, but what was that to him, who was never ill any where, so he could get bread and water? There was something flighty in his manner, but on the whole he was a fine old pilgrim, and one well suited to

'Repay with many a tale the nightly bed'.

A nightly bed, indeed, I had not to offer him, but he had as comfortable a birth by the fire as the sepoys could make him, and I heard his loud cheerful voice telling stories after his mess of rice and ghee, till I myself dropped asleep.

November 27.—I found Almorah a small but very curious and interesting town. It chiefly consists of one long street, running along the ridge of the mountain from the fort westward to a

---

[1] Gold coins, then worth 16 rupees each.

smaller block-house eastward, with scattered bungalows, chiefly inhabited by Europeans, to the right and left hand on the descent of the hill. The main-street has a gate at each end, and, on a small scale, put me in mind of Chester. The houses all stand on a lower story of stone, open to the street, with strong square pillars, where the shops are, looking like some of the rows. Above the buildings are of timber, exactly like those of Chester, in one or sometimes two very low stories, and surmounted by a sloping roof of heavy grey slate, on which many of the inhabitants pile up their hay in small stacks for winter consumption. The town is very neat, the street has a natural pavement of slaty rock which is kept beautifully clean: the stone part of the houses is well white-washed, and adorned with queer little paintings; and the tradesmen are not only a fairer but a much more respectable looking race than I had expected to see, from the filth and poverty of the agricultural Khasiyas.

We passed two or three little old pagodas and tanks, as well as a Mussulman burial-ground. The Mussulmans were treated with great rigour here during the Ghorkha government. They are now fully tolerated and protected, but their numbers are very small. Government, on the conquest of Almorah,[1] very liberally built a number of small bungalows in airy situations round it, for the accommodation, gratis, of any of their civil or military servants, who might come to reside here for their health. They are small low cottages of stone with slated roofs, and look extremely like the sea-bathing cottages on the Welch coast, having thick walls, small windows, low rooms, and all the other peculiarities (most different from the generality of Anglo-Indian houses) which suit a boisterous and cold climate.

Sunday, November 28.—This day I enjoyed the gratification of being the first Protestant Minister who had preached and administered the sacraments in so remote, yet so celebrated, a region.

[1] Almora had been captured from the Gurkhas in 1815.

Heber was concerned about the deforestation in the surrounding countryside.

November 29.—Great devastations are generally made in these woods, partly by the increase of population, building, and agriculture, partly by the wasteful habits of travellers, who cut down multitudes of young trees to make temporary huts, and for fuel, while the cattle and goats which browse on the mountains prevent a great part of the seedlings from rising. Unless some precautions are taken, the inhabited parts of Kemaoon will soon be wretchedly bare of wood, and the country, already too arid, will not only lose its beauty, but its small space of fertility. Of the inhabitants every body seems to speak well. They are, indeed, dirty to a degree which I never saw among Hindoos, and extremely averse to any improvement in their rude and inefficient agriculture, but they are honest, peaceable, and cheerful, and, in the species of labour to which they are accustomed, extremely diligent. There are hardly twelve convicts now in the gaol of Almorah; and the great majority of cases which come before Mr Traill are trifling affrays, arising from disputed boundaries, trespass, and quarrels at fair and market. The only serious public cases which are at all prevalent, are adultery, and, sometimes, carrying off women to marry them forcibly. They use their women ill, and employ them in the most laborious tasks, in which, indeed, a wife is regarded by the Khasiya peasant as one of the most laborious and valuable of his domestic animals. These people, though rigid Hindoos, are not so inhospitable as their brethren of the plain. Even Europeans travelling through the country, who will put up with such accommodations as the peasantry have to offer, are almost sure of being well received, and have no need of carrying tents with them, provided their journey is made at a time when the peasantry are at home to receive them, and not during the annual emigration to the plains.

[The Bishop received a visit from] the Pundit of the Criminal Court of Kemaoon, a learned brahmin, and a great astrologer. He had professed to Mr Traill a desire to see me, and asked if I were as well informed in the Vedas, Puranas, and other sacred books of the Hindoos, as another European Pundit whom he had heard preach some years before at the great fair of Hurdwar? He evidently meant the Baptist Missionary Mr Chamberlayne; and it pleased me to find that this good and able, though bigotted man, had left a favourable impression behind him among his auditors. Mr Traill told him that I had been only a short time in the country; but he was still anxious to see me, and I regretted much to find, when we met, that his utterance was so rapid and indistinct that I could understand less of his conversation than of most Hindoos whom I have met with. He explained to me, however, that three or four years before the British conquered Kemaoon he had, through his acquaintance with the stars, foretold the event, and that his calculation, signed and dated, was lodged with the Raja at Derea. He said he had now discovered three new stars, in the shape of a triangle, south-east of the great bear, which, by their position, assured the north an ascendancy over the east, and implied that we should triumph in our present struggle with the Birman empire. I asked him some questions about the form of the earth, the source of the Ganges, the situation of mount Meru, and received better answers than I expected. He said that, in old times, the Ganges was supposed to rise from mount Meru, but that modern Hindoos, at least the enlightened, gave the name of Meru to the North Pole, and were aware that the Gunga rose from the peaks, one of which I had seen above Gungotree, and south of the great snowy range, which he called, not Himalaya, but Himmachund. He laughed at the fancy of the elephant and tortoise, whom the Pundits of Benares placed as supporters to the earth, and said it was a part of the same system with that which made the earth flat, and girded in by six other worlds, each having its own ocean. I drew a diagram of the world with its circles, &c. and he recognized them with great delight, shewing me the sun's path along the ecliptic. He expressed a great desire to learn more of the European discoveries in astronomy and geography, and listened with much attention to my account (in which I frequently had recourse to Mr Traill as interpreter,) of the Copernican system, and the relative situations of England, Russia, Turkey, Persia, Arabia, and India. He asked if we had yet discovered the shorter way to India through the ice of the North

Pole, of which, he said, he had heard from a brahmin of Benares, who had his account from Colonel Wilford:[1] and he knew America under the name of 'the New World', and as one of the proofs that the earth was round. He was very anxious to obtain any Hindoo books containing the improved system of astronomy and geography...He is evidently a man of considerable talent, and extremely desirous to improve whatever opportunities of knowledge fall in his way; and, like all these mountaineers, he is of a lively cheerful turn, without any of the crouching manner and flattering address which is apparent in most of the Hindoos of Calcutta and Benares.

It is pleasing to see on how apparent good terms Mr Traill is with all these people. Their manner in talking to him is erect, open, and cheerful, like persons who are addressing a superior whom they love, and with whom they are in habits of easy, though respectful intercourse. He says he loves the country and people where he has been thrown, and has declined, as Sir Robert Colquhoun[2] told me, several situations of much greater emolument for the sake of remaining with them. He has probably, indeed, chosen wisely, since, though he may not return home so rich a man, he is far more likely to take with him the power of enjoying life and property. Almost the whole of the dry season he is travelling about in the discharge of his official duty, and it was a mere chance which gave me the advantage of meeting him now at Almorah.

Heber left Almora on 2 December and descended again to the plain. He travelled through Moradabad and Meerut, and before the end of the month was nearing Delhi.

[1] Francis Wilford (*c.* 1760–1822) had served in the Company's Engineers, spending the latter part of his life at Banaras. He studied ancient Indian geography and tried to show that the British Isles were mentioned in the *Puranas*.
[2] Commandant of the Kumaon Battalion, 1815–28.

Part VI

DELHI AND AGRA

December 28.—I set off from Meerut by Dâk, as far as Begumabad.
Here I mounted Nedjeed—did I ever tell you the name of my
little Arab horse before?—and pursued my journey, escorted by
five of Colonel Skinner's irregular cavalry, the most showy and
picturesque cavaliers I have seen since I was in the South of
Russia. They had turbans of dark red shawl, long yellow caftans
with dark red cummerbunds, and trowsers of the same colour.
The commander of the party had a long spear with a small yellow
pennon, the others had each a long matchlock-gun which they
carried on the right shoulder with the match ready lighted. They
had all, likewise, pistols, swords, and shields, and their caftans
and turbans so strongly quilted, as to secure them against most
sabre-cuts. Their horses were very tolerable in size and appearance, but hot and vicious, and the whole cavalcade had an
appearance remarkably wild and Oriental. They are reckoned, by
all the English in this part of the country, the most useful and
trusty, as well as the boldest body of men in India, and during the
wars both of Lord Lake[1] and Lord Hastings their services and
those of their chief were most distinguished. Colonel Alexander
Skinner is a good and modest, as well as a brave man. He has just
devoted 20,000 sicca rupees to build a Church at Delhi.[2] Unfortunately I shall not meet him there, as he is now on the frontier
with most of his men, fighting the rebellious clans of Seiks and
Mewatties. The Hindoostanees, who respect him very highly, call
him by a whimsical but not ill-applied corruption of his name,
'Secunder[3] Sahib', Lord Alexander.

[1] Lake played an important part in the Maratha War of 1803–5; it was his army
which captured Delhi from Sindhia.

[2] St James', Kashmir Gate. Skinner—whose Christian name was James, not
Alexander—had been born in 1778 of a Scottish father and a Rajput mother. He
died in 1841, and was buried in the church which he had founded in Delhi.

[3] This was a corruption of his surname.

224

Delhi and Agra

December 29.—The morning was clear and pleasant, and the air and soil delightfully refreshed by the rain. I rode Câbul, and arrived by about eight o'clock on the banks of the Jumna, on the other side of which I had a noble view of Delhi, which is a larger and finer city than I expected to see. The inhabited part of it, for the ruins extend over a surface as large as London, Westminster, and Southwark, is about seven miles in circuit, seated on a rocky range of hills, and surrounded by an embattled wall, which the English Government have put into repair and are now engaged in strengthening with bastions, a moat, and a regular glacis. The houses within are many of them large and high. There are a great number of mosques with high minarets and gilded domes, and above all are seen the palace, a very high and extensive cluster of gothic towers and battlements, and the Jumna Musjeed, the largest and handsomest place of Mussulman worship in India. The chief material of all these fine buildings is red granite, of a very agreeable though solemn colour, inlaid in some of the ornamental parts with white marble, and the general style of building is of a simple and impressive character, which reminded me, in many respects, of Carnarvon. It far exceeds any thing at Moscow.

December 30.—This morning Lushington and I rode to the tomb of the emperor Humaiöon,[1] six miles from the city, S.W. We passed, in our way to the Agra gate, along a very broad but irregular street, with a channel of water, cased with stone, conducted along its middle. This is a part of the celebrated aqueduct constructed by Ali Merdan Khân, a Persian nobleman in the service of the emperor Shahjehan,[2] then long neglected during the troubles of India and the decay of the Mogul power, and within these few years repaired by the English Government. It is conducted from the Jumna, immediately on leaving its mountains and while its stream is yet pure and wholesome, for a distance of about 120 miles; and is a noble work, giving fertility to a very large extent of country near its banks, and absolutely the sole source of vegetation to the gardens of Delhi, besides furnishing its inhabitants with almost the only drinkable water within their reach. When it was first re-opened, by Sir Charles Metcalfe, in

---

[1] Died 1556; see *infra*, p. 228, n. 1.   [2] Reigned 1627–58.

1820, the whole population of the city went out in jubilee to meet its stream, throwing flowers, ghee, &c. into the water, and calling down all manner of blessings on the British Government, who have indeed gone far, by this measure, to redeem themselves from the weight of, I fear, a good deal of impolicy.

It most unfortunately happened that, during the present year, and amid all the other misfortunes of drought and scarcity which this poor country has undergone, the Jumna changed its course, and the canal became dry! The engineer officer who superintends its works, was at the time labouring under the remains of a jungle fever; his serjeant was in the same condition, and consequently there was no one who, when the mischief was discovered, could go up to the hills to remedy it. The suffering of the people was very dismal; since the restoration of the canal they had neglected the wells which formerly had, in some degree, supplied their wants. The water which they drank was to be brought from a distance and sold at a considerable rate, and their gardens were quite ruined. That of the presidency had not at the moment when I saw it, a green thing in it, and those of the poor were in a yet worse condition, if worse were possible. It was not till the middle of November that the canal could be again restored, when it was hailed with similar expressions of joy to those which had greeted its former re-appearance.

Half-way along the street which I have been describing, and nearly opposite another great street with a similar branch of the canal, which runs at right angles to the former, stands the imperial palace,[1] built by the Emperor Shah Jehan, surrounded on this side by a wall of, I should think, sixty feet high, embattled and machicollated, with small round towers and two noble gateways, each defended by an outer barbican of the same construction, though of less height. The whole is of red granite, and surrounded by a wide moat. It is a place of no strength, the walls being only calculated for bows and arrows or musquetry, but as a kingly residence it is one of the noblest that I have seen. It far surpasses the Kremlin, but I do not think that, except in the durability of its materials, it equals Windsor.

Sentries in red coats (sepoys of the Company's regular army,)

---

[1] The Red Fort.

appear at its exterior, but the internal duties, and, indeed, most of the police duties of Delhi, are performed by the two provincial battalions raised in the emperor's name, and nominally under his orders. These are disciplined pretty much like Europeans, but have matchlock guns and the oriental dress, and their commanding officer, Captain Grant of the Company's service, is considered as one of the domestics of the Mogul and has apartments in the palace.

From the gate of Agra to Humaiöon's tomb is a very aweful scene of desolation, ruins after ruins, tombs after tombs, fragments of brick-work, freestone, granite, and marble, scattered every where over a soil naturally rocky and barren, without cultivation, except in one or two small spots, and without a single tree. I was reminded of Caffa in the Crimea, but this was Caffa on the scale of London, with the wretched fragments of a magnificence such as London itself cannot boast. The ruins really extended as far as the eye could reach, and our track wound among them all the way. This was the seat of old Delhi, as founded by the Patan kings,[1] on the ruins of the still larger Hindoo city of Indraput,[2] which lay chiefly in a western direction. When the present city, which is certainly in a more advantageous situation, was founded by the emperor Shahjehan, he removed many of its inhabitants thither; most of the rest followed, to be near the palace and the principal markets; and as during the Maharatta government[3] there was no sleeping in a safe skin without the walls, old Delhi was soon entirely abandoned. The official name of the present city is Shahjehan-poor, 'city of the king of the world!' but the name of Delhi is always used in conversation and in every writing but those which are immediately offered to the emperor's eye.

[Heber thought Humayun's tomb] a noble building of granite inlaid with marble, and in a very chaste and simple style of Gothic architecture. It is surrounded by a large garden with terraces and fountains, all now gone to decay except one of the latter, which

---

[1] This seems to be a reference to the buildings of the Turkish and Afghan rulers between the mid-fourteenth and mid-sixteenth centuries, including Firuz Shah Kotla.
[2] Indraprastha.
[3] The Delhi territory was under Sindhia's control from 1785 to 1803.

enables the poor people who live in the out-buildings of the tomb to cultivate a little wheat. The garden itself is surrounded by an embattled wall, with towers, four gateways, and a cloister within all the way round. In the centre of the square is a platform of about twenty feet high, and I should apprehend 200 feet square, supported also by cloisters, and ascended by four great flights of granite steps. Above rises the tomb, also a square, with a great dome of white marble in its centre. The apartments within are a circular room, about as big as the Ratcliffe library, in the centre of which lies, under a small raised slab, the unfortunate prince[1] to whose memory this fine building is raised. In the angles are smaller apartments, where other branches of his family are interred. From the top of the building I was surprised to see that we had still ruins on every side; and that, more particularly, to the westward and where old Indraput stood, the desolation apparently extended to a range of barren hills seven or eight miles off.

After breakfast we went with Mr and Mrs Elliott[2] to see a shawl manufactory carried on by Cashmerian weavers with wool brought from Himalaya, in the house of a wealthy Hindoo merchant, named Soobin-chund. The house itself was very pretty and well worth seeing as a specimen of eastern domestic architecture, comprising three small courts surrounded by stone cloisters, two of them planted with flowering shrubs and orange-trees, and the third ornamented with a beautiful marble fountain. I did not think the shawls which were shewn very beautiful, and the prices of all were high. I was more struck with the specimens of jewellery which they produced, which I thought very splendid, and some of the smaller trinkets in good taste. I was persecuted to accept a splendid nuzzur of shawls, &c. to the value, perhaps, of 1000 s. rupees, which of course I did not choose to take. My pleading my religious profession did not satisfy my Hindoo host, who said that I might at least give it to my 'Zennana';[3] luckily Mr Elliott suggested to me to say that I accepted it with gratitude,

---

[1] Humayun had to spend part of his reign as an exile in Iran. He recovered Delhi in 1555, but died a few months later as a result of a fall down the staircase of his library.

[2] Charles Elliott, the Governor-General's Agent at the Mughal Court 1823–6.

[3] Women.

but that I was a traveller and begged him to keep it for me: to which I added, that 'what was in the house of my friend I considered as in my own'. He quite understood this, and bowed very low, being, I believe, well pleased to get his compliment over at so easy a rate. The son, however, a lad who spoke a very little English followed me to the door with a Turkman horse, which he begged me to accept as his nuzzur. The horse was a pretty one, but not very valuable. I, however, got rid of the matter as well as I could by saying, that 'spirited horses were fittest for the young: that I accepted it cheerfully, but begged, as I had no other proper return to make, that he would do me the favour to take it back again!' He smiled and bowed, and we parted. In the narrow street where the house of Soobin-chund stands, we passed a little cluster of Cashmerian women, the wives, I suppose, of his workmen, distinguishable by their large and tall figures in comparison with the Hindoostanees, their fair complexions, and their peculiar head-dress which consisted of a large roll of turban under the usual veil...

We afterwards went to the Jumna Musjeed,[1] and the Kala Musjeed. The former is elevated very advantageously on a small rocky eminence, to full the height of the surrounding houses. In front it has a large square court surrounded by a cloister open on both sides, and commanding a view of the whole city, which is entered by three gates with a fine flight of steps to each. In the centre is a great marble reservoir of water, with some small fountains, supplied by machinery from the canal. The whole court is paved with granite inlaid with marble. On its west side, and rising up another flight of steps, is the mosque itself, which is entered by three noble gothic arches, surmounted by three domes of white marble. It has at each end a very tall minaret. The ornaments are less florid, and the building less picturesque, than the splendid groupe of the Imambara and its accompaniments at Lucknow; but the situation is far more commanding, and the size, the solidity, and rich materials of this building, impressed me more than any thing of the sort which I have seen in India. It is in excellent repair, the British Government having made a grant for this purpose, a measure which was very popular in Delhi.

[1] The Jami Masjid—built by Shah Jahan.

Delhi and Agra

The 31st *December* was fixed for my presentation to the Emperor, which was appointed for half-past eight in the morning. Lushington and a Captain Wade also chose to take the same opportunity. At eight I went accompanied by Mr Elliott with nearly the same formalities as at Lucknow, except that we were on elephants instead of in palanqueens, and that the procession was, perhaps, less splendid, and the beggars both less numerous and far less vociferous and importunate. We were received with presented arms by the troops of the palace drawn up within the barbican, and proceeded, still on our elephants, through the noblest gateway and vestibule which I ever saw. It consists, not merely of a splendid gothic arch in the centre of the great gate-tower,—but, after that, of a long vaulted aisle, like that of a gothic cathedral, with a small, open, octagonal court in its centre, all of granite, and all finely carved with inscriptions from the Koran, and with flowers. This ended in a ruinous and exceedingly dirty stable-yard! where we were received by Captain Grant, as the Mogul's officer on guard, and by a number of elderly men with large gold-headed canes, the usual ensign of office here, and one of which Mr Elliott also carried. We were now told to dismount and proceed on foot, a task which the late rain made inconvenient to my gown and cassock, and thin shoes, and during which we were pestered by a fresh swarm of miserable beggars, the wives and children of the stable servants. After this we passed another richly-carved, but ruinous and dirty gateway, where our guides, withdrawing a canvass screen, called out, in a sort of harsh chaunt, 'Lo, the ornament of the world! Lo, the asylum of the nations! King of Kings! The Emperor Akbar Shah![1] Just, fortunate, victorious!' We saw, in fact a very handsome and striking court, about as big as that at All Souls, with low, but richly ornamented buildings. Opposite to us was a beautiful open pavilion of white marble, richly carved, flanked by rose-bushes and fountains, and some tapestry and striped curtains hanging in festoons about it, within which was a crowd of people, and the poor old descendant of Tamerlane seated in the midst of them. Mr Elliott here bowed three times very low, in which we followed his example. This ceremony was repeated twice as we

---

[1] Akbar II: reigned 1806–37.

advanced up the steps of the pavilion, the heralds each time repeating the same expressions about their master's greatness. We then stood in a row on the right-hand side of the throne, which is a sort of marble bedstead richly ornamented with gilding, and raised on two or three steps. Mr Elliott then stepped forwards, and, with joined hands, in the usual eastern way, announced, in a low voice, to the emperor, who I was. I then advanced, bowed three times again, and offered a nuzzur of fifty-one gold mohurs in an embroidered purse, laid on my handkerchief, in the way practised by the baboos in Calcutta. This was received and laid on one side, and I remained standing for a few minutes, while the usual court questions about my health, my travels, when I left Calcutta, &c. were asked. I had thus an opportunity of seeing the old gentleman more plainly. He has a pale, thin, but handsome face, with an aquiline nose, and a long white beard. His complexion is little if at all darker than that of an European. His hands are very fair and delicate, and he had some valuable-looking rings on them. His hands and face were all I saw of him, for the morning being cold, he was so wrapped up in shawls, that he reminded me extremely of the Druid's head on a Welch halfpenny. I then stepped back to my former place, and returned again with five more mohurs to make my offering to the heir apparent, who stood at his father's left hand, the right being occupied by the Resident. Next, my two companions were introduced with nearly the same forms, except that their offerings were less, and that the Emperor did not speak to them.

The Emperor then beckoned to me to come forwards, and Mr Elliott told me to take off my hat which had till now remained on my head, on which the Emperor tied a flimsy turban of brocade round my head with his own hands, for which however, I paid four gold mohurs more. We were then directed to retire to receive the 'Khelâts' (honorary dresses) which the bounty of 'the Asylum of the World' had provided for us. I was accordingly taken into a small private room, adjoining the Zennana, where I found a handsome flowered caftan edged with fur, and a pair of common looking shawls, which my servants, who had the delight of witnessing all this fine show, put on instead of my gown, my cassock remaining as before. In this strange dress I had to walk back again, having my name announced by the criers (something in the same way that Lord Marmion's[1] was) 'as Bahadur, Boozoony, Dowlut-mund', &c. to the presence, where I found my two companions who had not been honoured by a private dressing room, but had their Khelâts put on them in the gateway of the court. They were, I apprehend, still queerer figures than I was, having their hats wrapped with scarfs of flowered gauze, and a strange garment of gauze, tinsel, and faded ribbands, flung over their shoulders above their coats. I now again came forward and offered my third present to the Emperor, being a copy of the Arabic Bible and the Hindoostanee Common Prayer, handsomely bound in blue velvet laced with gold, and wrapped up in a piece of brocade. He then motioned to me to stoop, and put a string of pearls round my neck, and two glittering but not costly ornaments in the front of my turban, for which I again offered five gold mohurs. It was, lastly, announced that a horse was waiting for my acceptance, at which fresh instance of imperial munificence, the heralds again made a proclamation of largesse, and I again paid five gold mohurs. It ended by my taking my leave with three times three salams, making up, I think, the sum of about threescore, and I retired with Mr Elliott to my dressing room, whence I sent to her Majesty the *Queen*, as she is generally called, though Empress would be the ancient and more proper title, a present of five mohurs more, and the Emperor's Chobdahs came eagerly up to know when they should attend to receive their bukshish. It must not, however, be supposed that this interchange of civilities was very expensive either to his Majesty or to me. All the presents which he gave, the horse included, though really the handsomest which had been seen at the court of Delhi for many years, and though the old gentlemen evidently intended to be extremely civil, were not worth much more than 300 s. rupees, so that he and his family gained at least 800 s. rupees by the morning's work, besides what he received from my two companions, which was all clear gain, since the Khelâts which they got in return, were only fit for May-day, and made up, I fancy, from the cast off finery of the Begum. On the other hand, since the Company have wisely ordered that all the presents given by

---

[1] W. Scott, *Marmion: a tale of Flodden Field.*

Native Princes to Europeans should be disposed of on the Government account, they have liberally, at the same time, taken on themselves the expense of paying the usual money nuzzurs made by public men on these occasions. In consequence none of my offerings were at my own charge, except the professional and private one of the two books, with which, as they were unexpected, the Emperor, as I was told, was very much pleased. I had, of course, several buckshishes to give afterwards to his servants, but these fell considerably short of my expenses at Lucknow. To return to the hall of audience. While in the small apartment where I got rid of my shining garments, I was struck with its beautiful ornaments. It was entirely lined with white marble, inlaid with flowers and leaves of green serpentine, lapis lazuli, and blue and red porphyry; the flowers were of the best Italian style of workmanship, and evidently the labour of an artist of that country. All, however, was dirty, desolate, and forlorn. Half the flowers and leaves had been picked out or otherwise defaced, and the doors and windows were in a state of dilapidation, while a quantity of old furniture was piled in one corner, and a torn hanging of faded tapestry hung over an archway which led to the interior apartments. 'Such', Mr Elliott said, 'is the general style in which this palace is kept up and furnished. It is not absolute poverty which produces this, but these people have no idea of cleaning or mending any thing.' For my own part I thought of the famous Persian line,

'The spider hangs her tapestry in the palace of the Caesars';

and felt a melancholy interest in comparing the present state of this poor family with what it was 200 years ago, when Bernier[1] visited Delhi, or as we read its palace described in the tale of Madame de Genlis.[2]

After putting on my usual dress, we waited a little, till word was brought us that the 'King of Kings!', 'Shah-in-Shah', had retired to his Zennana; we then went to the Hall of Audience, which I had previously seen but imperfectly, from the crowd of

[1] François Bernier (1620–88), a French physician and traveller, visited Delhi in 1663. For his impressions of the city, see his *Travels in the Mogul Empire*, 2nd ed., revised by V. A. Smith, 1914, 239 ff.

[2] *Nourmahal*, by Mme. de Genlis; *Nouvelle bibliotheque des romans*, II, Paris, 1802.

people and the necessity of attending to the forms which I had to go through. It is a very beautiful pavilion of white marble, open on one side to the court of the palace, and on the other to a large garden. Its pillars and arches are exquisitely carved and ornamented with gilt and inlaid flowers, and inscriptions in the most elaborate Persian character. Round the frieze is the motto, recorded, I believe, in Lalla Rookh,[1]

> 'If there be an Elysium on earth,
> It is this, it is this!'

The marble floor, where not covered by carpets, is all inlaid in the same beautiful manner with the little dressing-room, which I had quitted.

The gardens, which we next visited, are not large, but, in their way, must have been extremely rich and beautiful. They are full of very old orange and other fruit trees with terraces and parterres on which many rose bushes were growing, and, even now, a few jonquils in flower. A channel of white marble for water, with little fountain pipes of the same material carved like roses, is carried here and there among these parterres, and at the end of the terrace is a beautiful octagonal pavilion, also of marble, lined with the same Mosaic flowers as in the room which I first saw, with a marble fountain in its centre, and a beautiful bath in a recess on one of its sides. The windows of this pavilion, which is raised to the height of the city wall, command a good view of Delhi and its neighbourhood. But all was, when we saw it, dirty, lonely, and wretched: the bath and fountain dry: the inlaid pavement hid with lumber and gardener's sweepings, and the walls stained with the dung of birds and bats.

We were then taken to the private mosque of the palace, an elegant little building, also of white marble and exquisitely carved, but in the same state of neglect and dilapidation, with peepuls allowed to spring from its walls, the exterior gilding partially torn from its dome, and some of its doors coarsely blocked up with unplaistered brick and mortar.

We went last to the 'Dewanee aûm', or hall of public audience, which is in the outer court, and where on certain occasions the

---

[1] Thomas Moore, *Lalla Rookh, an Oriental romance*, 1817, 328.

great mogul sate in state, to receive the compliments or petitions of his subjects. This also is a splendid pavilion of marble, not unlike the other hall of audience in form, but considerably larger and open on three sides only; on the fourth is a black wall, covered with the same Mosaic work of flowers and leaves as I have described, and in the centre a throne raised about ten feet from the ground, with a small platform of marble in front, where the vizier used to stand to hand up petitions to his master. Behind this throne are Mosaic paintings of birds, animals, and flowers, and in the centre, what decides the point of their being the work of Italian, or at least European artists, a small groupe of Orpheus playing to the beasts.[1] This hall, when we saw it, was full of lumber of all descriptions, broken palanqueens and empty boxes, and the throne so covered with pigeon's dung, that its ornaments were hardly discernible. How little did Shahjehan, the founder of these fine buildings, foresee what would be the fate of his descendants, or what his own would be![2] 'Vanity of vanities!' was surely never written in more legible characters than on the dilapidated arcades of Delhi!

After breakfast I had a numerous attendance of persons who either wished to be confirmed themselves, or to have my explanation of the nature and authority of the ceremony. In the afternoon I went with Mr and Mrs Elliott a drive round a part of the city. Its principal streets are really wide, handsome, and, for an Asiatic city, remarkably cleanly, and the shops in the bazars have a good appearance. The chief street down which we drove, is called the 'chandnee chokee', or silversmith's street, but I did not see any great number of that trade resident there. It is about as wide as Pall-Mall, and has a branch of the aqueduct running along its centre. Half-way down its length is a pretty little mosque with three gilt domes, on the porch of which, it is said, Nader Shah[3] sat from morning to evening to see the work of massacre which

[1] These mosaics were originally made in Italy 'and in the course of commercial relations found their way to India to be acquired as objects of art by someone at the Mughal court'—*Cambridge History of India*, IV, 558.

[2] Shah Jahan's third son Aurangzeb seized the throne during the course of a civil war in 1658 and imprisoned his father in the Agra Fort, where he died eight years later.

[3] The ruler of Iran, who invaded the Mughal Empire and sacked Delhi in 1738–9.

his army inflicted on the wretched citizens. A gate leading to a bazar near it retains the name of 'coonia durwazu', slaughter-gate! The chandnee chokee conducted us to the gate of Lahore, and we went along the exterior of the town to the gate of Cashmere, by which we returned to the Residency. The city wall is lofty and handsome, but, except ruins and sun-burnt rocks, there is nothing to be seen without the ramparts of Delhi. The Shelimar gardens, extolled in Lalla Rookh, are completely gone to decay. Yet I am assured by every body that the appearance of things in the province of Delhi is greatly improved since it came into our hands! To what a state must the Maharattas have reduced it!

January 1 1825.—We went to see Koottab-sahib, a small town about twelve miles south-west of Delhi, remarkable for its ruins, and, among the Mussulmans, for its sanctity.

Our route lay over a country still rocky and barren, and still sprinkled with tombs and ruins, till, on ascending a little emi-nence, we saw one of the most extensive and striking scenes of ruin which I have met with in any country. A very tolerable account of it is given in Hamilton's India,[1] and I will only observe that the Cuttab Minar,[2] the object of principal attraction, is really the finest tower I have ever seen, and must, when its spire was complete, have been still more beautiful. The remaining great arches of the principal mosque, with their granite pillars, covered with inscriptions in the florid Cufic character, are as fine, in their way, as any of the details of York Minster. In front of the principal of these great arches is a metal pillar[3]..., and several other remains of a Hindoo palace and temple, more ancient than the foundation of the Koottab, and which I should have thought striking, if they had not been in such a neighbourhood. A multi-tude of ruined mosques, tombs, serais, &c. are packed close round, mostly in the Patan style of architecture, and some of them very fine. One, more particularly, on a hill, and surrounded by a wall with battlements and towers, struck me as peculiarly suited, by

---

[1] W. Hamilton, *A geographical, statistical, and historical description of Hindostan*, London, 1820, I, 423–4.

[2] Built in the early thirteenth century by the Turkish sultans.

[3] Probably dating from the fourth century A.D. It is of almost pure iron.

its solid and simple architecture, to its blended character, in itself very appropriate to the religion of Islam, of fortress, tomb, and temple. These Patans built like giants and finished their work like jewellers. Yet the ornaments, florid as they are in their proper places, are never thrown away, or allowed to interfere with the general severe and solemn character of their edifices. The palace of the present imperial family is at some little distance behind these remains. It is a large but paltry building, in a bad style of Italian architecture, and with a public road actually leading through its court-yard. A little beyond and amid some other small houses, near a very fine tank, we alighted at rather a pretty little building belonging to Bukshi Mahmoud Khân, the treasurer of the palace, where a room and a good breakfast were prepared for us.

After breakfast, the day being cool and rather cloudy, we went to see the ruins, and remained clambering about and drawing till near two o'clock. The staircase within the great Minar is very good, except the uppermost story of all, which is ruinous and difficult of access. I went up, however, and was rewarded by the very extensive view, from a height of 240 feet, of Delhi, the course of the Jumna for many miles, and the ruins of Toghlikabad, another giantly Patan foundation, which lay to the south-west.

We returned in the evening to Delhi, stopping by the way to see Sufter Jung's tomb.[1] It is very richly inlaid with different kinds of marble, but has too much of the colour of potted meat to please me, particularly after seeing buildings like those of Kootab-sahib. We were received here, to my surprise, by the son of baboo Soobin Chund, who is, it seems, the agent of the King of Oude in Delhi, and consequently has the keeping of this place entrusted to him. He had actually brought a second and finer horse for my acceptance; and I had great difficulty in convincing him of two things; first, that I had no power to render him any service which could call for such presents; and secondly, that my declining his presents was not likely to diminish my goodwill towards him, supposing me to have such power. I succeeded at last, however, in silencing, if not convincing him,

---

[1] Safdar Jang was the second Nawab of Oudh, and Wazir of the Empire until he was overthrown in 1753. He died the following year.

and we returned to the Residency, passing in our way by the Observatory,[1] a pile of buildings much resembling those at Benares, and built by the same person, Jye Singh, Raja and founder of Jyepoor in Rajpootana.

Acbar Shah has the appearance of a man of 74 or 75: he is, however, not much turned of 63,[2] but, in this country, that is a great age. He is said to be a very good-tempered, mild old man, of moderate talents, but polished and pleasing manners. His favourite wife, the Begum, is a low-born, low-bred, and violent woman, who rules him completely, lays hold on all his money, and has often influenced him to very unwise conduct towards his children, and the British Government. She hates her eldest son, who is, however, a respectable man, of more talents than native princes usually shew, and happily for himself, has a predilection for those literary pursuits which are almost the only laudable or innocent objects of ambition in his power. He is fond of poetry, and is himself a very tolerable Persian poet. He has taken some pains in the education of his children, and, what in this country is very unusual, even of his daughters. He too, however, though not more than thirty-five, is prematurely old, arising partly from the early excesses into which the wretched follies of an Eastern court usually plunge persons in his situation,—and partly from his own subsequent indulgence in strong liquors. His face is bloated and pimpled, his eyes weak, and his hand tremulous. Yet, for an Eastern prince, as I have already observed, his character is good, and his abilities considered as above the common run.[3]

There are, perhaps, few royal families which have displayed during their power so many vices and so few virtues as the house of Timour. Their power had been gradually declining ever since the time of Aurungzebe,[4] and at present, Mr Elliott once observed to me, that he could not perceive the least chance, that, supposing our empire in the east to be at an end, the King of Delhi could for a moment recover any share of authority. He did not even think

---

[1] The Jantar Mantar; see also *supra*, p. 140.   [2] In fact he was 70.

[3] This prince, who was in fact about fifty at the time of the Bishop's visit, succeeded Akbar II in 1837 as Bahadur Shah II, and reigned until the time of the Mutiny. He died in exile in Rangoon in 1862.

[4] Reigned 1658–1707.

that the greater Princes of India, who would fight for our spoils, would any of them think it worth their while to make use of the Emperor's name as a pageant to sanction their own ambitious views; and he observed that, all things considered, few captive and dethroned Princes had ever experienced so much liberality and courtesy as they had from British hands, and that they could not reasonably hope to gain by any diminution of our influence in India. Yet their present circumstances are surely pitiable, as well as an aweful instance of the instability of human greatness. The gigantic genius of Tamerlane, and the distinguished talents of Acbar,[1] throw a sort of splendour over the crimes and follies of his descendants: and I heartily hope that Government will reverence the ruins of fallen greatness, and that, at least, no fresh degradation is reserved for the poor old man whose idea was associated in my childhood with all imaginable wealth and splendour, under the name of 'the Great Mogul!'

January 3.—This morning early I sent off my tents and baggage to Furreedabad, a little town about fifteen miles from Delhi, and in the afternoon followed them on horseback, escorted by five of Skinner's horse, and accompanied by Mr Lushington and Dr Smith....[2]

Furreedabad offers nothing curious except a large tank with a ruined banqueting-house on its shore; it has a grove of tamarind and other trees round it, but no mangoes; few of these, indeed, grow in the province of Delhi, owing to the unusual multitude of white ants, to whose increase the ruins and the dry sandy soil are favourable, and who attack the mangoes in preference to any other tree. The whole country, indeed, is barren and disagreeable, and the water bad. That of the Jumna acts on strangers like the Cheltenham waters, and the wells here are also extremely unpalatable. One might fancy oneself already approaching the confines of Persia and Arabia. Our camp is, however, plentifully supplied with all necessaries and comforts, and a servant of the Raja of Bullumghur brought us some fine oranges, and at the same time told us, that his master would not suffer him to receive

[1] Akbar I, 1556–1605.
[2] A doctor who had joined the Bishop's party at Meerut.

either payment or present for any of the supplies furnished, and only hoped that I would call at his house next morning in my way, which I readily promised to do.

The Raja of Bullumghur holds a considerable territory along this frontier as a feudatory of the British Government, on the service of maintaining 2000 men to do the ordinary police duties, and guard the road against the Mewattee and other predatory tribes. The family and most of their people are of the Jât race, and they have for many generations been linked by friendship and frequent intermarriages with the neighbouring Raja of Bhurtpoor, who is now our friend, but whose gallant and successful defence of his castle against Lord Lake during the Maharatta war, has raised the character of the Jâts, previously a very low caste, to considerable estimation for their valour in all this part of India.[1] The present acting Raja of Bullumghur is only Regent, being guardian to his nephew, a boy now educating at Delhi. I had heard the Regent and his brother described as hospitable and high-spirited men, and was not sorry to have an opportunity of seeing a Hindoo court.

January 4.—A little before day-break we set off as usual, through a country something, and but little, more fertile than that we had passed. It improved, however, gradually as we approached Bullumghur, which, by its extensive groves, gave evidence of its having been long a residence of a respectable native family. I was not, however, at all prepared for the splendour with which I was received. First we saw some. . . wild-looking horsemen. . ., posted as if on the look-out, who, on seeing us, fired their matchlocks and gallopped off as fast as possible. As we drew nearer we saw a considerable body of cavalry with several camels and elephants, all gaily caparisoned, drawn up under some trees, and were received by the Raja himself, a fat and overgrown man, and his younger brother, a very handsome and manly figure, the former alighting from a palanqueen, the other from a noble

---

[1] In fact the Jats of Bharatpur had been a force to be reckoned with since the time of Aurangzeb. The Raja reigning at the time when Heber passed through was not he who had defended the fortress successfully against Lake in 1804–5, but Baldev Singh, who reigned only for eighteen months and died on 26 February 1825; whereupon his cousin Durjun Sal usurped the throne from his six-year-old son—see also Introduction, p. 26.

Persian horse, with trappings which swept the ground. I alighted from my horse also and the usual compliments and civilities followed. The elder brother begged me to excuse his riding with me as he was ill, which indeed we had heard before, but the second went by my side, reining in his magnificent steed, and shewing off the animal's paces and his own horsemanship. Before and behind were camels, elephants, and horsemen, with a most strange and barbarous music of horns, trumpets, and kettle-drums, and such a wood of spears that I could not but tell my companion that his castle deserved its name of Fort of Spears. As we drew nearer we saw the fort itself, with high brick walls, strengthened with a deep ditch and large mud bastions, from which we were complimented with a regular salute of cannon. Within we found a small and crowded, but not ill-built town, with narrow streets, tall houses, many temples, and a sufficient number of Brahminy bulls to shew the pure Hindoo descent of the ruler. The population of the little capital was almost all assembled in the streets, on the walls, and on the house-tops, and salamed to us as we came in. We passed through two or three sharp turns, and at length stopped at the outer gate of a very neat little palace, built round a small court planted with jonquils and rose bushes, with a marble fountain in the centre, and a small open arched hall, where chairs were placed for us. Sitringees[1] were laid, by way of carpet, on the floor, and the walls were ornamented with some paltry Hindoo portraits of the family, and some old fresco paintings of gods, goddesses, and heroes encountering lions and tygers.

After we had been here a few minutes a set of dancing-girls entered the room followed by two musicians. I felt a little uneasy at this apparition, but Dr Smith, to whom I mentioned my apprehensions, assured me that nothing approaching to indecency was to be looked for in the dances or songs which a well-bred Hindoo exhibited to his visitors. I sat still, therefore, while these poor little girls, for they none of them seemed more than fourteen, went through the same monotonous evolutions which I had heard my wife describe, in which there is certainly very little grace or interest, and no perceptible approach to indecency. The chief part of the figure, if it can be called so, seemed to consist

---

[1] A kind of checked or striped mat.

in drawing up and letting fall again the loose wide sleeves of their outer garments, so as to shew the arm as high as the elbow, or a very little higher, while the arms were waved backwards and forwards in a stiff and constrained manner. Their dresses were rich, but there was such an enormous quantity of scarlet cloth petticoats and trowzers, so many shawls wrapped round their waists, and such multifarious skirts peeping out below each other, that their figures were quite hidden, and the whole effect was that of a number of Dutch dolls, though the faces of two or three out of the number were pretty. Two sung each a Persian and a Hindoostanee song with very pleasing though not powerful voices, after which, as the demands both of curiosity and civility were satisfied, I gave them a gratuity, as I understood was usual on such occasions, as a token of their dismissal.

After this some cake and Persian grapes were brought in, and I took leave, having in the civilest and most cordial way I could, declined the usual present of shawls, and accepted one of fruit and sweetmeats. On going away I told the Raja's jemautdar to come to the camp in the evening, and he and his fellow-servants should have the usual bukshish, but he answered that neither he nor any of the Raja's people, except the dancing-girls to whom it was an usual token of approbation, dared accept any thing of the kind, the first instance which I had met with of a Hindoo refusing money. Soon after I had taken leave, and while we were still escorted by the Bullumghur cavalry, a message come from the Raja to say that he had heard of my intended liberality to his people, but that it was his particular request that I would give nothing either to his servants or to the suwarrs, whom he intended, with my leave, to send on with me as far as Muttra. Surely this is what in England would be called high and gentle-manly feeling.

On our approach to Sikre, where the tents were pitched, I found we had entered another little feudal territory, being received by about twenty horsemen, with a splendid old warrior at their head, who announced himself as the jaghiredar of the place, and holding a little barony, as it would be called in Europe, under the Company, intermixed with the larger territories of Bullumghur. Cassim Ali Khân, the Nawâb of Sikre, who thus introduced himself, was a figure which Wouverman or Rubens would have delighted to paint, a tall, large, elderly man, with a fine countenance, and a thick and curly but not long grey beard, on a large and powerful white Persian horse, with a brocade turban, a saddle-cloth of tyger's skin with golden tassels which almost swept the ground, sword, shield, and [pistols mounted]with silver, and all the other picturesque insignia of a Mussulman cavalier of distinction. He said that he had been a tusseeldar in command of 200 horse in Lord Lake's war, and had been recompensed at the end of the contest with a little territory of ten villages, rent and tax free. The Raja, he said, who had 250 villages, nearly enclosed him, but they were good friends. The Raja certainly, though his brother is a fine young man, had nothing in his whole cavalcade to equal the old Nawâb's figure, which was perfect as a picture, from his bare muscular neck and his crisp grey mustachios, down to his yellow boots and the strong brown hand, with an emerald ring on it, the least turn of which on his silver bridle seemed to have complete mastery over his horse, without too much re-pressing its spirit. He afterwards shewed me his certificates of service from Lord Lake and others, and it appeared that his character in all respects had corresponded with his manly and intelligent appearance.

At Sikre I found a letter from Mr Cavendish,[1] Collector and Magistrate of this district, saying that he was encamped in the neighbourhood and intended to call on me next morning at our next station, at Brahminy Kerar.

January 5.—The country between Sikre and Brahminy Kerar is uninteresting enough, though rather more fertile than in the neighbourhood of Delhi. Half-way, near a village named Pulwul, we passed Mr Cavendish's encampment, and were met by an escort of his suwarrs. I had long since had my eyes pretty well accustomed to the sight of shields and spears, but I have not failed to observe that, along this frontier which has not been till of late in a settled or peaceable state, and where hard blows are still of no unfrequent occurrence, even the police troopers sit their horses better, and have a more martial air by far, than persons in the

---

[1] Richard Cavendish, in charge of the Southern Division of the Delhi territories 1824–8.

same situation in the Dooab or even in Rohilcund. I begin, indeed, to think better of the system on which the province of Delhi has been governed since its conquest, from all which I hear of its former state. This neighbourhood, for instance, is still but badly cultivated, but fifteen years ago it was as wild, I am assured, as the Terrai, as full of tygers, and with no human inhabitants but banditti. Cattle-stealing still prevails to a great extent, but the Mewattees are now most of them subject either to the British Government or that of Bhurtpoor, and the security of life and property afforded them by the former, has induced many of the tribes to abandon their fortresses, to seat themselves in the plain and cultivate the ground like honest men and good subjects, while the tranquillity of the border, and the force maintained along it, prevents the Bhurtpoor marauders from renewing their depredations so often as they used to do. Highway robberies also sometimes occur, generally attended with murder; but, on the whole, the amendment has been great, and an European, under ordinary circumstances, may pass in safety through any part of the district. The lands are not now highly assessed, and Government has liberally given up half the year's rent in consideration of the drought. Still, however, something more is wanting, and every public man in these provinces appears to wish that a settlement for fourteen or even twenty years could be brought about, in order to give the Zemindars[1] an interest in the soil and an inducement to make improvements.

January 6.—We went on eight coss to Horal. The country along the road-side is jungly, but cultivation seems rapidly gaining on it. The road-side is, in India, always the part last cultivated, the natives being exposed to many injuries and oppressions from sepoys and travellers. I was told that for every bundle of grass or faggots which the thannadar, or other public officer, brought to my camp, he demanded as much more from the poor peasants, which he appropriated to his own use; and that, even if I paid for what I got, it required much attention, and some knowledge of the language, to be sure that the money was not intercepted in its way to the right owner. But the common

---

[1] In the Delhi territory this term denoted groups of village proprietors.

practice of the thannadar was, to charge nothing for what was furnished to the traveller, both from wishing to make a compliment to the latter, (which costs him nothing,) and also to take, without the means of detection, his own share of the plunder. The best way is to insist on a written bill, and request the collector afterwards to enquire of the Ryuts whether the money had been paid.

At Horal is a very pretty native house now uninhabited but used as a court of justice, with a fine tank near it, both the work of a former Hindoo jemautdar, in memory of whom a small temple is raised in the neighbourhood. Within I saw the representation of four human feet, one pair larger than the other, on a little altar against the wall, and was told that it was the customary way of commemorating that the favourite wife had burnt herself with her husband. This horrible custom, I am glad to find, is by no means common in this part of India; indeed, I have not yet found it *common* any where except in Bengal, and some parts of Bahar.

January 11.—This morning we arrived at Secundra,[1] nine coss from Furrah, a ruinous village and without a bazar, but remarkable for the magnificent tomb of Acbar, the most splendid building in its way which I had yet seen in India. It stands in a square area of about forty English acres, enclosed by an embattled wall, with octagonal towers at the angles surmounted by open pavilions, and four very noble gateways of red granite, the principal of which is inlaid with white marble, and has four high marble minarets. The space within is planted with trees and divided into green alleys, leading to the central building, which is a sort of solid pyramid surrounded externally with cloisters, galleries, and domes, diminishing gradually on ascending it, till it ends in a square platform of white marble, surrounded by most elaborate lattice-work of the same material, in the centre of which is a small altar tomb, also of white marble, carved with a delicacy and beauty which do full justice to the material, and to the graceful forms of Arabic characters which form its chief ornament. At the bottom of the building, in a small but very lofty vault, is the real tomb of this great monarch, plain and unadorned, but also of white marble. There are many other ruins in the

---

[1] Sikandra.

vicinity, some of them apparently handsome, but Acbar's tomb leaves a stranger little time or inclination to look at any thing else. Government have granted money for the repair of the tomb, and an officer of engineers is employed on it. A serjeant of artillery is kept in the place, who lives in one of the gateways; his business is to superintend a plantation of sissoo-trees made by Dr Wallich. He says the soil does not appear to suit them; they grow, however, but by no means rapidly. For fruit trees, particularly the orange, the soil is very favourable, and the tall tamarinds and the generally neglected state of the garden afford more picturesque points of view than large buildings usually are seen in.

On 12 *January Heber arrived at Agra.*

Archdeacon Corrie's celebrated convert, Abdul Musseeh,[1] breakfasted this morning at Mr Irving's;[2] he is a very fine old man with a magnificent grey beard, and much more gentlemanly manners than any Christian native whom I have seen. His rank, indeed, previous to his conversion, was rather elevated, since he was master of the jewels to the court of Oude, an appointment of higher estimation in Eastern palaces than in those of Europe, and the holder of which has always a high salary. Abdul Musseeh's present appointments, as Christian Missionary, are sixty rupees a month, and of this he gives away at least half! Who can dare to say that this man has changed his faith from any interested motives? He is a very good Hindoostanee, Persian, and Arabic scholar, but knows no English. There is a small congregation of native Christians, converted by Mr Corrie when he was Chaplain at Agra,[3] and now kept together by Abdul Musseeh. The earnest desire of this good man is to be ordained a Clergyman of the Church of England, and if God spares his life and mine, I hope, during the Ember weeks in this next autumn, to confer orders on him.[4] He is every way fit for them, and is a most sincere Christian,

---

[1] In fact it was Henry Martyn rather than Corrie who was responsible for Abdul Masih's conversion.

[2] John Irving: appointed chaplain at Agra in 1822.

[3] See Introduction, p. 5.

[4] Abdul Masih was ordained by Heber in December 1825, but he died little more than a year later—see also Introduction, p. 27.

quite free, so far as I could observe, from all conceit or enthusiasm. His long eastern dress, his long grey beard, and his calm resigned countenance, give him already almost the air of an apostle.

January 13.—I went to see the celebrated Tage-mahal, of which it is enough to say that, after hearing its praises ever since I had been in India, its beauty rather exceeded than fell short of my expectations. There was much, indeed, which I was not prepared for. The surrounding garden, which as well as the Tage itself, is kept in excellent order by Government, with its marble fountains, beautiful cypresses and other trees, and profusion of flowering shrubs, contrasts very finely with the white marble of which the tomb itself is composed, and takes off, by partially concealing it, from that stiffness which belongs more or less to every highly finished building. The building itself is raised on an elevated terrace of white and yellow marble, and having at its angles four tall minarets of the same material. The Tage contains, as usual, a central hall about as large as the interior of the Ratcliffe library, in which, enclosed within a carved screen of elaborate tracery, are the tombs of the Begum Noor-jehan, Shahjehan's beloved wife, to whom it was erected, and by her side, but a little raised above her, of the unfortunate Emperor himself. Round this hall are a number of smaller apartments, corridors, &c. and the windows are carved in lattices of the same white marble with the rest of the building, and the screen. The pavement is in alternate squares of white and, what is called in Europe, sienna marble, the walls, screens, and tombs are covered with flowers and inscriptions, executed in beautiful Mosaic of cornelians, lapis-lazuli, and jasper; and yet though every thing is finished like an ornament for a drawing-room chimney-piece, the general effect produced is rather solemn and impressive than gaudy. The parts which I like least are the great dome and the minarets. The bulbous swell of the former I think clumsy, and the minarets have nothing to recommend them but their height and the beauty of their materials. But the man must have more criticism than taste or feeling about him, who could allow such imperfections to weigh against the beauties of the Tage-mahal. The Jumna washes one side of the garden, and there are some remains of a bridge which was designed by Shah-jehan with the intention, as the story goes, to build a second Tage of equal beauty for his own separate place of interment, on the opposite side of the river. . . .

During the rest of my stay at Agra I was confined by a feverish cold, and was barely able to go out on Friday to hold a Confirmation, with a voice more completely lost than I ever remember happening to me before. . . .

The number of persons confirmed was about forty, half of whom were native Christians, mostly old persons and converts of Mr Corrie's during his residence here. Abdul Musseeh told me there were a good many more scattered up and down in the neighbouring towns of Coel, Allyghur, and Etwah, whither he went from time to time, but who were too far off to attend on this occasion. Of several he spoke as elderly persons, who had been in the Maharatta service during Penn's[1] time, of European extraction, but who knew no language but Hindoostanee, and were very glad to have religious instruction afforded them in that language. Many of them gladly attend on his and Mr Irving's ministry, but others are zealous Roman Catholics and adhere closely to the Priest of Agra.

One of these Indo-Europeans is an old Colonel of French extraction, but completely Indian in colour, dress, language, and ideas. He is rich and has a large family of daughters, two or three of whom he has married, rather advantageously, to some of the wealthy country-born English. But no man is allowed to see any of these young ladies till he has had his offer accepted by the father, and till it is perfectly understood that he is pledged to marry one of them. He is then introduced behind the purdahs of the Zennana, and allowed to take his choice! The poor girls, of course, are never once consulted in the transaction. Mr Irving celebrated one of these marriages, at which, except the bride, no female was visible, though he was told that the rest were allowed to peep from behind the curtains.

I took this opportunity of enquiring in what degree of favour the name of the French stood in this part of India, where, for so many years together, it was paramount. I was told that many people were accustomed to speak of them as often oppressive and

[1] Heber probably meant the French adventurer Perron, who commanded Sindhia's army from 1796 to 1803, and who died in France in 1834.

avaricious, but as of more conciliating and popular manners than the English Sahibs. Many of them, indeed, like this old Colonel, had completely adopted the Indian dress and customs, and most of them were free from that exclusive and intolerant spirit, which makes the English, wherever they go, a caste by themselves, disliking and disliked by all their neighbours. Of this foolish, surly, national pride, I see but too many instances daily, and I am convinced it does us much harm in this country. We are not guilty of injustice, or wilful oppression, but we shut out the natives from our society, and a bullying, insolent manner is continually assumed in speaking to them.

Part VII

RAJPUTANA

January 17.—I sent off my tents this morning to a small village about nine miles from Agra, and two on the Agra side of the little town of Kerowlee, and drove over myself in the afternoon. I had found it necessary, during my stay at Agra, to make many alterations in, and some additions to my usual domestic arrangements, preparatory to leaving the Company's territory for my long journey through the independent states of Rajpootana, Meywar, &c. My tents were only adapted for cold weather, and would prove a very insufficient protection against either the sun or the storms of central India, being of European construction, and formed simply of one fold of thin canvas lined with baize. The necessity being admitted by all parties, I purchased two, which were on sale in the city, on the Company's account, there being none of any sort at the Depôt. My new lodgings were not so roomy or convenient as my old, but they answered very well, and every body tells me I shall find the advantage when the hot winds begin to blow. Another necessary was a fresh supply of live-stock. I had before been content to carry a few fowls on the back of one of the camels, and to trust to the supplies which the villages afforded for a kid or a sheep occasionally. But we were now going to countries where no Mussulmans are found, where there are few great cities, and a very scattered population of villagers, who consume no animal food themselves,—who have no supplies of the kind for strangers;—and, above all, who are now in a state of absolute famine. And though by myself, it must be a desolate country indeed where I should feel want, I was bound to consider that I was not alone, and that my companions also required attention. I was advised to buy some sheep, which were to be driven with us and killed as they were wanted. These, with some

salt beef and tongues, were thought sufficient to carry us to
Guzerat. At Nusseerabad[1] no supplies of any kind are to be
looked for. A solar hat and green shade were next recommended,
and pressed on my acceptance by the kindness of Mrs Irving.
A spare saddle, and a store of horse-shoes, were also declared to
be necessary, and, in short, so many things were to be procured,
that, had I been actually going into the interior of Africa, a
less formidable preparation might, I should have thought, have
sufficed. Some of my bearers, too, declared they neither would nor
dared go beyond the limits of the Company's Raj! This was at
first likely to be the greatest difficulty of all, since there were at
Agra none to be obtained who would undertake to go further than
Nusseerabad, and there, there are absolutely none to be had. A
small advance of wages, however, induced most of them to
promise anew they would 'follow me to the world's end'. The
very deep and difficult wells which I am told to expect in our
progress to the south-west, made it necessary for me to hire
another bheestie,[2] to draw water for myself and my horses. All
these difficulties I had little doubt that I should find extremely
exaggerated; but I was compelled, in my local ignorance, to
follow the opinions of those who had local knowledge, and who
evidently considered my journey as one of an arduous nature.

January 18.—We went on this morning to Futtehpoor-sicri,[3]
about ten miles, through a verdant and tolerably well-cultivated
country, but with few trees. . . . The approach to Futtehpoor is
striking; it is surrounded by a high stone wall, with battlements
and round towers, like the remaining part of the city walls at
Oxford. Within this is a wide extent of ruined houses and mosques,
interspersed with fields cultivated with rice and mustard, and a
few tamarind trees, and nearly in the middle, on a high ridge of
rocky hills, is a range of ruinous palaces, serais,[4] and other public
buildings, in the best style of Mussulman architecture; and to
form the centre of the picture, a noble mosque, in good repair,
and in dimensions equal, I should think, to the Jumna Musjeed of
Delhi.

---

[1] Nasirabad—a cantonment near Ajmer.
[2] Water-carrier.   [3] Fatehpur Sikri.   [4] Inns.

Rajputana

This town was the favourite residence of Acbar, and here, in his expeditions, he usually left his wives and children, under the care of his most trusted friend, Sheikh Soliman.[1] The mosques, the palace, and the ramparts, are all Acbar's work, and nearly in the same style with the castle of Agra and his own tomb at Secundra. The two former, are, however plainer than this last, and there is a far less allowance of white marble.

We found our tents pitched among the ruins and rubbish, about a bow-shot from the foot of the hill, and in full view of the great gate of the mosque, which is approached by the noblest flight of steps I ever saw. The morning was still cool, and we determined to see the curiosities without loss of time. The steps of which I have spoken lead to a fine arch[2] surmounted by a lofty tower; thence we pass into a quadrangle of about 500 feet square, with a very lofty and majestic cloister all round, a large mosque surmounted by three fine domes of white marble on the left hand, and opposite to the entrance two tombs of very elaborate workmanship, of which that to the right contains several monuments of the imperial family; that to the left a beautiful chapel of white marble, the shrine of Sheikh Soliman, who had the good fortune to be a saint as well as a statesman.

The impression which this whole view produced on me will be appreciated when I say, that there is no quadrangle either in Oxford or Cambridge fit to be compared with it, either in size, or majestic proportions, or beauty of architecture. It is kept in substantial repair by the British Government, and its grave and solid style makes this an easier task than the intricate and elaborate inlaid work of Secundra and the Taje Mahal. The interior of the mosque itself is fine, and in the same simple character of grandeur, but the height of the portal tower, and the magnificence of the quadrangle had raised my expectations too high, and I found that these were the greatest as well as the most striking beauties of Futtehpoor.

A little to the right is the palace, now all in ruins except a small part which is inhabited by the tusseeldar of the district. We

[1] This must be a reference to Sheikh Salim Chishti, a Muslim *pir* (saint) who lived at Sikri. Akbar's eldest son, later Emperor with the name Jahangir, was born in his cell in 1569 and named after him.

[2] The Buland Darwaza.

rambled some time among its courts and through a range of stables worthy of an Emperor, consisting of a long and wide street, with a portico on each side fifteen feet deep, supported with carved stone pillars in front, and roofed with enormous slabs of stone, reaching from the colonnade to the wall. There are four buildings particularly worthy of notice, one a small but richly ornamented house, which is shewn as the residence of Beerbal the Emperor's favourite minister,[1] whom the Mussulmans accuse of having infected him with the strange religious notions with which, in the latter part of his life, he sought to inoculate his subjects.

6   Buland Darwaza, Fatehpur Sikri

Another is a very beautiful octagonal pavilion in the corner of the court, which appears to have been the zennana, and was variously stated to us to have been the Emperor's private study, or the bed-chamber of one of his wives who was a daughter of the Sultan of Constantinople. It has three large windows filled with an exquisite tracery of white marble, and all its remaining wall is carved with trees, bunches of grapes, and the figures of different kinds of birds and beasts, of considerable merit in their execution, but the two last disfigured by the bigotry of Aurungzebe, who, as is well known, sought to make amends for his own abominable cruelty and wickedness towards his father and brothers, by a more than

[1] Birbal was a courtier and poet who subscribed to Akbar's syncretistic religion *Din-i-Illahi*.

usual zeal for the traditions and observances of Islam. The third is a little building which, if its traditional destination be correct, I wonder Aurungzebe allowed to stand. It consists merely of a shrine or canopy supported by four pillars, which the Mussulman ciceroni of the place pretend was devoted by Acbar to the performance of magical rites. Whatever its use may have been, it is not without beauty. The fourth is a singular pavilion,[1] in the centre of which is a pillar or stone pulpit richly carved, approached by four stone galleries from different sides of the room, on which the Emperor used to sit on certain occasions of state, while his subjects were admitted below to present their petitions. It is a mere capriccio, with no merit except its carving, but is remarkable as being one of the most singular buildings I have seen, and commanding from its terraced-roof a very advantageous view of the greater part of the city, and a wide extent of surrounding country.

Of this last much appears to have been laid out in an extensive lake, of which the dam is still to be traced, and the whole hill on which the palace stands bears marks of terraces and gardens, to irrigate which an elaborate succession of wells, cisterns, and wheel appears to have been contrived adjoining the great mosque, and forcing up the water nearly to the height of its roof. The cisterns are still useful as receptacles for rain-water, but the machinery is long since gone to decay. On the whole, Futtehpoor is one of the most interesting places which I have seen in India, and it was to me the more so, because, as it happened, I had heard little about it, and was by no means prepared to expect buildings of so much magnitude and splendour.[2]

Mr Lushington was forced to leave me to return to Lucknow, and we parted with mutual hopes that we might often meet again, but in India how many chances are there against such hopes being accomplished! If his health is spared he will, I hope and believe, be a valuable man in this country, inasmuch as he has memory, application, good sense, excellent principles both religious and moral; and, what I have seldom seen in young Indian civilians, a strong desire to conciliate the minds and improve the condition of the inhabitants of the country.

[1] The Diwan-i-khas.
[2] Akbar lived in his new city for less than twenty years and then deserted it.

After dinner I again walked to the mosque and went to the top of the gateway tower, which commands a very extensive view. The most remarkable object in the distance was the rampart of Bhurtpoor, eight coss from us, and hardly to be distinguished by the naked eye, but sufficiently visible with a pocket telescope.

January 19.—We rode this morning ten miles through a tolerably cultivated country, but strangely overspread with ruins, to a large dilapidated village named Khanwah. In our way we had a heavy shower of rain, and rain continued to fall at intervals through the greater part of the day. On my arrival at Khanwah, I found that this place, though laid down in Arrowsmith's map as within the British boundary, was in truth a part of the territory of Bhurtpoor, and that for the two following marches I should also be under the Raja's authority.

January 20.—From Khanwah to Pharsah is reckoned seven coss. The coss in this neighbourhood are long, and the distance, so far as I could judge, is above fourteen miles. The country, though still bare of wood, has more scattered trees than we had seen for many days back, and notwithstanding that the soil is sandy and only irrigated from wells, it is one of the best cultivated and watered tracts which I have seen in India. The crops of corn now on the ground were really beautiful, that of cotton, though gone by, shewed marks of having been a very good one; what is a sure proof of wealth, I saw several sugar-mills and large pieces of ground where the cane had just been cleared, and contrary to the usual habits of India, where the cultivators keep as far as they can from the high-way, to avoid the various molestations to which they are exposed from thieves and travellers, there was often only a narrow path-way winding through the green wheat and mustard crop, and even this was crossed continually by the channels which conveyed water to the furrows. The population did not seem great, but the few villages which we saw were apparently in good condition and repair, and the whole afforded so pleasing a picture of industry, and was so much superior to any thing which I had been led to expect in Rajpootana, or which I had seen in the Company's territories since leaving the southern parts of Rohilcund, that I was led to suppose that either the Raja of Bhurtpoor was an extremely exemplary and parental governor, or that the system of management adopted in the British provinces was in some way or other less favourable to the improvement and happiness of the country than that of some of the Native states.

What the old jemautdar of Khanwah said as to the rent he paid to Government, and the answers which he made to some questions put to him, were not, however, such as would lead one to expect an industrious or prosperous peasantry. No certain rent is fixed by Government, but the state takes every year what it thinks fit, leaving only what, in its discretion, it regards as a sufficient maintenance for the Zemindars and Ryuts. This is pretty nearly the system which has produced such ruinous effects in Oude, but which is of course tempered in these smaller states by the facility of bringing complaints to the ear of the Sovereign, by the want of power in the Sovereign himself to withstand any general rising to which his tyranny might in the long run drive his subjects, and most of all, by the immediate and perceptible loss of income which he would sustain, if by dealing too hard with any particular village, he made its inhabitants emigrate to the territories of his neighbour. Nor must the old hereditary attachment be lost sight of, which makes the rulers or subjects of a Jât or Rajpoot state regard each other as kindred, and feel a pride, the one in the power and splendour of a chief who is the head of his clan, the other in the numbers and prosperity of those who constitute his society and court in time of peace, and in war his only army.

At present there seems no doubt that all the smaller princes of this part of India have been great gainers by the rise of the British power on the ruins of that of Sindia and Holkar. They have all of them peace and tranquillity, which for many years they had never enjoyed for three months together. Many have had additional territory given them, and all have their revenues in a more flourishing state than they had been in the memory of man. The organization, therefore, of this new confederacy, if it may be called so, may seem to be the most brilliant and successful measure of Lord Hastings' administration, and one from which, as yet, almost unmingled good has flowed to the people and nobles of Western and Central Hindostan. I confess I am tempted to wish that more of the country over which our influence extends were divided into similar fiefs and petty feudal lordships.

Sir David Ochterlony,[1] who, as agent to the Governor General, is the common arbitrator and referree in the disputes of these little sovereigns, is said to maintain an almost kingly state. His income from different sources is little less than 15,000 s.rup. monthly, and he spends it almost all. Dr Smith, in his late march from Mhow to Meerut, passed by Sir David's camp. The 'burra sahib', or great man was merely travelling with his own family and personal followers from Delhi to Jyepoor, but his retinue, including servants, escort, European and native aides-de-camp, and the various nondescripts of an Asiatic train, together with the apparatus of horses, elephants, and camels,—the number of his tents, and the size of the enclosure hung round with red cloth, by which his own and his daughter's private tents were fenced in from the eyes of the profane, were what an European, or even an old Indian, whose experience had been confined to Bengal, would scarcely be brought to credit. All this is at least harmless, and so far as it suits the habits and ideas of the natives themselves, it may have a good effect. But in Agra and Delhi, though Sir David is uniformly spoken of as a kind, honourable, and worthy man, I was shocked to find that the venality and corruption of the people by whom he is surrounded, was a matter of exceeding scandal. Against one of his moonshees it appears he had been frequently warned without effect, till at length, in the course of a casual conversation with the Emperor's treasurer, Sir David found to his astonishment, that his own name stood as a pensioner on the poor old sovereign's civil list to the amount of 1000 rupees monthly! The moonshee had demanded it in his master's name; to refuse was out of the question, and delicacy had prevented the Emperor from naming the subject to the person whom, as he supposed, he was laying under an obligation! So careful ought

---

[1] Ochterlony had succeeded Metcalfe as Resident at Delhi in 1819, and was subsequently appointed Agent in Rajputana and Malwa. He was deeply hurt by Amherst's refusal to act upon his advice in the Bharatpur crisis (see Introduction, p. 26), and died shortly after his resignation, in July 1825.

public men in India to be that their servants do not abuse their authority. But, how great must be the difficulties attendant on power in these provinces, when, except Sir John Malcolm, I have heard of no one whom all parties agree in commending. His talents, his accessibility, his firmness, his conciliating manners, and admirable knowledge of the native language and character, are spoken of in the same terms by all.[1]

January 21.—From Pharsah to Wuerh[2] is five long coss, during which we gradually approached one of the chains of low hills I have mentioned; they are very naked and sandy.. . .

We overtook a body of people going to a marriage, with a couple of large banners, two kettle-drums on a camel, several horns and other musical instruments, and two or three hackeries full of men with pink turbans and holiday faces. Our falling in with them was lucky, since we had lost our way, and none of our horsemen could give any guess at the situation of Wuerh. About a mile further, however, an extensive line of groves came into view, and shewed that we were approaching a place of some consequence, while the care with which every foot of ground was enclosed and improved, spoke well for the industry of its inhabitants. We found it a large town, surrounded by a high mud rampart, at the gate of which we were stopped by a decent-looking elderly man, who salamed to me, and said that I should find my tents by following a path which he pointed out among the orchards and gardens outside the wall. The truth, however, appeared to be that he did not like us to enter his fortress, for it was not till we had nearly gone half round the town, that we found the tents pitched in a fine tope at a short distance from a gate directly opposite to that at which he had prevented us from entering. If he feared to put us in possession of the plan of his castle, he could not, as it happened, have taken a better way to enable us to gain all the military knowledge which was necessary, since our path wound close under the wall, and we saw all its principal flanks and lines of defence. The wall is of earth, high and steep, well flanked

---

[1] Malcolm was responsible for the settlement of Malwa during the three years following the peace of 1818. From 1827 to 1830 he was Governor of Bombay; he died in 1833.

[2] Wer.

by semi-circular bastions, with a wide but shallow ditch filled up
in several places, and without a glacis. If well defended, it would
scarcely yield to a coup de main, but might be breached, I should
think, in a few hours. There were loop-holes for musquetry in the
parapets of the bastions, but I saw no cannon. The rampart was
in many places much decayed, but bore evident marks of having
recently received considerable repairs,—a measure which may
have been suggested either by the disastrous reports with regard
to the British arms in the east,[1] which had been so industriously
circulated, or still more likely, by the quarrel between the Rannee
of Jyepoor and the British Resident, and the retreat of the latter
from the city. It is not necessary to suppose, as some of the
Europeans in Agra do, that if our Government had really tottered
the Raja of Bhurtpoor would have rejoiced in an opportunity of
helping it down the hill. However well he may wish us, (and he
has been, certainly, a gainer by our predominance,) in a time of
universal war and trouble, such as would probably follow our
evacuation of this part of the country, it would be highly desirable
that his castles should be found in a state of good repair. And this
is a sufficient motive for the repairs which I saw at Wuerh.

As we wound round the rampart to reach the camp, we passed
a number of huts occupied by the 'chumars' (leather-dressers)
and other Hindoos of low-caste, who follow professions regarded
as unclean by the majority of their countrymen, and are therefore
not admitted into any of their towns. Leprous persons lie under
the same exclusion, and many Gypseys are usually found among
this mingled and refuse population, which is generally as im-
moral as it is degraded and unfortunate. The suburbs of the
ancient cities of the Jews seem to have been almost similarly
inhabited, and I was forcibly struck to-day (as I rode through the
huts of which I have spoken and saw the filthy swine, the dogs
gnawing the carcases of different animals, and the flaunting dress
and unequivocal air of the miserable, ragged, and dirty females,)
with that passage in the Revelations which, though figuratively
applied to the pure discipline of the Christian Church in its state
of glory, is obviously taken from the police of a well-regulated

---

[1] The Burma War.

earthly city in that age and country. 'There shall in no wise enter into it any thing that defileth.' 'For without are dogs, and sorcerers, and whore-mongers, and murderers, and idolators, and whoseoever loveth and maketh a lie.'

January 24.— We proceeded to Maunpoor, eight long coss, through an open sandy country. About half-way we passed a chain of hills at a place called Balaherry. The hill tops are thickly studded with castles, some of them of a considerable size and extremely like buildings of the same kind in England. We passed no fewer than seven in the day's march.

Maunpoor is a small town on the plain surrounded by a mud wall, with eight semicircular bastions, and a ditch now dry, but the works are in bad repair. If the present tranquillity were to last ten or fifteen years, it is to be doubted whether any mud forts would remain in the country, save those which the old families of rank and feudal pride might still keep up as monuments of old times. Still there are every year quarrels among some or other of these Rajpoot nobles, and no season, I am told, has yet passed in which the troops at Nusseerabad have not been called out as peace-makers, or to inflict chastisement.

January 27.—This morning we marched eight long coss to Mohunpoora. In the way I had an opportunity of seeing some part of the magnificence which Dr Smith had described, for we passed Sir David Ochterlony and his suite on his road to Bhurtpoor. There certainly was a very considerable number of led horses, elephants, palanqueens, and covered carriages, belonging chiefly, I apprehend, (besides his own family,) to the families of his native servants. There was an escort of two companies of infantry, a troop of regular cavalry, and I should guess forty or fifty irregulars, on horse and foot, armed with spears and matchlocks of all possible forms; the string of camels was a very long one, and the whole procession was what might pass in Europe for that of an eastern prince travelling. Still, neither in numbers nor splendour did it at all equal my expectation. Sir David himself was in a carriage and four, and civilly got out to speak to me. He is a tall and pleasing-looking old man, but was so wrapped up in shawls, kincob, fur, and a Mogul furred cap, that his face was all that was visible. I was not sorry to have even this glimpse of an old officer whose exploits in India have been so distinguished. His history is a curious one. He is the son of an American gentleman who lost his estate and country by his loyalty during the war of the separation. Sir David himself came out a cadet, without friends, to India, and literally fought his way to notice. The most brilliant parts of his career were his defence of Delhi against the Maharatta army, and the conquest of Kemaoon from the Ghorkhas. He is now considerably above seventy, infirm, and has been often advised to return to England. But he has been absent from thence fifty-four years; he has there neither friend nor relation,—he has been for many years habituated to eastern habits and parade, and who can wonder that he clings to the only country in the world where he can feel himself at home? Within these few days I had been reading Coxe's Life of Marlborough,[1] and at this moment it struck me forcibly how little it would have seemed in the compass of possibility to any of the warriors, statesmen, or divines of Queen Anne's time, that an English General and an English Bishop would ever shake hands on a desert plain in the heart of Rajpootana!

January 28.—This morning was dusky and close, with heavy clouds, which however gradually dispersed and were succeeded by a good deal of wind. Our march to Jyepoor was one I should think of nearly twenty miles. The early part of it was over a desolate plain of deep sand, traversed by a nullah, the windings of which we twice fell in with. About eight miles from Jyepoor we came to a deep water-course, apparently the work of art, and with a small stream in it flowing from the hills to which we were approaching. Round its edge some little cultivation was visible, though nothing could exceed the dry and hungry nature of the sand which was under us and around us, and which now began to be interspersed with sharp stones and bits of rock. The hills, as we drew near, appeared higher and steeper than those which we had hitherto crossed, but entirely of rock, shingle, and sand,

---

[1] W. Coxe, *Memoirs of John, Duke of Marlborough*, London, 1818.

without a blade of vegetation of any kind, except a very little grass edging here and there the stony, ragged water-course which we ascended, and which was our only road. The desolation was almost sublime, and would have been quite so had the hills been of a more commanding elevation. The pass grew narrower, the path steeper and more rugged as we proceeded along it, and the little stream which we were ascending, instead of dimpling amid the grass and stones, now leapt and bounded from crag to crag like a Welch rivulet. Still all was wild and dismal, when, on a turn of the road, we found ourselves in front of a high turretted and battlemented wall, pierced with a tier of arched windows, shewing us beyond them the dark green shades of a large Oriental garden. A grim-looking old gateway on one side built close to the road, and seeming almost to form a part of it, shewed us the path which we were to pursue, and I was thinking of Thalaba on 'the bridleless steed' at the gate of Aloaddin's paradise, and felt almost ready to look round for the bugle-horn suspended in the portal,[1] when the English uniform appeared to dissolve the illusion, and Colonel Raper,[2] who had good-naturedly come out thus far to meet me, rode up to welcome me.

On seeing him I at first hoped that we had already arrived at the gate of Jyepoor, but he told me that we had still four miles of very bad road before us. The rampart which we now passed is intended to guard the approach, and the garden which I mentioned is one of several attached to different temples founded in this wild situation by the same sovereign, Jye Singh, who built the city. Of these temples we passed through a little street, with very picturesque buildings on each side of it, and gardens perpetually green from the stream which we were now leaving, and which derives its source from a considerable pool higher up in the bosom of the hills. Our own track emerged on an elevated but sandy and barren plain, in which, nevertheless, some fields of wheat were seen, and, what surprised me, some fine peepul-trees. This plain, which seems to have been once a lake, is surrounded on three sides by the same barren stony hills, and has in its centre the city

[1] This is a reference to Book VI of *Thalaba the destroyer*, a long poem with an Oriental theme by Southey.
[2] F. V. Raper, Resident at Jaipur 1824-6.

of Jyepoor, a place of considerable extent, with fortifications so
like those of the Kremlin, that I could almost have fancied myself
at Moscow.

Heber stayed at Jaipur for five days, but on 31 *January he made an
excursion to Amber* (*Umeer*), *the old capital of the state.*

After leaving the city we proceeded by a wide sandy road, through
a succession of gardens and garden-houses, some of the latter of
which were very handsome, to the banks of a large lake, covered
with water-fowl, and with a small island in the midst on which
were the ruins of a palace. The mere supplies the stream which
we had passed in our way up the ghât;[1] it has on this side every
appearance of being a natural sheet of water; its banks are more
woody and wild than any thing which I had seen since I left
Kemaoon, and the steep and rugged road by which we ascended
the hill beyond it, contributed to raise my expectation of a
beautiful view from the top.

 This road led us through an ancient gate-way in an embattled
and turretted wall which connected the two hills, like that which
I described on the other side of Jyepoor, and within we found a
street like that also, of temples and old buildings of the same
character, one of which was pointed out to me as a shrine whither
the young Raja is carried weekly to pay his devotions, and another
as the house where he puts up his horses and reposes on such
occasions. Beyond was a still steeper ascent to a second gate,
which introduced us to a very wild and romantic valley, with a
small lake at the bottom,—the crests of the hills on either side
crowned with walls and towers, their lower parts all rock and
wood interspersed with ruined buildings, in front, and on the
margin of the lake, a small ruinous town, overgrown with trees,
and intermingled with towers and temples, and over it, but a
little to the left hand, a noble old fortified palace, connected by
a long line of wall and tower with a very large castle on the
highest part of the hill. We now descended the ghât by a similar
road to that which had conducted us thither, among some fine old
trees, fragments of rock, and thickets of thorny underwood, till

---

[1] In this context, a hill.

we reached the town which almost entirely consisted of temples, and had few inhabitants but grim and ghastly Yogis, with their hair in elf-knots and their faces covered with chalk, sitting naked and hideous, like so many ghoules, amid the tombs and ruined houses. A narrow winding street led us through these abodes of superstition, under a dark shade of peepul-trees, till we found ourselves on another steep ascent paved with granite and leading to the palace. We wound along the face of the hill, through, I think, three gothic gateways, alighted in a large moss-grown quadrangle surrounded by what seemed to be barracks and stables, and followed our guides up a broad and long flight of steps, through another richly ornamented gateway, into the interior courts of the building, which contain one very noble hall of audience, a pretty little garden with fountains, and a long succession of passages, cloisters, alcoves, and small and intricate apartments, many of them extremely beautiful, and enjoying from their windows, balconies, and terraces, one of the most striking prospects which can be conceived. The carving in stone and marble, and the inlaid flowers and ornaments in some of these apartments, are equal to those at Delhi and Agra, and only surpassed by the beauties of the Tage-mahal. My companions, none of whom had visited Umeer before, all declared that, as a whole, it was superior to the castle of Delhi. For myself, I have seen many royal palaces containing larger and more stately rooms, —many, the architecture of which was in a purer taste, and some which have covered a greater extent of ground, (though in *this*, if the fortress on the hill be included, Umeer will rank, I think, above Windsor,)—but for varied and picturesque effect, for richness of carving, for wild beauty of situation, for the number and romantic singularity of the apartments, and the strangeness of finding such a building in such a place and country, I am able to compare nothing with Umeer; and this, too, was the work of Jye Singh! The ornaments are in the same style, though in a better taste, than those of his palace at Jyepoor, and the size and number of the apartments are also similar. A greater use has been made of stained glass here, or else, from the inaccessible height of the window, the glass has remained in better preservation. The building is in good repair, but has a solitary and deserted aspect;

and as our guide, with his bunch of keys, unlocked one iron-clenched door after another, and led us over terraces and up towers, down steep, dark, sloping passages, and through a long succession of little silent courts, and dim vaulted chambers, seen only through coloured glass, and made more gorgeously gloomy by their carving, gilding, and mirrors, the idea of an enchanted castle occurred, I believe, to us all; and I could not help thinking what magnificent use Ariosto or Sir Walter Scott would have made of such a building. After all we saw only part of it. Higher up the hill was another grim-looking ward, with few external windows, but three or four elegantly carved kiosks projecting from its roof, and a few cypresses peeping over its walls, which they said was the zennana, and not allowed to be seen; and above this again, but communicating by a succession of gates and turrets, was the castle which I have mentioned, grimmer and darker still, with high towers and machicollated battlements, with a very few ornamented windows, many narrow loop-holes, and one tall minaret rising above the whole cluster. The interior of this, of course, was not shewn; indeed, it is what the government of Jyepoor considers as their last resource. The public treasure used to be laid up here; and here, it is said, are many state prisoners, whose number is likely to be increased if the present rule continues.

On returning to the stable-yard, our conductor asked us if we wished to see the temple? I answered of course 'any thing more that was to be seen', and he turned short and led us some little distance up the citadel, then through a dark low arch into a small court, where, to my surprise, the first object which met my eyes was a pool of blood on the pavement, by which a naked man stood with a bloody sword in his hand. The scenes through which we had passed were so romantic, that my fancy had almost been wound up to expect an adventure, and I felt, I confess, for an instant my hand instinctively clench more firmly a heavy Hindoostanee whip I had with me, the butt end of which would, as a last resource, have been no despicable weapon. The guide, how-ever, at the same instant, cautioned me against treading in the blood, and told me that a goat was sacrificed here every morning. In fact a second glance shewed me the headless body of the poor animal lying before the steps of a small shrine, apparently of Kali.[1] The brahmin was officiating and tinkling his bell, but it was plain to see, from the embarrassment of our guide, that we had intruded at an unlucky moment, and we therefore merely cast our eyes round the court without going nearer to the altar and its mysteries. The guide told us in our way back that the tradition was that, in ancient times, a man was sacrificed here every day; that the custom had been laid aside till Jye Singh had a frightful dream, in which the destroying power appeared to him and asked him why her image was suffered to be dry? The Raja, afraid to disobey, and reluctant to fulfil the requisition to its ancient extent of horror, took counsel and substituted a goat for the human victim, with which the

> Dark goddess of the azure flood,
>   Whose robes are wet with infant tears,
> Scull-chaplet wearer, whom the blood
>   Of man delights three thousand years,

was graciously pleased to be contented.

Heber left Jaipur finally on 2 February.

The escort now sent with me were very attentive to their duty, and evidently picked men; indeed I have seldom seen finer or taller young fellows than they most of them were. Their horses and arms likewise were good and in good order, but their clothes extremely ragged and dirty, and their wild riding, their noisy whooping and hallooing, and the air of perfect equality with which they were disposed to treat us, were remarkably contrasted with the profound respect, the soldierly calmness, and handsome equipments of Skinner's cavaliers. I was, indeed, prepared to expect a much greater simplicity and homeliness of manner in the Rajpoots and tribes of Central India, than in those who had been subjects of the Mogul empire, and, even at the court of Jyepoor, I was struck with the absence of that sort of polish which had been apparent at Lucknow and Delhi. The Hindoos seem every where, when left to themselves and under

---

[1] The great Earth-mother, usually identified with the forces of terror and death; a consort of Siva.

their own sovereigns, a people of simple tastes and tempers, inclined to frugality, and indifferent to show and form. The subjects of even the greatest Maharatta prince sit down without scruple in his presence, and no trace is to be found in their conversation of those adulatory terms which the Mussulmans introduced into the northern and eastern provinces.

February 3.—We arrived at Mouzabad, another rather large town, with a ruined wall, a mosque, some good gardens, and several temples. The largest of these was called by the Rannee's suwarr, 'Bunyan ka Mandur', The Trader's Temple, belonging to the sect of Jains,[1]. . . who are numerous in all the west of India, where they nearly engross the internal traffic of the country. This building was externally richly carved, and appeared. . . to contain several apartments; but we were not permitted to see the inside, though the suwarrs, without scruple, took us into the court, and up to the terraced roof, walking with their shoes on, in high contempt (as became the Rajpoot 'children of the sun',) both of the tradesmen and their deity. I have no doubt that they would, at a word speaking, have made a way for us to the very sanctuary; but as the Jains seemed evidently in pain, and anxious that we should go no further, I thought it both uncivil and inhuman to press the point. A small but richly-carved dome rises in the centre of this building, and beyond this again and, as I conceive, immediately over the image of Painnâth, three high pyramids of carved stone are raised. . . .

February 4.—From Mouzabad we went to Hirsowlee, six coss, over a country little different from what we had traversed since Jyepoor, equally level, equally ill cultivated and ill inhabited.

Dr Smith, in the course of the day, gave [the sowars] what they considered a great treat, that is, a lump of Malwah opium. All the Rajpoots indulge in this practice, and many to a great excess, but as the remainder of their food is so simple, and they touch no other stimulant of any kind, it of course does them less harm than Europeans. Our Rajpoot escort had now got into so high

---

[1] A sect founded in the sixth century B.C. by the reformer Mahavira. Jains stress the sanctity of all life, and place special emphasis on non-violence.

good humour with us, that nothing could surpass their attention and attendance, and though their style of attention was very different from the polished and profound respect of the Hindoostanees, it had so much apparent cordiality in it that I began to be much pleased with them. They reminded me of the Tchernoymorsky Cossacks. They are certainly a fine-looking people, and their complexion the fairest that I have seen in India.

Heber proceeded through Ajmer and Nasirabad, and on 17 *February he entered the state of Udaipur.*

A 'Bhât' or Bard came to ask a gratuity. I desired him first to give a specimen of his art, on which he repeated some lines of so pure Hindoo, that I could make out little or nothing except 'Bhadrinâth', 'Duccun', and other words expressive of immense extent, and of the different parts of the compass; the poetry was in praise of the vast conquests of the British. He only repeated a very few lines, and seemed unwilling to go on, on which one of the bystanders, a Dâk peon, reproached him for his idleness, and rattled off twenty lines of the same language in high style and with much animation, as a sort of challenge to an Amœbæan contest. He spoke so rapidly that I caught even less of his meaning than of the bard's before, but the measure struck me as very nearly approaching to the hexameter. The bard rejoined with considerable vehemence, and I perceived that like the corresponding contests of the shepherds in Theocritus and Virgil, the present trial of skill would soon degenerate into a scolding match, and therefore dismissed both parties (according to the good old custom of Daphnis and other similar arbiters) giving each a small gratuity.

The Bhâts are a sacred order all through Rajpootana. Their race was especially created by Mahadeo[1] for the purpose of guarding his sacred bull; but they lost this honourable office through their cowardice. The god had a pet lion also, and as the favourite animals were kept in the same apartment, the bull was eaten almost every day in spite of all the noise which the Bhâts could make, greatly to the grief of Siva, and to the increase of his trouble, since he had to create a new bull in the room of every one

---

[1] Lit. 'the great god'; a title of Siva.

which fell a victim to the ferocity of his companion. Under these circumstances the deity formed a new race of men, the Charuns, of equal piety and tuneful powers, but more courageous than the Bhâts, and made them the wardens of his menagerie. The Bhâts, however, still retained their functions of singing the praises of gods and heroes, and, as the hereditary guardians of history and pedigree, are held in higher estimation than even the brahmins themselves, among the haughty and fierce nobles of Rajpootana. In the yet wilder districts to the south-west, the more warlike Charun, however, take their place in popular reverence. A few years back it was usual for merchants or travellers going through Malwah and Guzerât to hire a Charun to protect them, and the sanctity of his name was generally sufficient. If robbers appeared, he stepped forwards waving his long white garments, and denouncing, in verse, infamy and disgrace on all who should injure travellers under the protection of the holy minstrel of Siva. If this failed he stabbed himself with his dagger, generally in the left arm, declaring that his blood was on their heads; and, if all failed, he was bound in honour to stab himself to the heart, a catastrophe of which there was little danger, since the violent death of such a person was enough to devote the whole land to barrenness, and all who occasioned it to an everlasting abode in Padalon.

The Bhâts protect nobody; but to kill or beat one of them would be regarded as very disgraceful and ill-omened; and presuming on this immunity and on the importance attached to that sort of renown which it confers, they are said often to extort money from their wealthy neighbours by promises of spreading their great name, and threats of making them infamous and even of blasting their prospects. A wealthy merchant in Indore, some years since, had a quarrel with one of these men, who made a clay image which he called after the merchant's name, and daily in the bazar and in the different temples addressed it with bitter and reproachful language, intermixed with the most frightful curses which an angry poet could invent. There was no redress, and the merchant, though a man of great power and influence at court, was advised to bribe him into silence; this he refused to do, and the matter went on for several months, till a number of the merchant's friends subscribed a considerable sum, of which, with much submission and joined hands, they intreated the Bhât to accept. 'Alas!' was his answer, 'why was not this done before? Had I been conciliated in time your friend might yet have prospered. But now, though I shall be silent henceforth, I have already said too much against him, and when did the imprecations of a bard, so long persisted in, fall to the ground unaccomplished?' The merchant, as it happened, was really overtaken by some severe calamities, and the popular faith in the powers of the minstrel character is now more than ever confirmed.

. . . I can perceive . . . in the crowds of women and children who come out to see us, that Dr Smith and I are lions of the first magnitude; and an instance which happened this day shews that we are reckoned formidable lions too. A girl of about twelve years old, whom we met in our walk round the town, stopped short and exclaimed in a voice almost amounting to a cry, 'Alas, mighty sir, ('maharaja') do not hurt me! I am a poor girl and have been carrying bread to my father.' What she expected me to do to her I cannot tell, but I have never before been addressed in terms so suitable to an Ogre.

February 20.—Ummeerghur is a good sized town, in the centre of which are three very pretty temples ranged in a line, and built on an uniform plan, with a tomb on their right hand, where repose the ashes of a rich merchant their founder. A considerable manufactory of chintz seemed going on, and the place bore the marks of apparent prosperity. Above it, on a high rock, stands a castle, which was conquered last year for the Ranah[1] from a rebellious Thakoor.[2] The Ranah, with 3000 men, had besieged it three months before he asked for the help of British troops. Finding, however, that he made no progress, he applied to the Brigadier at Neemuch,[3] and two battalions and a few mortars settled the affair in little more than one day. This was told me by the Khamdar[4] of the town, and confirmed with a sort of exultation by the jemautdar of a troop of irregular cavalry, who, as his corps is under a British officer, and he himself had served in our army

---

[1] Of Udaipur. [2] Rajput chieftain.
[3] A British cantonment; see *infra*, p. 278. [4] Governor.

against Asseerghur, seemed to pique himself on being a British, not an Oodeypoor soldier.

We have not yet passed any Bheel villages, but I am told that we are getting into their neighbourhood....During the period which is emphatically called by all the people of this country 'the years of trouble', these savages were one among the many scourges which laid waste the fields, and made travelling a desperate adventure. The revival of the Rajpoot Governments, and the better system of police which English influence has introduced among them, together with the aid which they receive on all serious occasions from the garrisons of Mhow and Neemuch, have put a stop in a great degree to these depredations; and the judicious measures of firmness and conciliation pursued towards the Bheel chiefs, who have had lands granted them tax-free, in order to bring them into regular habits, and have been many of them enrolled, like the Puharrees and Mhairs, in local corps for the defence of the roads, have gone far to make the savages themselves sensible of their true interests, and the kind intentions of the English towards them. Still, however, there are occasional excesses, though they are chiefly indulged in against the Hindoos. A few months since, one of the bazars at Neemuch was attacked and plundered by a body of the hill people, who succeeded in getting off with their booty before the troops in the neighbouring cantonment would overtake them. And there are, doubtless, even in the plains, many who still sigh after their late anarchy, and exclaim, amid the comforts of a peaceable government,

> 'Give us our wildness and our woods,
> Our huts and caves again!'

The son of Mr Palmer, Chaplain of Nusseerabad, a clever boy, who speaks the native languages very fluently, while travelling lately with his father and mother in their way from Mhow, observed some Bheels looking earnestly at a large drove of laden bullocks which were drinking in a ford of the Bunass. He asked one of the men if the bullocks belonged to him? 'No', was the reply, 'but a good part of them would have been ours if it were not for you Sahib Log, who will let nobody thrive but yourselves!'

Rajputana

February 22.—From Gungrowr to Chittore is between twelve and thirteen miles, a wild but interesting road winding through woods at the foot of some fine rocky hills. The situation of Chittore is conspicuous from a considerable distance by the high rock on which the fortress stands, and which, from its scarped sides, and the buildings scattered along its crest, sufficiently denote its nature, even before the precise forms of the buildings themselves are distinguishable.

The Kamdar of the town, a very well-mannered man, in a splendid dress, called on me, and offered to conduct me to see the castle, which was a great favour, as it is a thing of which they are very jealous, and which probably not ten Europeans had seen out of all the number who have visited and lived in India. I proposed accompanying him at four in the evening, but he begged it might not be later than three, and that we would come on horseback, since it was, he said, nearly two coss to the top of the hill. We accordingly joined the Thakoor in the market-place of the little old city, where he was already mounted and ready to accompany us. Chittore was once the capital of this principality, and is still what would be called in England a tolerably large market-town, with a good many pagodas, and a meanly built but, apparently, busy bazar. The population seem chiefly weavers and dealers in grain. The fortress rises immediately above the town, and extends for a considerable distance to the right and left of it. The rock, where not naturally precipitous, has been scarped by art all round the summit to the height of from 80 to 120 feet, and is surmounted by a rude wall with semicircular bastions, enclosing, as our guide the Thakoor assured us, a circuit of six coss, or twelve miles. Of course it does not contain an area proportionate to this circumference, since the form is extremely irregular, and the ridge of the hill in many places narrow. But the length I can easily believe to be above two coss, and the measurement of the wall is, probably, not much exaggerated. The approach is by a zig-zag road, of very easy slope, but stony and in bad repair, passing under six gateways with traverses and rude out-works, before we arrive at the main entrance of the castle. The whole face of the hill, except the precipice, is covered with trees and brushwood, and the approach is therefore very picturesque and interesting. It is certainly, however, not two coss in gradual ascent, though it may perhaps be not far short of one. In advance of the castle gate is an out-work, or barbican, with a colonnade internally of octagonal pillars and carved imposts, supporting a flat terrace, and with a hall in the interior, which our guide pointed out to us as resembling the hall of audience at Delhi! If he had said the Emperor's stables, he would have been nearer the truth, but I did not think it necessary to contradict him. The gateway itself is very lofty and striking, with a good deal of carving, in the genuine style of ancient Hindoo architecture, with no Mussulman intermixture, and more nearly resembling the Egyptian than any thing I have seen since my arrival in this country. On entering, we first passed through a small street of very ancient and singular temples, then through a narrow and mean bazar, then, and so long as day-light lasted, through a succession of most extraordinary and interesting buildings, chiefly ruinous, but some still in good repair. The temples were the most numerous, none of them large, but several extremely solemn and beautiful. There were two or three little old palaces, chiefly remarkable for the profusion of carving bestowed on rooms of very small dimensions, and arranged with no more regard to convenience than a common prison. One of these, which is seated on a rock in the midst of a large pool, was pointed out as the residence of a very beautiful Rannee, whose fame induced the Emperor Acbar to demand her in marriage, and, on her father's refusal, to lay siege to Chittore, like another Agramant, in order to win the hand of this Eastern Angelica. After a long siege he succeeded in undermining a part of the wall, on which the princess in question persuaded all her country-women in the garrison to retire with her and her children into this palace, where they were, at their own desire, suffocated with the smoke of fuel heaped up in the lower apartments, only two remaining alive. The garrison then sallied out on the enemy, and all died fighting desperately, neither giving nor accepting quarter. The two female survivors of the carnage were found by Acbar, and given in marriage to two of his officers. I give this story as I heard it from the Thakoor Myte Motee Ram. With the exception of the romantic cause assigned for Acbar's invasion of

Oodeypoor, it is indeed 'an ower true tale', the horrible circumstances of which may be found in Dow's History of Hindostan.[1] It is extremely probable that there may have been some one high-spirited princess who urged her companions to submit cheerfully to slaughter, rather than to the wretched lot of female captives; but it is certain that all the women and children were slaughtered nearly in the manner described, which, in the blood-stained history of India, was of no uncommon occurrence, and known by the technical name of 'Joar',[2] being an act of devotion to Kali, to which men had recourse in the last extremity.

The palace on the lake has, however, no appearance of having suffered by fire, though the ruins of a long range of apartments to the north of the lake may very probably have been the scene of this sacrifice, and in this, perhaps, I may have misunderstood my informant. Just above, and on the crest of the hill, as if connected with this event, stands the largest temple in the fort, dedicated to the destroying powers, with the trident of Siva in front, and within, lighted by some lamps, in its furthest dark recess, a frightful figure of the blood-drinking goddess,[3] with her lion, her many hands full of weapons, and her chaplet of skulls. A tyger's skin was stretched before her, and the pavement was stained with the blood of sacrifices from one end to the other. On one side, on a red cloth, sate three brahmins, the principal of whom, a very handsome man of about 35, was blind, and seemed to be treated by the other two, and by all the bystanders, with great deference. On my entering the temple, which is very beautiful, I gave a rupee to the brahmin next me, who with a very humble obeisance laid it at the foot of his superior, telling him at the same time that it was the gift of a 'belattee[4] Raja'. He took no notice, however, of either it or me, merely raising his calm melancholy face and sightless eyes at the sound of my voice, and again turning them towards the shrine, while he kept telling the beads of his rosary. A large peepul grows in the court of the temple, and there are many others scattered on different parts of the hill. In this and all the other temples, I was much struck with the admirable masonry and

[1] A. Dow, *The history of Hindostan*, London, 1770, II, 257–9.
[2] *Jauhar*. This siege took place in 1567–8.
[3] Durga, the slayer of demons; like Kali, a form of the great Mother-goddess.
[4] British.

judicious construction of the domes which covered them, as well as with the very solemn effect produced by their style of architecture. A Gothic or Grecian building of the same size would merely have been beautiful, but these, small as they are, are aweful, the reason of which may be found in the low and massive proportion of their pillars, in the strong shadow thrown by their projecting cornices and un-pierced domes, in the long flights of steps leading to them, which give a consequence to structures of very moderate dimensions, and in the character of their ornaments, which consist either of mythological bas-reliefs, on a very minute scale, so as to make the buildings on which they are found seem larger, or in an endless repetition and continuation of a few very simple forms, so as to give the idea of a sort of infinity. The general construction of all these buildings is the same, a small court-yard, a portico, a square open building supported by pillars and surmounted by a dome, and behind this a close square shrine, surmounted by an ornamented pyramid. . . .

There are, besides the pool which I have already noticed, many beautiful pools, cisterns, and wells, in different parts of this extraordinary hill, amounting, as we were assured, to 84, of which, however, in the present singularly dry season, only twelve have water. One of these last, cut in the solid rock, and fed by a beautiful spring with a little temple over it, is a most picturesque and romantic spot. It has high rocks on three sides, crowned with temples and trees; on the fourth are some old buildings, also of a religious character, erected on the edge of the precipice which surrounds the castle, a long flight of rock-hewn steps leads down to the surface of the water, and the whole place breathes coolness, seclusion, and solemnity. Below the edge of the precipice, and with their foliage just rising above it, grow two or three plaintains of a very large size, which were pointed out to me as great curiosities. The Kamdar assured me that they were 300 years old, and that they every year produced excellent fruit, though, as he truly said, there could be very little earth on the ledge where they were rooted. They probably derive moisture from the water filtering through the rampart, which here forms a dam to the pool. For their great age I have only his authority.

The most extraordinary buildings in Chittore are two minarets or tower temples, dedicated to Siva. The smaller of these we only saw from a distance, and were told it was now ruinous; the largest, which resembles it in form, is a square tower nine stories high, of white marble most elaborately carved, surmounted by a cupola, and the two highest stories projecting, balcony-wise, beyond those beneath them, so that it stands on its smaller end. There is a steep and narrow but safe staircase of marble within,

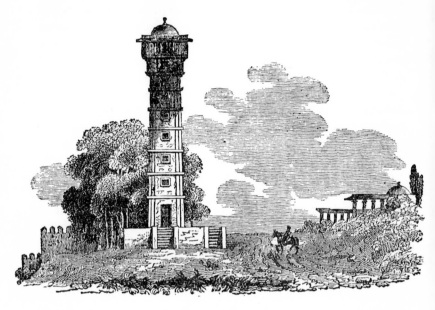

7　The tower temple at Chittor

conducting to seven small and two large apartments, all richly and delicately carved with mythological figures, of which the most conspicuous and most frequently repeated are, Siva embracing Parvati,[1] and Siva in his character of destroyer, with a monstrous Cobra di Capello in each hand. Our guides said that the building was 500 years old, but from its beautiful state of preservation, I should not suppose it half that age. It is, so far as I could judge by the eye, about 110 or 120 feet high. The view from the top is very extensive, but, at the present season of the year, there is so

[1] A consort of Siva.

276

much dust and glare that a distant prospect cannot be seen to advantage in this part of India.

On our return from the fort I found the killadar[1] with a number of people round him, seated on the roof of the colonnade which I have mentioned. I paid him some compliments in passing on the magnificence and strength of his castle, which he received in a surly manner enough, barely standing up to return my civilities. I suspect that, though compelled by the order of his superiors to admit me, he was not well pleased at seeing Feringees within his castle, and perhaps still less so, that they came by the invitation of another person. We returned down the hill by torch-light, greatly pleased with our visit.

We did not see much of the rampart, but were struck by the very slight appearance of precaution or defence at the gates which we passed. There was only one clumsy piece of cannon visible, and the number of armed men did not altogether amount to sixty. A considerable population resides within the fort, but they seemed all brahmins, weavers, and market-people. If well garrisoned by a British force, the place would, with the addition of some case-mates, be very nearly impregnable. Its situation is such that to batter it could be of little use, and, from its great extent, shells would not occasion much danger to the garrison. But to man its walls, even in the most imperfect manner, would require a moderate army.

February 23.—Sawa is a good-sized town, walled, and containing two or three well-looking houses, four handsome pagodas, and two very beautiful boolees.[2] An unusual number of drunken men, four or five shewed themselves in the course of the day; they came in two parties to ask justice against some Brinjarrees,[3] who, they said, had beaten and robbed them. It appeared on cross-examination, that in the Brinjarree encampment spirits were (in the language of the Calcutta market-book) 'procurable'. These men had been there, and got into some quarrel in which they had been soundly beaten, and very possibly robbed too, though this last seemed doubtful, as they had still their usual Rajpoot orna-

---

[1] Commandant of the fort.   [2] Pools or wells.
[3] Travelling merchants.

ments of silver about them, which would, I should think, have gone first. I told them I was not the sovereign of the land, and bade them go to the Kamdar of the town. I had seen very few drunken men in India before, but the time of 'Hoolee'[1] is now coming on, which is the Hindoo carnival, and in which the people of central India more particularly indulge in all kinds of riot and festivity. The sepoys of my guard have begun to assail the women whom they pass on their march with singing and indecent language, a thing seldom practised at other times. This is also the season for pelting each other with red powder, as we have seen practised in Calcutta.

February 25.—Neemuch itself differs in no conspicuous respect from any of the other large cantonments of the Bengal army. It is a stationary camp of thatched bungalows and other buildings, open on all sides, and surrounded by a fine plain for the performance of military evolutions. The soldiers are employed in building a sort of fort, as a shelter to the women, children, and stores, in time of need. There is a fine house here built by Sir David Ochterlony, and well furnished, but which he has never occupied. These buildings, with the surrounding slip of Meidân, constitute the entire British territory in this neighbourhood, the small town of Neemuch, and most of the surrounding country, belonging to Sindia. The cantonment itself is in fact on his ground, but was sold or ceded by him, though with considerable reluctance, at the last peace. Not even Swabia, or the Palatinate, can offer a more chequered picture of interlaced sovereignties than Meywar, and indeed all Malwah, of which Meywar, in common parlance, is always reckoned a part. In the heart of the territory which on our English maps bears Sindia's colour, are many extensive districts belonging to Holkar, Ameer Khân, the Raja of Kotah, &c.; and here scarcely any two villages together belong to the same sovereign. Sindia, however, though all this is usually reckoned beyond his boundary, has the lion's share. Never was an arrangement better calculated to ensure protection and impunity to robbers, even if there had not been abundance of jungle and inaccessible rocks, inhabited by a race (the Bheels)

---

[1] Holi—the spring festival, in honour of Krishna and the *gopis* (milkmaids).

whose avowed profession, from the remotest antiquity, has been plunder. The presence of a powerful army in the midst of such a territory, under officers anxious and interested in the maintenance of good order, has of course contributed greatly to repress these disorders, and must, as I should apprehend, be regarded as a real benefit and blessing to the country by all its peaceable and industrious inhabitants.

I was very hospitably entertained at Neemuch by Captain Macdonald,[1] political agent for this part of India.

The character of the Rajpoots, and their Government, Captain Macdonald represented in unfavourable terms. The people who are grievously oppressed, and have been, till very lately, engaged in incessant war, have the vices of slaves added to those of robbers, with no more regard to truth than the natives of our own provinces, exceeding them in drunkenness, fondness for opium, and sensuality, while they have a blood-thirstiness from which the great mass of Hindoos are very far removed. Their courage, however, and the gallant efforts they made to defend their territories against the Maharattas, deserve high praise; and some effects of a favourable nature have been produced among them by the intercourse which they have had with the English. The specimens of our nation which they have hitherto seen, have on the whole, been very favourable. None of the King's regiments have yet been sent here, and few Europeans of any description except officers. They have, therefore, seen little of the drunkenness and violence of temper which have made the natives of our own provinces at once fear and despise a Feringee soldier, and they still, Captain Macdonald says, admire us more and wonder more at the difference of wisdom, morals, and policy, which they perceive between us and them, than any other people with whom he has had intercourse in India. And he is of opinion that their present state of feeling affords by no means an unfavourable soil for the labours of a missionary.

The Bheels were regarded both by him and the other officers with whom I conversed, as unquestionably the original inhabitants of the country, and driven to their present fastnesses and their

---

[1] Alexander Macdonald (1789–1825).

present miserable way of life by the invasion of those tribes, wherever they may have come from, who profess the religion of Brahma.

The difficulties which the English Residents have to encounter in their attempts to improve the condition either of Bheels or Hindoos, are in this country very great. All interference in the internal concerns of the petty sovereigns who are the Company's feudatories, is naturally viewed with a jealous eye by the native rulers themselves, and except in the way of advice or indirect influence, is, in all ordinary cases, discouraged by the Supreme Government. The Rajas of these states are the most ignorant and degraded of men, incompetent to judge of their own true interests, and uninfluenced by any other motive which might induce them to consult the happiness of their people.

The Ranah of Oodeypoor[1] is surrounded and governed by minions of the most hateful description, who drain his treasury, force him to contract new debts, and squeeze his people to the utmost. The heir apparent of Pertaubghur,[2] who had till lately been the efficient sovereign of the country, is now in confinement by order of the English Government, in consequence of his having committed, in about three years' time, no fewer than six murders with his own hands, or, at least, sanctioned them by his presence. His father, the Raja,[3] who was entirely unable to restrain him but pleaded with many tears for his liberty, is a poor old man, past every thing except a strong affection for his unworthy son, and a spirit of avarice which seems to know no bounds, and will not be convinced that he would increase his revenues, eventually, by allowing his waste lands to be cultivated at easy rents. The Raja of Banswarra[4] is a very young and weak prince, and the Rajas of Lunewarra and Doongerpoor are, in fact, without power to do good; the territories of the former never having recovered from the cruelty of the Pindarrees, and, consequently, are become jungle from one end to the other, and the poor prince of Doongerpoor being in the hands of a party of rebels who have shut up

[1] Rana Bhim Singh: reigned 1778–1828.
[2] Kour Dip Singh: d. May 1826.   [3] Sawant Singh: d. 1844.
[4] Bhawani Singh: reigned 1819–39.

themselves and him in a strong castle, where they are at this moment besieged by a body of the Bombay army, who, finding themselves unequal to their work, have applied for help to Neemuch.[1]

In such a state of society, and in a country previously reduced by Maharattas and Pindarrees to a state of universal misery, such as no country besides has known, little can be done in the way of advice or influence by young men stationed at different courts, and obliged to apply for directions to a Government 1000 miles off. It is even probable that too frequent or too arbitrary inter-ference would defeat its own ends, and that such a close connection as subsists with Oude, for instance, would, as in that case, by no means add to the happiness of the people whom we seek to benefit.

Captain Macdonald agreed with Dr Gibb in speaking of the Mussulman Governors as wiser and better than the Hindoos; their religion, in fact, is better, and their education is something superior. But it should seem, by what he says, that Sindia's terri-tories, and Holkar's, are also better governed than those of these Western Princes, whose misfortunes and long-continued degra-dation seem to have done any thing but taught them wisdom. Sindia[2] is, himself, a man by no means deficient in talents or good intentions; but his extensive and scattered territories have never been under any regular system of controul, and his Maharatta nobles, though they too are described as a better race than the Rajpoots, are robbers almost by profession, and only suppose themselves to thrive when they are living at the expence of their neighbours. Still, from his well-disciplined army and numerous artillery, his government has a stability which secures peace, at least, to the districts under his own eye; and as the Pindarrees feared to provoke him, and even professed to be his subjects, his country has retained its ancient wealth and fertility to a greater degree than most other parts of Central India. The territories of Holkar were as badly off as any, but for their restoration they had

[1] Peace was restored shortly afterwards, but the ruler (Jaswant Singh) was deposed later in 1825.
[2] Daulat Rao Sindhia: reigned 1794–1827.

the advantages of Sir John Malcolm's advice and commanding influence. The ministers who have ruled the country during the young Raja's[1] minority, are of his choice; the system of administering justice and collecting the revenue, recommended by him, has been preserved, and, by all which I can learn, the beautiful valley of the Nerbuddah has enjoyed, during the last ten years, a greater degree of peace and prosperity than it perhaps ever did before within the limits of Hindoo history.

Besides the Rajpoots, Bheels, and Jains, a good many Jâts are scattered up and down these provinces, chiefly as cultivators of the land. There are also more Mussulmans than I expected to find, of whom the majority are of Patan race and of the Sunnite sect. The smaller, but by far the wealthier and more industrious party, are here called Boras,—a sect whose opinions are but imperfectly ascertained. They approach nearest to the Sheeahs, with a tendency towards Sooffeism,[2] and are believed by Captain Macdonald to be a remnant of the old sect of Hussunus, or as they are called in European History, 'Assassins'.[3] They have nothing, however, at present of the sanguinary and warlike temper which distinguished the followers of the 'Old Man of the Mountain'.[4] They are in general very peaceable and orderly merchants and tradesmen, and have considerable influence and privileges in most of the cities of Central India, agreeing far better with both Jains and Rajpoots than their fiery Sunnite rivals. Between these last and them, however, blood has been lately shed. A new Sunnite teacher in the city of Mundissore, a few weeks since, thought proper to distinguish himself by a furious attack on the Sheeite heresy from the pulpit, and by exhorting the true believers to cast out such wretches from dwelling among them. In consequence some wealthy Boras were insulted in the bazar by the Patans, and a fray ensued, in which the Boras, peaceable as they generally are, had the advantage. The Sunnite preacher was killed, but his body was buried by his friends with all the honours

---

[1] Mulhar Rao Holkar: reigned 1811–33.

[2] *Sufis* are Muslim mystics.

[3] This sect was founded by Hassan bin Sabbah (d. 1124), and occupied various hill-fortresses especially in Syria. Macdonald was not far wrong, as both Assassins and Bohras are Ismaili—and therefore Shia—communities.

[4] A title given by the Crusaders to a twelfth-century chief of the Assassins.

of martyrdom. The fray was again renewed, when the Patans killed several Boras and drove the rest from the place, declaring that they would pursue their advantage in all the neighbouring towns till the accursed were rooted from the earth. It ended in two companies of British sepoys being sent to keep the peace, and in the arresting of one or two ringleaders. Had not a large force been at hand, it is probable that a grand war would have begun between the parties in half the towns of Malwah; so easily is blood shed where all hands are armed and all laws feeble.

March 4.—We marched seven coss, or about sixteen miles, to Amba Ramba, or, as it is generally called, Ambera. The country during this march becomes more rugged and woody, but is still tolerably well-cultivated; and after passing a low but rocky chain of hills, I was glad to see that the people were at work in their poppy-grounds, and that the frost, to all appearance, had not extended far in this direction. The opium is collected by making two or three superficial incisions in the seed-vessel of the poppy, whence a milky juice exudes, which is carefully collected. The time of cutting them seems to be as soon as the petals of the flower fall off, which is about the present season. Sugar-mills are seen in every village, but no canes are now growing. The crops of barley and wheat are very thin, and the whole country bears marks of drought, though not by any means so decidedly and dismally as Jyepoor.

I was to-day talking with Dr Smith on the remarkably diminutive stature of the women all over India,—a circumstance extending, with very few exceptions, to the female children of Europeans by native mothers; and observed that one could hardly suppose such little creatures to be the mothers or daughters of so tall men as many of the sepoys are. He answered, that the women whom we saw in the streets and fields, and those with whom only, under ordinary circumstances, Europeans could form connexions, were of the lowest caste, whose growth was stinted from an early age by poverty and hard labour, and whose husbands and brothers were also, as I might observe, of a very mean stature. That the sepoys, and respectable natives in general, kept their women out of our way as much as possible; but that he, as a medical man, had frequently had women of the better sort brought to him for advice, whose personal advantages corresponded with those of their husbands, and who were of stature equal to the common run of European females.

March 6.—The country, though still as wild as wild could be, had improved both in greenness and beauty during this morning's ride, and, on the other side of Panchelwas, became extremely pretty. We crossed a river, the Mhye,[1] which, notwithstanding its distance from the sea, though shallow, was still broad, and not stagnant, with rocks on each side crowned with wood and some ruined temples, while the hills were not only greener and better wooded than any we had lately seen, but assumed a certain degree of consequence of size and outline. At last, our path still winding through the wood, but under the shade of taller and wider spreading trees, and over a soil obviously less burnt and barren, we came to a beautiful pool, with some ruined temples, and a stately flight of steps leading to it, overhung by palms, peepuls, and tamarinds; and beyond it, on the crown of a woody hill, the towers of a large castle. This was the palace of Banswarra, and on advancing a little further the town came in sight at its foot, with its pagodas, ramparts, and orchards.

The walls of Banswarra include a large circuit, as much, I should think, as those of Chester; but in the one, as well as the other instance, a good deal of space is taken up with gardens. There are some handsome temples and an extensive bazar, in which I saw a considerable number of Mussulmans. We took up our abode without the walls in a little old palace, with a pretty garden and a large cistern of water, now dry, which has been appropriated by the Rawul to the use of Captain Macdonald. From this house is an advantageous view of the city and palace, the trees are finer, and the view more luxuriant than any thing... which we have seen since our leaving Bhurtpoor.

The Rawul came to call on me in the afternoon with his Khamdar, and a considerable train of vassals, whom he presented

[1] Mahi.

to me as a highland chief would have done the gentlemen of his clan, and describing them in the same manner as the Thakoors of his house. They were mostly good-looking stout men, of a rustic but manly figure. The Rawul himself is a small, thin, and effeminate young man, of no prepossessing appearance. He was plainly dressed, except that he had a very handsome sword, a most voluminous red turban, and great gold anklets.

The Rawul said his age was just twenty-one, and he had been on the musnud since the year 1816.[1] Both he and his minister spoke

8   The palace of Banswara

much of the oppression and cruelty formerly exercised on them by the Maharattas and Pindarrees. They said that ours was a good Government for peace, and putting down thieves, but complained of the opium laws, and asked where all the opium went which was monopolized. They listened with much attention to Dr Smith's account of the empire of China, and the quantity of opium which was consumed there, but were still more interested on his telling them that on my voyage from Bombay to Calcutta I must pass by Lanca, (the name given to Ceylon in the Hindoo books, and respecting which they have many extravagant legends.) They would scarcely believe him when he said that it was now under the British Government, and that he had been there, and asked

[1] 1819, in fact.

eagerly 'if the principal city was surrounded by a wall of solid gold?' He answered that this was an old tradition, but that they themselves knew that many things mentioned in old books had not their like on earth now; that Lanca was still a rich country, but not so fine as it had been represented, which seemed to satisfy them.

In the afternoon Dr Smith strolled out by himself, and had some conversation with a few old men whom he had found under the shade of a tree. They seemed well satisfied with the present peaceable times, and answered his questions very readily about the internal politics of their country. The Khamdar, they said, was a Jain, and seemed to hold him cheap accordingly; with the Rawul they did not seem well pleased. He was twenty-one, they said, and yet not married, a circumstance always discreditable among the Hindoos, but here particularly so where it is a matter of much difficulty for girls of high blood to obtain suitable matches. We were objects of great curiosity in this place. A crowd was assembled all day before my gate, observing every movement within; and when I walked in the evening I had as great a crowd after me as I have seen after a Persian ambassador, or other such outlandish person, in the streets of London.

Part VIII

GUJARAT

March 14.—[In the principality of Baria,] containing about 270 villages, a very large proportion were almost without inhabitants; and in the course of our afternoon's walk through the little town, I for the first time saw some of the horrors of an Indian famine. The town had been, to all appearance, neat and substantially built, but a great many houses were uninhabited, and falling to decay. The cattle which they were driving in from the jungle for the night were mere skeletons, and so weak that they could hardly get out of the path. There were few beggars, for it seemed as if they had either died off or gone to some other land; but all the people, even the bunyans, who generally look well fed, were pictures of squalid hunger and wretchedness; and the beggars who happened to fall in my way! alas! I shall never forget them! for I never before could have conceived life to linger in such skeletons. To one of these, an elderly man, naked except a little rag fastened with a packthread round his waist, I gave all the pice I could collect from my own pocket or the servants who were with me; and after all, they, I am sorry to say, amounted to only two or three anas. The man clasped them in his hands, burst into a ghastly laugh, and ran off as if in a hurry to buy food immediately. A little further was a still more dreadful figure, a Bheel, who did not beg, but was in a state of such visible starvation that I called to him, and bid him go to the khânsaman for something to eat. I followed him to my tents, and found that he had already had some scraps given him by the sweeper. I added to these a shoulder of mutton and a seer of flour, as well as, I am ashamed to say *how* little money, all which the poor wretch tried to fold in the rag which he took from his loins. He seemed quite past every thing, and even indifferent to what I was doing for him. Some famishing children now came up, a poor man who said he was a butcher, but had no employ, and a black, who described himself as a Mussulman Fakir, and a native of Masuah in Abyssinia. I gave a few anas to each, reproaching myself all the time for giving so little, but apprehending that I should shortly have half the population round me, and that if I gave what I felt inclined to do, I should not leave myself enough for my own expences to Baroda, as well as for the many similar objects of distress which I might see by the way.

The misery of this immediate neighbourhood has been materially augmented by superstition. The calamity is want of water, yet there is a fine boolee close to the city, which, even now, is nearly full, but of which no use is made. A man fell into it and was drowned, two years ago, and the people not only desisted from drinking the water themselves, (which for a certain time was not unnatural,) but from giving it their cattle, or irrigating their ground from it. For want of being stirred it is now, of course, putrid and offensive, but would soon recover if drawn off liberally for the fields, and become again useful both for beast and man. But they would starve, and in fact were starving, rather than incur this fancied pollution. The agricultural implements, and every thing else in this country, seem behind those of their Hindoostanee neighbours. The carts and ploughs are ruder and worse constructed, and their wells have not even the simple machinery, if it deserves the name, for raising the water, which I never saw one without in Upper India, and which is always found in the wildest parts of Malwah, and the valley of the Nerbudda. We were as yet, however, in the jungles, and it would not have been fair to judge of Guzerât in general from the specimen which we now had seen.

[On March 15 Heber saw] the finest banyan-tree which I had ever seen, literally a grove rising from a single primary stem, whose massive secondary trunks, with their straightness, orderly arrangement, and evident connection with the parent stock, gave the general effect of a vast vegetable organ. The first impression which I felt on coming under its shade was, 'What a noble place of worship!' I was glad to find that it had not been debased, as I expected to find it, by the symbols of idolatry, though some rude earthen figures of elephants were set up over a wicket leading to it, but at a little distance. I should exult, in such a scene, to collect a Christian congregation. The banks of the Mhysree are steep and rocky, and the granite rock is seen every where through the country, peeping out, or rising in large insulated masses, above the scanty soil.

March 17.—We were overtaken this morning by the principal moonshee of the Residency, a shrewd Maharatta brahmin, accompanied by two others, aides-du-camp to the Guicwar,[1] who had some days been in quest of me with letters, having marched to meet me via Godra, and thus gone as far as Doodeah before they found their mistake. They had with them two of Mr Williams's[2] chobdars, and two of the Raja's, with divers irregular horse, a standard, nagari,[3] and four regular cavalry. There was a good deal of parade, but not equal in grave and orderly magnificence to what I had seen in Hindostan. Still I found that in Guzerât, as well as elsewhere in India, pomp *was* attended to. I was agitated with a delight, not unmixed with painful anxiety, on hearing that my dear wife was probably already at sea on her way to meet me, with one of my little ones, having been compelled, alas! to leave the other in Calcutta.

March 18.—From Kunjerree to Jerrdda is twelve miles, through an open and, in less unfavourable years, a well cultivated country. Even now I saw some fields of flourishing sugar-cane watered from wells, on examining which I found, to my surprise, that the water was very near the surface, and that had the people possessed more capital, for industry I do not suspect them of wanting, they might have, in a great degree, defied the want of rain. We found Archdeacon Barnes'[4] tent here, and he himself arrived at breakfast time. I had not seen him since he left Oxford, and found him less changed by the lapse of seventeen years, ten of them spent in India, than I expected. In other respects he is scarcely altered at all, having the same cheerful spirits and unaffected manner which he used to have when a young Master of

[1] The ruler of Baroda.
[2] James Williams: appointed Resident at Baroda 1821; d. 1837.
[3] Kettle-drum.
[4] George Barnes, Archdeacon of Bombay 1814–25.

Arts. From him I learned that Mr Williams and the Guicwar Raja both meant to come out to meet me the next day, at some little distance from Baroda.

I walked in the afternoon with him and Dr Smith, to look at the Maharatta horse, who had accompanied the Raja's vakeel and Mr Williams's dewan. They were fifty in number, the horses much better, both in size and spirit, than those usually ridden by the irregular cavalry of Hindostan, the men inferior in height, good looks, and dress; the arms and appointments of both pretty nearly the same; some had spears, most had matchlocks, shields, and swords.

March 19.—From Jerrdda to Baroda is thirteen miles over a bare and open country, the roads much cut up. Expecting to meet 'great men' we made our march in regular order, the nagari beating and Maharatta standard flying before us, followed by my chobdars and a chobdar of the Resident's, who gave the word for marching in a sort of shrill cry, 'Chŭlō Maharatta!' Forward Maharattas! The vakeels and the dewan followed with the chief part of my escort. After marching about eight miles, we were met by a body of horse in Persian dresses, under a young officer splendidly mounted on a dapple-grey Arab horse, with the most showy accoutrements which I had seen in India, and a shield of rhinoceros-hide as transparent as horn, and ornamented with four silver bosses. He announced himself as sent by the Resident to enquire after my health, and advanced in a very graceful manner to embrace me.... After this ceremony, and a little more conversation with the dewan, the young officer, who was evidently a dandy of the first brilliancy in his own way, began to ride before me, shewing off his horse and horsemanship in all the usual manége of the East, curvetting, wheeling, galloping forwards, and stopping short. He did all this extremely well, but some of his followers in imitating him were not so skilful or so fortunate, and one of them got a pretty rude fall in crossing some of the deep ruts with which the road was intersected. This gave me a good excuse for desiring them to ride gently, a measure desireable on more accounts than one, since the dust was almost intolerable. About a mile further Mr Williams met us, with several other gentlemen, and an escort of regular troopers, one of whom carried an union-jack before him, a custom which is common, he told me, in Guzerât and the Deckan, though not practised, as far as I have seen, in other parts of India. He told me that 'his highness' had just left his palace as he passed the gate of the town, and that we should find him without the gates under some trees. We therefore quickened our pace as much as was compatible with the comfort of our attendants on foot, and with the movements of the suwarree elephant, who was, I found, considered an essential part of the show, and was directed to follow me closely, though with an empty howdah. On the spot designated we found a numerous body of cavalry, camels, whose riders had each a large bundle of rockets, and infantry armed with matchlocks and swords, of whom a large proportion were Arabs. These troops made a long lane, at the end of which were seen several elephants, on one of which, equipped with more than usual splendour, I was told was the Maharaja. The whole shew greatly exceeded my expectations, and surpassed any thing of the kind which I had seen, particularly as being all Asiatic, without any of the European mixture visible in the ceremonies of the court of Lucknow. We here dismounted and advanced up the lane of foot, when different successive parties of the principal persons of the city advanced to meet us, beginning with a young man whom Mr Williams introduced to me as secretary to the Raja and son of the brahmin Vakeel Shastree, whom the Peishwa, Bajee Rao, murdered by the advice of Trimbukjee,[1] and thence proceeding through the different gradations of bankers and financial men, military officers, (of whom many were Patans,) according to their ranks, Vakeels of foreign states, ministers, ending with the prime minister, (all of whom were brahmins) the Raja's brother-in-law, his nephew, a little boy of six years old, the Raja's brother, the heir-apparent, a child also of about six, and the Maharaja himself, a short stout-built young man, of twenty-seven years old.[2] The usual forms of introduction and enquiries after health followed, and his Highness, after asking when I would

---

[1] Trimbakji was the favourite of Baji Rao II, the last Peshwa. In 1815 he arranged for the murder of Gangadhar Shastri, the envoy of the Company's ally the Gaikwar, for which the Resident at Poona insisted upon his arrest and imprisonment. He escaped in 1816; but was later re-arrested and imprisoned at Chunar.

[2] Syaji Rao Gaikwar: reigned 1819–47.

come to see him, for which I fixed Monday evening, remounted his elephant, and we proceeded different ways into the city, which is large and populous, with tolerably wide streets and very high houses, at least for India, chiefly built of wood, which I had not seen for a long time, with tiled sloping roofs, and *rows* along the streets something like those of Chester. The palace, which is a large shabby building, close to the street, four stories high, with wooden galleries projecting over each other, is quite a specimen of this kind. There are some tolerable pagodas, but no other building which can be admired. The streets are dirty, with many swine running up and down, and no signs of wealth, though, as I was told, there was a good deal of its reality, both among the bankers and principal tradesmen. The Residency is a large ugly house without verandahs, and painted blue, as stuccoed houses sometimes are in England. It was at this time under repair, and Mr Williams, with his sister, were encamped in a grove of mangoes about a mile from the city; our tents were pitched near his. In passing through the city I saw two very fine hunting tygers in silver chains, and a rhinoceros (the present of Lord Amherst to the Guicwar) which is so tame as to be ridden by a mohout, quite as patiently as an elephant. There were also some very striking groupes of the native horsemen, who thronged the street like a fair; one of them, a very tall and large man on a powerful horse, was cased completely in chain armour, like the figure representing a crusader at the exhibition of ancient armour in Pall-Mall. He had also a long spear shod with silver, a very large shield of transparent rhinoceros-hide, also with silver studs, and was altogether a most shewy and picturesque cavalier. Many of the others had helmets, vant-braces, gauntlets, &c. but none were so perfectly armed as he was.

During our ride Mr Williams introduced to me more particularly the officer with the splendid equipment who came to meet me, by the name of Namdar Khân, a native of Persia, and Commander of the Residency escort. He had been aide-du-camp to Sir John Malcolm during the Pindarree war, and was a man of very distinguished and desperate bravery, though, certainly, the greatest coxcomb, as he was also one of the handsomest young men I ever saw. Nothing could exceed the smartness of his embroidery, the spotless purity of his broad belts, the art with which his eyelids were blackened with antimony, his short curling beard, whiskers, and single love-lock, polished with rose-oil, or the more military and becoming polish of his sword, pistols, and dagger; he held his bridle with his right hand, having lost the other by the bursting of a gun. He had, however, an artificial hand made in Baroda, which, so far as show was concerned, and when covered like the other with a white military glove, did very well, but which enhanced the merit of its wearer's excellent horsemanship, since it must have made the management of his charger more difficult. In his instance, and in that of many other natives of rank who had been introduced to me this morning, I already perceived what I had afterwards abundant opportunity of observing, that they associated with Europeans and were treated by them on much more equality and familiarity than is usual in Hindostan. Some of this may arise from the frank and friendly manner which distinguishes Mr Williams individually, as well as the unusual fluency with which he speaks Hindoostanee. But I apprehend that more may be attributed to the lively temper and neglect of forms which are general among the Maharattas themselves, and which are remarkably opposed to the solemn gravity of a Mussulman court, as well as to the long and recent wars in which the Guicwar and the English have been allies, and in which the principal officers of both nations were forced into constant and friendly intercourse.

The Bombay sepoys were long remarkable for their very low stature; at present they have had so many recruits from Hindostan that the difference is greatly removed, and their grenadier companies have a full proportion of tall men among them. Their battalion companies are, indeed, still under-sized. Nor have they, like the regiments in Hindostan, drawn recruits from the purer castes alone. Many of their number are Kholees,[1] some are Boras, and no inconsiderable number Jews, of whom a great number is found on the coast of Cattywar, Cambay, &c.[2] Their pay and allowances are considerably better than those of the Bengal

[1] See *infra*, pp. 300 ff.
[2] Jewish communities have existed on the west coast of India possibly since before the time of Christ.

Presidency, and, altogether, the taller men among them have more the appearance of English troops than even the fine strapping soldiers of Hindostan. They are said, indeed, to fall far short of these in sobriety and peaceable temper and obedience to their officers. In bravery they are surpassed by no troops in the world, and this is fortunate, since no army can have a more troublesome country to manage.

The Guicwar is said to be a man of talent, who governs his states himself, his minister having very little weight with him, and governs them well and vigorously. His error is too great a fondness for money, but as he found the state involved in debt, even this seems excuseable. His territory is altogether considerable, both in Cutch, Cattywar, and Guzerât, though strangely intersected and cut up by the territories of Britain, Sindia, and several independant Rajas. Those of Lunewarra and Doongurpoor, which used to hold of Sindia, now pay him tribute also, as do the Rajas of Palhanpoor and Cattywar. Still his income, amounting to no less than eighty lacks, or, nearly, £800,000, exceeds greatly any thing which might have been expected from the surface under his rule, and the wild and jungly nature of some parts of it, and can only be accounted for by the remarkable population and fertility of those districts which are really productive. Out of these revenues he has only 3000 irregular horse to pay, his subsidiary force being provided for out of the ceded territory, and he is therefore, probably, in more flourishing circumstances, and possesses more real power than any sovereign of India except Runjeet Singh. Sindia, and, perhaps, the Raja of Mysore, might have been excepted, but the former, though with three times his extent of territory, has a very imperfect controul over the greater part of it, and, indeed, cannot govern his own house: and the latter is, apparently, intent on nothing but amusing himself, and wasting his income on costly follies of state coaches and gimcracks, to which the Guicwar wisely prefers the manner of living usual with his ancestors.

March 21.—In the evening we went in all the state which we could muster, to pay our visit to the Guicwar, who received us, with the usual Eastern forms, in a long narrow room, approached by a very mean and steep stair-case. The hall itself was hung with red cloth, adorned with a great number of paltry English prints, lamps, and wall-shades, and with a small fountain in the centre. At the upper end were cushions piled on the ground as his Highness's musnud,[1] with chairs placed in a row on his left hand for the Resident and his party. The evening went off in the usual form, with Nâch girls, Persian musicians, &c. and the only things particularly worthy of notice were, that his Highness went through the form of giving the Resident and myself a private audience in his own study, a little hot room up sundry pair of stairs, with a raised sofa, a punkah, and other articles of European comfort, as well as two large mirrors, a print of Buonaparte, and another of the duke of Wellington. He there shewed me a musical snuff-box with a little bird, in which he seemed to take much pride, and an imperfect but handsome copy of the Shah Nameh, of which he desired me to accept. The rest of our conversation consisted of enquiries after the Governor General, the war, the distance from Calcutta, and other such princely topics, till, a reasonable time for our consultation having elapsed, we returned down stairs again. The next thing that struck me was the manner in which the heir apparent, the little boy before mentioned, made his appearance in the durbar, announced by nearly the same acclamations as his father, and salaming, as he advanced, to the persons of rank, with almost equal grace, and more than equal gravity. After bending very low, and touching the ground before his father's seat, he went up to Mr Williams with the appearance of great pleasure, climbed upon his knee, and asked him for a pencil and paper with which he began to scribble much like my own dear little girl. The third circumstance I remarked was the general unconstrained, and even lively conversation which was carried on between the Raja, his courtiers, and Mr Williams, who talked about their respective hunting feats, the merits of their elephants, &c., much as, mutatis mutandis, a party in England might have done. The Raja was anxious to know whether I had observed his rhinoceros, and his hunting tygers, and offered to shew me a day's sport with the last, or to bait an elephant for me, a cruel amusement which is here not uncommon.

[1] Cushions used as throne.

He had a long rallying dispute with one of the Thakoors as to an elephant which, the Raja said, the Thakoor had promised to give him for this sport; and I do not think he understood my motives for declining to be present at it. A Mussulman, however, who sat near him, seemed pleased by my refusal, said it was 'very good', and asked me if any of the English clergy attended such sports. I said it was a maxim with most of us to do no harm to any creature needlessly; which was, he said, the doctrine of their learned men also. Mr Williams told me that this sort of conversation, which was very little disturbed by the most strenuous efforts which the poor singers and dancing-girls could make to attract attention, was characteristic of a Maharatta durbar, and that he had known the most serious business carried on by fits and starts in the midst of all this seeming levity. At last, about eight o'clock, the Raja told us that he would keep us from our dinner no longer; and the usual presents were brought in, which were, however, much more valuable than any which I had seen, and evidently of a kind, very few of which were within the compass of my redeeming from the Company. About nine we got back to dinner, hungry enough, and a little tired, but for my own part both amused and interested.

The Raja offered to return my visit next day; but, knowing that Tuesday is, in the estimation of all Hindoos, unlucky, I named Wednesday in preference, telling him my reason. He answered very politely, that he should account every day lucky in which he had the opportunity of cultivating my acquaintance, but was evidently well pleased. He had already, out of civility, and in consequence of being informed that I received no visits on Sunday, waved one prejudice in my favour; since the day on which I arrived, being the last day of their month, was one on which he usually never stirred from home.

March 23.—Several of the principal Thakoors of the court, as well as some Patan military chiefs, and some wealthy shroffs[1] of the city, sent messages to Mr Williams to express a desire to call on me, and become better acquainted than was possible at a public Durbar. This was a sort of interest, Mr Williams said, which he

---

[1] Bankers.

had never known them shew before: and he therefore proposed that I should give up the morning to see native company, good-naturedly promising to stay with me, both to introduce my visitors, and to help my imperfect knowledge of the language. About twenty persons called, comprising the greater part of those to whom I had been introduced the day of my arrival. Three of them were very young men, or rather boys, the sons of the late minister, Shastree, who, as I have already stated, was assassinated at Poonah by the suggestion of Trimbukjee. The youngest, a very fine and interesting lad, was learning English, which he spoke very well and with but little foreign accent. I asked him what English work he studied, and he answered, 'I am reading the book of Elegant Extracts'. His tutor is a Parsee. Some little time since he had picked up, Mr Williams said, a New Testament, and read it with delight; till his Brahmin Gooroo, finding the nature of the book, took it from him. This is the first instance of such jealousy which has fallen in my way, and for this, I suspect that the insinuations of the Parsee tutor (all of whose nation are very suspicious about Christianity), were rather to blame than the prejudices of the simple Hindoo. I hope to send him another book from Bombay, which may offend prejudice less, and yet may eventually, by God's blessing, be of some use to him.

There were two or three Patans who asked many questions about the present state of Rohilcund, and listened with great interest to the account which I gave them. . . .

A Cuttywar Raja asked much about Meru and Badrinâth, and meandered on, at some length, about Indra's Heaven which lay beyond them. I did not understand much of his story, which was at length cut short by some contemptuous ejaculations of his Mussulman neighbour from Rohilcund, who said that he remembered the hills very well, but that all this was nonsense. Mr Williams observed that the Lord Sahib had also seen 'Kâf'. 'Aye', said the Mussulman, 'those *are* famous hills! There is the Mount Al Judi (Ararat) and the Ark of Huzrut Noah (St Noah) may be seen there to this day. There are also Hajiuge and Majiuge (Gog and Magog).' I told him that I had seen Kâf, but had not been so far as Mount Ararat; though I believed that the 'burra Sahib' (Mr Williams) had seen it, which he confirmed, having been in Persia with Sir John Malcolm; but that I had seen Kâf from Russia, which lay on the other side. Another Mussulman here expressed a surprise, which was both natural and shewed his intelligence. 'Did you see it in this journey? I thought that both Kâf and Russia were a very great distance from any part of Hindostan.' I explained to him, of course, where my former travels had been, and found that he was well acquainted with the names both of Russia and Ustumboul, which last he explained, of his own accord, to be 'Cunstuntinoopla', though he did not seem to know much about their relative situations. This was a young man, whom the other called 'Nawâb', but whose name I could not catch. . . .

About sun-set the Raja came in state, and was received accordingly by Mr Williams in a very large dinner tent, where nearly the same forms took place (mutatis mutandis) as occurred during my visit to him. The little boy was put on my knee to-day, partly, I believe, as a compliment, and partly to give the Guicwar an opportunity of talking over some private business with Mr Williams, (as I afterwards learned) whom he informed in a low voice, that he had a daughter a year older than this little boy, whom, consequently, it was high time he should bestow in marriage; that he had an excellent match for her in the son of a Raja in the Deckan, but that he had no money to pay the necessary expences; and hoped, therefore, that the Government would join him in a security for five lacs of rupees, in order that he might obtain them at more reasonable interest than he could otherwise hope to do. Mr Williams, in the same voice, told him that the Government, he much feared, would never consent to such a measure; on which the Raja came down in his request to four and even three lacs, his wish to obtain which last sum Mr Williams promised to transmit to Government. This, Mr Williams afterwards told me, is a specimen of the way in which important business was often introduced and discussed in the midst of crowds and ceremonial parties. On my observing that the wish to obtain money did not tally with all which I had heard of the Raja's wealth and covetousness, he answered that the Raja always distinguished his personal savings from the national property; that he expected his daughter to be portioned out by the state; but that if he could get sufficient security, he was able and likely, under a borrowed name, himself to lend the money. While this conversation was going on, I was doing my best to entertain my little friend, to whom, in addition to the present destined for him on account of the Company, I gave a huge native coloured drawing on vellum, of the Howa Mahil at Jyepoor, with which he seemed greatly pleased, and which, by the explanation of the different objects which it contained, afforded more conversation than it would have been otherwise easy for me to keep up with him, though he was really a lively and forward boy. He was fond of riding both horses and elephants, but the 'Sircar', Sovereign, (meaning his father) had not yet taken him out hunting. He had begun to read and write in Maharatta, but in no other language, and was fonder of drawing pictures than letters, the same word, 'likna', being used both for drawing and writing. His father, who engaged as he was on the other side, contrived very dexterously to bestow all necessary attention on me, bid him ask me about my journey, but I do not think he knew any of the names of places which I mentioned, except, perhaps, Calcutta and Delhi. All the rest of the world was, in his vocabulary, 'Belattee'.

There was a good deal of Persian singing and instrumental music, the character of which does not seem a want of harmony, but dullness and languor. The airs were sung sotto voce; the instruments, chiefly guitars, were low-toned and struck in a monotonous manner; and the effect intended to be produced seemed rather repose and luxurious languor, than any more ardent or animated feeling. One man, a native of Lucknow, had a good natural voice, and two of the women sang prettily. The tunes had first parts only. The Nâch women were, as usual, ugly, huddled up in huge bundles of red petticoats; and their exhibition as dull and insipid to an European taste as could well be conceived. In fact nobody in the room seemed to pay them any attention, all being engaged in conversation, though in an under voice, and only with their near neighbours. About eight the Raja went away; and we sate down to dinner, but not till I had discovered that the greater part of the camels which the Raja had promised to lend me for my journey had not yet arrived, and that it would be impossible for me to send off, as I had intended, my baggage and servants that night. I now regretted that I had dismissed the Hindoostanee elephants and camels, but there was no use in repining.

March 24.—This morning Dr Smith and I were up at four o'clock, and, with a good deal of exertion, succeeded in assembling the camels and bearers and fairly setting our servants on their way. We ourselves remained till the evening, and then set off to join the camp. Archdeacon Barnes accompanied me, and Mr Williams and several other gentlemen rode out with me three or four miles to a boolee, at which I found, to my surprise that, in addition to the four Bombay troopers whom he had sent me before, we were joined by Bappoojee Maharatta (his Dewan) with six silver sticks and spear-men, and above fifty Guicwar horse, with their standard and nagari. I pleaded that these were really unnecessary, considering the numerous guard of sepoys, fifty men, whom I had sent on with the baggage. He answered, however, that though less might do in Hindostan, here these outward forms were both desirable and necessary! To this I could say nothing, and proceeded on my march; though I could not help thinking that since the days of Thomas a Becket or Cardinal Wolsey, an English Bishop had seldom been so formidably attended.

March 25.—We resumed our march at the usual hour, and went, through a well-cultivated, enclosed, and prettily wooded country, eleven miles to Emaad, a small village with a large tank not quite dry. In our way we were met by twenty of the Chuprassees, or, to use the language of the country, the sepoys, of the Collector Mr Williamson,[1] all of the Kholee caste, rather short but broad-set and muscular men, with a harshness, not to say ferocity, in the countenances of many of them which remarkably differed from the singularly mild and calm physiognomy usually met with in the other side of India. They were well and smartly dressed in green and scarlet kirtles, with black turbans, had every man his small round buckler and sheaf of arrows at his back, his sword and dagger by his side, and long bow in his hand, and excepting in their dusky complexions, were no bad representa-

---

[1] Thomas Williamson, Collector of Kaira 1824–8.

tives of Robin Hood and his sturdy yeomen. About half-way we were overtaken by Mr Williamson himself, who rode with us to our camp, as did also Captain Ovans,[1] who was encamped near and employed in taking a survey of the country. This gentleman brought with him some specimens of his maps, which are extremely minute, extending to the smallest details usually expressed in the survey of a gentleman's property in England, with a copious field book, and a particular statement of the average number of farms, tanks, hills, orchards, &c. in each townland. The execution of the maps is very neat, and their drawing said to be wonderfully accurate, though the mapping, measurement, and angles are, as well as the drawing, by native assistants. All which Captain Ovans seems to do is generally to superintend their operations, to give them instructions in cases of difficulty, to notice any error which he may discover in their calculations, and to cover with ink and finish for the inspection of Government the maps which they delineate in pencil. Their neatness, delicacy, and patience in the use of the different instruments and the pencil, he spoke of as really extraordinary; and he was no less satisfied with their intelligence, acuteness, and readiness in the acquisition of the necessary degree of mathematical science. From these gentlemen I gleaned several interesting facts about the inhabitants of this country.

Its wilder parts are pretty generally occupied by the Bheels, concerning whom I am able to add little to what I said before. The other and more settled inhabitants are either Mussulmans, of whom the number is but small; Hindoo bunyans; Rajpoots of a degenerate description, and chiefly occupied in cultivating the soil; Maharattas, who are not by any means numerous except in and about the Guicwar's court; and Kholees, or, as they are pretty generally called, Coolies. These last form perhaps two-thirds of the population, and are considered by public men in Guzerât as the original inhabitants of the country, a character which, I know not why, they refuse to the Bheels, who here, as in Malwah, seem to have the best title to it. I suspect, indeed, myself, that the Coolies are only civilized Bheels, who have laid aside some of the

[1] Charles Ovans (1793–1858) was engaged on the revenue survey of Gujarat from 1820 to 1829.

wild habits of their ancestors, and who have learned, more particularly, to conform in certain respects, such as abstinence from beef, &c. to their Hindoo neighbours. They themselves pretend to be descended from the Rajpoots, but this is a claim continually made by wild and warlike tribes all over India, and it is made, more particularly, by the Puharree villagers at the foot of Rajmahal who have embraced the Hindoo religion; and that the Coolies themselves do not believe their claim, is apparent from the fact that they neither wear the silver badge, nor the red turban. Be this as it may, they are acknowledged by the Hindoos as their kindred, which the Bheels never are; and though their claim of being children of the sun is not allowed by the Rajpoots who live among them, there have been instances in which intermarriages have taken place between Maharattas of high rank and the families of some of their most powerful chieftains.

Their ostensible and, indeed, their chief employment, is agriculture, and they are said to be often industrious farmers and labourers, and, while kindly treated, to pay their rent to Government as well, at least, as their Rajpoot neighbours. They live, however, under their own Thakoors, whose authority alone they willingly acknowledge, and pay little respect to the laws, unless when it suits their interest, or they are constrained by the presence of an armed force. In other respects they are one of the most turbulent and predatory tribes in India, and with the Bheels, make our tenure of Guzerât more disturbed, and the maintenance of our authority more expensive there, than in any other district of the Eastern empire. The cutcherries, and even the dwelling-houses of the civil servants of the Company, are uniformly placed within, instead of without, the cities and towns, a custom ruinous to health and comfort, but accounted a necessary precaution against the desperate attacks to which they might otherwise be liable. The magistrates and collectors have a larger force of armed men in their employ than any others of the same rank whom I have met with; and the regular troops, and even the European cavalry are continually called out against them. Yet in no country are the roads so insecure,—in none are forays and plundering excursions of every kind more frequent; or a greater proportion of, what would be called in Europe, the gentry and landed proprietors addicted to acts of violence and bloodshed. In these plundering parties they often display a very desperate courage; and it is to their honour, that, rude and lawless as they are, they do not apparently delight in blood for its own sake, and neither mutilate, torture, nor burn the subjects of their cupidity or revenge, like the far worse 'decoits' of Bengal and Ireland.

Some good had been done, Mr Williamson said, among many of these wild people, by the preaching and popularity of the Hindoo reformer, Swaamee Narain,[1] who had been mentioned to me at Baroda. His morality was said to be far better than any which could be learned from the Shaster. He preached a great degree of purity, forbidding his disciples so much as to look on any woman whom they passed. He condemned theft and bloodshed; and those villages and districts, which had received him, from being among the worst, were now among the best and most orderly in the provinces. Nor was this all, insomuch as he was said to have destroyed the yoke of caste,—to have preached one God, and, in short, to have made so considerable approaches to the truth, that I could not but hope he might be an appointed instrument to prepare the way for the Gospel.

While I was listening with much interest to Mr Williamson's account of this man, six persons came to the tent, four in the dress of peasants or bunyans, one, a young man, with a large white turban, and the quilted lebada[2] of a Coolie, but clean and decent, with a handsome sword and shield, and other marks of rustic wealth; and the sixth, an old Mussulman, with a white beard, and pretty much the appearance, dress, and manner of an ancient serving-man. After offering some sugar and sweetmeats as their nuzzur, and, as usual, sitting down on the ground, one of the peasants began, to my exceeding surprise and delight, 'Pundit Swaamee Narain, sends his salaam', and proceeded to say that the person whom I so much desired to see was in the neighbour-

---

[1] Swami—a Hindu holy man or monk. Swami Narayan had been born at Ayodhya in 1781. He was an exponent of *bhakti*—a movement which developed in all parts of India from the eleventh century onwards, and whose basic feature was devotion to a personal god, generally Krishna or Rama conceived as *avatars* (incarnations) of Vishnu. Swami Narayan was opposed to *sati* and infanticide, and in favour of the education of women. He died in 1830.

[2] Cotton tunic.

hood, and asked permission to call on me next day. I, of course, returned a favourable answer, and stated with truth, that I greatly desired his acquaintance, and had heard much good of him. I asked if they were his disciples, and was answered in the affirmative. The first spokesman told me that the young man now in company was the eldest son of a Coolie Thakoor, whose father was one of the Pundit's great friends, that he was himself a Rajpoot and ryut, that the old man in green was a Mussulman sepoy in the Thakoor's service, and sent to attend on his young master. He added, that though of different castes, they were all disciples of Swaamee Narain, and taught to regard each other as brethren. They concluded by asking me when I was to go next day, and appointed, in their teacher's name, that he would visit me at Nerriad in the forenoon; they then took their leave, I having first embraced the Thakoor, and sent my salaam both to his father and his Gooroo.

On asking Mr Williamson about the state of knowledge in this province, and the facility which it afforded for establishing schools, he said that there were large schools in most of the principal towns, where the children of the bunyans learnt writing, reading, accounts, and such portions of the national religion as their caste is allowed to receive. But there was no gratuitous instruction; and the ryuts from poverty, and the Coolie Thakoors from indifference, very seldom, if ever, sent their children. They had no objection, however, except that of expence; and he did not doubt that if Government, or any religious society, would institute schools, they would be attended with thankfulness and punctuality.

I asked him if the Government were popular; he did not think that it was particularly otherwise, and ascribed the various tumults and rising of the Guzerâttees to their famines, which frequently reduced whole families and villages to the state of 'broken men', and to their long previous habits of misrule and anarchy, rather than to any political grievances. The valuation of their lands, he said, was moderate; it was only from year to year, but in a country where the crops were so precarious, a longer settlement was not desired by the people themselves. Even according to the present system, Government were often compelled to make great abatements, and, on most occasions, had shewn themselves indulgent masters.

Gujarat

The greatest evil of the land here, as elsewhere in India, is the system of the Adawlut Courts, their elaborate and intricate machinery, their intolerable and expensive delays and the severity of their debtor and creditor laws. Even in the Adawlut, however, a very essential improvement had been introduced by Mr Elphinstone[1] in discarding the Persian language, and appointing all proceedings to be in that of Guzerât. Still there remained many evils, and in a land so eaten up by poverty on the one hand, and usury on the other, the most calamitous results continually followed, and the most bitter indignation was often excited by the judgements, ejectments, and other acts of the Court, which though intended only to do justice between man and man, yet frequently depopulated villages, undid ancient families, pulled down men's hereditary and long-possessed houses over their heads, and made the judges hated and feared by the great body of the people as practising severities in the recovery of private debts, which none of the native governors, however otherwise oppressive, either ventured to do, or thought of doing. One good effect has, indeed, followed, that by making a debt more easy to recover, the rate of interest has been lessened. But this is a poor compensation for the evils of a system which, to pay a debt, no matter how contracted, strips the weaver of his loom, the husbandman of his plough, and pulls the roof from the castle of the feudal chieftain, and which, when a village is once abandoned by its inhabitants in a time of famine, makes it next to impossible for those inhabitants, who are all more or less in debt, to return, in better times, to their houses and lands again.

March 26.—About eleven o'clock I had the expected visit from Swaamee Narain, to my interview with whom I had looked foward with an anxiety and eagerness which, if he had known it, would, perhaps, have flattered him. He came in a somewhat different style from all which I expected, having with him near 200 horsemen, mostly well-armed with matchlocks and swords, and several of them with coats of mail and spears. Besides them he had a large rabble on foot, with bows and arrows, and when I considered that I had myself an escort of more than fifty horse,

[1] Mountstuart Elphinstone, Governor of Bombay 1819–27.

and fifty musquets and bayonets, I could not help smiling, though my sensations were in some degree painful and humiliating, at the idea of two religious teachers meeting at the head of little armies, and filling the city, which was the scene of their interview, with the rattling of quivers, the clash of shields, and the tramp of the war-horse. Had our troops been opposed to each other, mine, though less numerous, would have been, doubtless, far more effective from the superiority of arms and discipline. But, in moral grandeur, what a difference was there between his troop and mine. Mine neither knew me, nor cared for me; they escorted me faithfully, and would have defended me bravely, because they were ordered by their superiors to do so, and as they would have done for any other stranger of sufficient worldly rank to make such an attendance usual. The guards of Swaamee Narain were his own disciples and enthusiastic admirers, men who had voluntarily repaired to hear his lessons, who now took a pride in doing him honour, and who would cheerfully fight to the last drop of blood rather than suffer a fringe of his garment to be handled roughly. In the parish of Hodnet there were once, perhaps, a few honest countrymen who felt something like this for me; but how long a time must elapse before any Christian Teacher in India can hope to be thus loved and honoured! Yet surely there is some encouragement to patient labour which a Christian Minister may derive from the success of such men as these in India,—inasmuch as where others can succeed in obtaining a favourable hearing for doctrines, in many respects, at variance with the general and received system of Hindooism,— the time may surely be expected, through God's blessing, when *our* endeavours also, may receive their fruit, and our hitherto almost barren Church may 'keep house and be a joyful mother of children'.

The armed men who attended Swaamee Narain were under the authority, as it appeared, of a venerable old man, of large stature, with a long grey beard and most voluminous turban, the father of the young Thakoor who had called on me the day before. He came into the room first, and, after the usual embrace, introduced the holy man himself, who was a middle-sized, thin, and plain-looking person, about my own age, with a mild and diffident expression of countenance, but nothing about him indicative of any extraordinary talent. I seated him on a chair at my right-hand, and offered two more to the Thakoor and his son, of which, however, they did not avail themselves without first placing their hands under the feet of their spiritual guide, and then pressing them reverently to their foreheads. Others of the principal disciples, to the number of twenty or thirty, seated themselves on the ground, and several of my own Mussulman servants, who seemed much interested in what was going on, thrust in their faces at the door, or ranged themselves behind me. After the usual mutual compliments, I said that I had heard much good of him, and the good doctrine which he preached among the poor people of Guzerât, and that I greatly desired his acquaintance; that I regretted that I knew Hindoostanee so imperfectly, but that I should be very glad, so far as my knowledge of the language allowed, and by the interpretation of friends, to learn what he believed on religious matters, and to tell him what I myself believed, and that if he would come and see me at Kairah, where we should have more leisure, I would have a tent pitched for him and treat him like a brother. I said this because I was very earnestly desirous of getting him a copy of the Scriptures, of which I had none with me, in the Nagree character, and persuading him to read them; and because I had some further hopes of inducing him to go with me to Bombay, where I hoped that by conciliatory treatment, and the conversations to which I might introduce him with the Church Missionary Society established in that neighbourhood, I might do him more good than I could otherwise hope to do.

I saw that both he and, still more, his disciples, were highly pleased by the invitation which I gave him, but he said, in reply, that his life was one of very little leisure, that he had 5000 disciples now attending on his preaching in the neighbouring villages, and nearly 50,000 in different parts of Guzerât, that a great number of these were to assemble together in the course of next week, on occasion of his brother's son coming of age to receive the brahminical string, but that if I staid long enough in the neighbourhood to allow him to get this engagement over, he would gladly come again to see me. 'In the mean time,' I said, 'have you any objection to communicate some part of your doctrine now?' It was evidently what he came to do, and his disciples very visibly exulted in the opportunity of his, perhaps, converting me. He began, indeed, well, professing to believe in one only God, the Maker of all things in Heaven and earth, who filled all space, upheld and governed all things, and, more particularly, dwelt in the hearts of those who diligently sought him; but he alarmed me by calling the God whom he worshipped Krishna, and by saying that he had come down to earth in ancient times, had been put to death by wicked men through Magic, and that since his time many false revelations had been pretended, and many false divinities set up. This declaration, I say, alarmed me, because notwithstanding the traits of resemblance which it bore to the history of our Lord, traits which are in fact to be found in the midst of all the uncleanness and folly in the popular legends respecting Krishna, I did not like the introduction of a name so connected with many obscene and monstrous follies. I observed, therefore, that I always had supposed that Hindoos called the God and Father of all, not Krishna but Brihm,[1] and I wished, therefore, to know whether his God was Brihm, or somebody distinct from him? The name of Brihm appeared to cause great sensation among his disciples, of whom some whispered with each other, and one or two nodded and smiled as if to say 'that is the very name'. The pundit also smiled and bowed, and with the air of a man who is giving instruction to a willing and promising pupil, said, 'a true word it is that there is only one God who is above all and in all things, and by whom all things are. Many names there may be, and have been, given to him who *is* and is the *same*, but whom we also as well as the other Hindoos call Brihm. But there is a Spirit in whom God is more especially, and who cometh from God, and is with God, and is likewise God, who hath made known to men the will of the God and Father of all, whom we call Krishna and worship as God's image, and believe to be the same as the sun "Surya".'

I now thought a fair opportunity was given me, and said, with rather more fluency than I had hoped to do, 'O pundit, it is a true

[1] Brahma—God, the Absolute, the Supreme Spirit; an impersonal being, to be distinguished from Brahmā, the Creator (the first person of the Hindu triad).

saying and to be received of all men, that God is every where, that there is no other besides him, that he dwells in the heart and prompts every good thought and word.' 'Ullah Acbar', said one of the Mussulmans. 'It is also true as you have well said, that it is by his Word, whom we call his Son, who is with the Father, and in whom the Father dwells, that the invisible God has made himself and his will known to mankind.' Here one of the Mussulmans left the room; perceiving which, and being anxious to keep the remainder a little longer, I said, addressing the old Mussulman sepoy who came with the Thakoor, 'you, sir, know what I mean, for you know what Mohammed has written of Jesus the Son of Mary, that he was the Breath of God and born of a virgin. But is not the breath of a man, the son of his mouth? is not the word of a man his breath, reduced to form and produced by him? When therefore we say that Jesus son of Mary is the Son of God, we mean that he is his Word, his Breath, proceeding from him and one with him from all eternity. But we cannot believe', I returned to the pundit, 'that the sun which we see in the sky can be either God, or that Word who is one with him, since the sun rises and sets, is sometimes on this side of the world and sometimes on that. But God is every where at once, and fills all things.' The Pundit replied, if I understood him right, that the sun is not God, but even as God for brightness and glory. But he said that their belief was, that there had been many avatars of God in different lands, one to the Christians, another to the Mussulmans, another to the Hindoos in time past, adding something like a hint, that another avatar of Krishna, or the Sun, had taken place in himself. I answered, 'O Pundit-jee! God has spoken in many ways and at many times by Prophets; but it is hard to believe that a single avatar might not be sufficient for the whole world. But on this and many other points, we may, if it please God, talk hereafter.' I then asked if he could read the Persian character, and on his answering in the negative, I expressed my concern that I had no copies of our Sacred Books with me in the Nagree, but said that if he would accept a volume or two, by way of keeping me in his remembrance, I would send them to him either from Kairah or Bombay. I then asked in what way he and his followers worshipped God, and finding that the question seemed to perplex him, I made Abdullah read the Lord's Prayer in Hindoostanee to shew what I meant, and as a specimen of what we repeated daily. I found, however, that he supposed me to ask in what form they worshipped God, and he therefore unrolled a large picture in glaring colours, of a naked man with rays proceeding from his face like the sun, and two women fanning him; the man white, the women black. I asked him how that could be the God who filled every thing and was every where? He answered that it was not God himself, but the picture or form in which God dwelt in his heart: I told him, as well as I could, (for to say the truth my fluency had begun to fail) what Christians and Mussulmans thought as to the worship of images; but did not decline receiving some paltry little prints of his divinity in various attitudes, which I said I should value as keepsakes. I asked about castes, to which he answered, that he did not regard the subject as of much importance, but that he wished not to give offence; that people might eat separately or together in this world, but that above 'oopur', pointing to heaven, those distinctions would cease, where we should be all 'ek ekhee jât', (one like another). A little further conversation of no great consequence followed, which was ended by my giving attar and pawn to the pundit, the two Thakoors, and some of the other more distinguished disciples whom he pointed out to me. We mutually took down each other's names in writing. I again pressed him to let me see him once more before I left the country, which he promised if possible; and we bad adieu with much mutual good-will, and a promise of praying for each other, which by God's help I mean to keep. On the whole it was plain that his advances towards truth had not yet been so great as I had been told, but it was also apparent that he had obtained a great power over a wild people, which he used at present to a good purpose; and though I feared to alarm him by beginning too rashly, I could not but earnestly desire further means and opportunity of putting him in a yet better way than he was now pursuing; but I thought from all which I saw that it would be to no advantage to ask him to accompany me to Bombay.

In the evening Dr Barnes and I proceeded eleven miles more in our palanqueens to Kairah, bearers having been sent from that place to meet us.

Gujarat

During my continuance in Kairah, I received a petition from Swaamee Narain, which, unfortunately, marked but too clearly the smallness of his advances beyond the usual limits of Hindooism. It was written in very good English, but signed by him in Nagree, and was brought to me by two of the persons whom I had seen among his disciples. Its purport was to request my influence with Government to obtain an endowment for a temple which he was building to Luckshmee Narain, the goddess of plenty, and also for a hospital and place of reception, which he wished to institute in the same neighbourhood, for pilgrims and poor travellers. I was at some pains to explain to these people that I was only a traveller and with no authority in the Government, and that, as being a Christian, I could not attempt any thing which was to encourage the worship of images. I told them, however, that I would convey their petition to Mr Elphinstone, so far as regarded the alms-house and relief of poor travellers, and that I would report, as I was bound to do, the good account which I heard from all quarters of the system of morals preached by Swaamee Narain and acted on by his disciples. From Mr Ironside,[1] who knows him well, and who speaks very favourably of him, I found that when expostulated with on the worship of images, the pundit often expressed his conviction of their vanity, but pleaded that he feared to offend the prejudices of the people too suddenly, and that, for ignorant and carnal minds, such outward aids to devotion were necessary. These opinions are, indeed, no more than some Christians of the Romish Church express; but since I have heard them, I confess I have thought less favourably of his simplicity and honesty of character, and have entertained fewer hopes of being able to render him any spiritual service. Still, as loosening prejudices, his ministry may, by God's mercy, be useful to his countrymen.

April 9.—We went thirteen miles more to a village called Tekaria . . . The country still, and, indeed, all the way to Broach, was chiefly cultivated with cotton, the roads very bad and worn into deep ruts, the trees less tall, spreading, and numerous than we had been accustomed to see.

[1] Edward Ironside: appointed Fourth Judge of the *Sadr Diwani* and *Sadr Faujdari Adalat* in 1821; retired from the service 1837.

Gujarat

Mr Boyd, the Collector of Broach, kindly sent two revenue officers, a tussildar, and an inferior functionary with some suwarrs to act as guides, and to procure us the usual supplies. The tussildar and his assistant were old men of the Mahommedan sect of Boras, and, whether justly so or no, seemed regarded as usurers and oppressors by the people under their care. The Boras in general are unpopular, and held in the same estimation for parsimony that the Jews are in England. Abdullah said, translating the expressions of some of the common people concerning them, that they were 'an abominable nation'.

April 10.—This day we reached Broach, a large ruinous city on the northern bank of the Nerbudda.

April 12.—We rode to Kim Chowkee, about sixteen miles, through a wilder country than we had lately seen, with a good deal of jungle and some herds of deer; at Kim Chowkee is a large serai, called here 'Durrumsallah', which is kept in good repair, having a picquet of sepoys to protect passengers from robbers; and, in one angle of the building, a roomy but hot and ill-contrived bungalow for European travellers. We found here (that is in the lower corridores and verandahs of the building) a considerable crowd of Borah inhabitants of Surat, who had come out thus far to meet the Moullah of their sect, whose usual residence is in the city, but who had now been on a spiritual journey into Malwah, where he had narrowly escaped death in the quarrel between his sect and the Patans at Mundissore. The Patans, indeed, had declared, in revenge for the death of their own preacher, whose slaughter I have already mentioned,[1] that the Moullah should never return to Surat alive, and the news of his near approach, and of his being on the safe side of the Nerbudda had called out an enthusiasm in his people, such as the sober and money-making Boras seem to be not often susceptible of.

The men whom we met here to-day were grave, wealthy-looking burghers, travelling in covered carts drawn, each of them, by two of the large and handsome Guzerâttee oxen, and ornamented and equipped in a style which made them by no means inconvenient or inelegant vehicles. One which was destined to

[1] See *supra*, p. 282.

312

receive the Moullah on his arrival, was a sort of miniature coach or palanqueen carriage shaped like a coach, with Venetian blinds, and very handsomely painted dark green. The oxen had all bells round their necks, and the harness of many was plated with massive silver ornaments. The Moullah did not arrive so soon as he was expected, otherwise the Serai would have offered the spectacle of a curious mixture of creeds; as it was, we had Mussulmans of three different sects (Omar, Ali, and Hussun)[1] Hindoos of almost every caste from brahmins to sweepers, divers worshippers of fire,[2] several Portugueze Roman Catholics, an English Bishop and Archdeacon with one lay-member of their sect, a Scottish Presbyterian, and two poor Greeks from Trebizond, who were on a begging journey to redeem their families from slavery. The whole number of lodgers in and about the Serai, probably, did not fall short of 500 persons. What an admirable scene for Eastern romance would such an inn as this afford!

April 13.—From Kim Chowkee to the river Taptee is almost fourteen miles, through a country still wild, and ill-cultivated, though, apparently, not unfruitful. This district is one of those recently acquired by the Company from the ruins of the Peishwah's empire; and it struck me that its neglected state was indicative of internal misgovernment; but I afterwards learned, that this apparent desolation does not extend far from the road-side, and that, in point of fact, the Collectorship is a very productive one. The banks of the Taptee are prettily edged with gardens, and here, at length, the coco-nut tree re-appeared. The tide was out, and we passed the stream by fording; on the other bank we were met by Mr Romer,[3] the Senior Judge of the Adawlut, a very clever and agreeable man, who had kindly asked us to his house, and had now brought carriages to meet us.

From the river-side to the gates of Surat are four miles and a half, through gardens and a deep sandy lane; thence we drove through the city, nearly two miles, to Mr Romer's house, where we found spacious, but very hot, apartments provided for us.

[1] Heber meant Sunnis, Shias and Bohras respectively.
[2] Parsis.
[3] John Romer: appointed Chief Judge and Political Agent at Surat in 1822; retired 1832.

Gujarat

Surat, or as the natives pronounce it, Soorut, (beauty) is a very large and ugly city, with narrow winding streets, and high houses of timber-frames filled up with bricks, the upper stories projecting over each other. The wall is entire and in good repair, with semicircular bastions and battlements like those of the Kremlin. Its destruction, or abandonment to ruin, has been more than once talked of; but the feeling of security which the natives derive from such a rampart, and the superior facilities which it affords to the maintenance of a good police, and the collection of the town duties, have, with good reason, preponderated in favour of supporting it. The circuit of the city is about six miles in a semicircle, of which the river Taptee or Tâpee forms the chord; near the centre of this chord, and washed by the river, stands a small castle, with round bastions, glacis, and covered way, in which a few sepoys and European artillerymen are stationed, and which is distinguished by the singularity of two flagstaves, on one of which is displayed an union-jack, on the other a plain red flag, the ancient ensign of the Emperors of Delhi. This arrangement was adopted, I believe, in courtesy, at the time when the East India Company conquered the fort from the Nawâb of Surat, and has never since been discontinued, though the Nawâb, like the Emperor himself, is now only a pensioner on the bounty or justice of the Government.[1] In the neighbourhood of this fort are most of the English houses, of a good size, and surrounded by extensive compounds, but not well contrived to resist heat, and arranged with a strange neglect both of tatties and punkahs. Without the walls are a French factory, containing some handsome and convenient buildings, but now quite deserted by their proper owners, and occupied by different English officers who pay a rent to some country-born people, who pretend to have an interest in them, and a Dutch factory, also empty, the chief of which is only waiting the orders of his Government to surrender this, like the other Dutch settlements, to the English.[2] The

[1] The Nawabs of Surat were the successors to the Mughal governors of the port, who had in the second quarter of the eighteenth century attained a *de facto* independence. But in 1759 the East India Company seized the fort and for the next forty years ruled through the Nawab as its puppet; then in 1799 Wellesley pensioned the Nawab, and direct British rule started.

[2] This actually took place in 1825.

French factory had been restored to that nation at the peace, and a governor and several officers came to take possession. The diseases, however, of the climate attacked them with unusual severity. The governor died, and his suite was so thinned that the few survivors returned to the Isle of Bourbon, whence nobody has been sent to supply their place.

The trade of Surat, indeed, is now of very trifling consequence, consisting of little but raw cotton, which is shipped in boats for Bombay. All the manufactured goods of the country are undersold by the English, except kincob and shawls, for which there is very little demand; a dismal decay has consequently taken place in the circumstances of the native merchants; and an instance fell under my knowledge in which an ancient Mussulman family, formerly of great wealth and magnificence, were attempting to dispose of their library, a very valuable one, for subsistence. There is a small congregation of Armenians in a state of decay and general poverty; but the most thriving people are the Borahs (who drive a trade all through this part of India as bunyans and money-lenders) and the Parsees. These last are proprietors of half the houses in Surat, and seem to thrive where nobody else but the Borahs can glean even a scanty maintenance. The boats which lie in Surat river are of thirty or forty tons, half-decked, with two masts and two very large lateen sails; vessels of greater draught must lie about fifteen miles off, below the bar, at the mouth of the Taptee, but except the ketches in the Company's service, few larger vessels ever come here. The English society is unusually numerous and agreeable, as this city is the station not only of a considerable military force, but of a Collector, a Board of Custom, a Circuit Court, and the Sudder Adawlut for the whole Presidency of Bombay, which for the greater conveniency of the people, and on account of its central situation, Mr Elphinstone has wisely removed hither. There is a very neat and convenient Church, which I consecrated on Sunday, April 17th, as well as an extensive and picturesque burial-ground, full of large but ruinous tombs of the former servants of the Company; most of these are from 120 to 180 years old, and in the Mussulman style of architecture, with large apartments surmounted by vaults, and containing within two or three tombs, exactly like those of the Mahometans, except that the bodies lie East and West, instead of North and South. . . .

I neither saw nor could hear of any distinguished Mussulman or Hindoo building in Surat. The Nawâb's residence is modern, but not particularly handsome; he has no territory, but a pension of a lack and a half per annum. He sent me some civil messages, but did not call. He is said to be a young man, much addicted to low company, and who shuts himself up even from the most respectable families of his own sect. I received civil messages and offers of visits from the Borah Moullah,—the Mogul Cazi, and other learned Mussulmans, but excused myself, being in fact fully occupied, and a good deal oppressed by the heat which almost equalled that in Kairah, and exceeded any thing which I had felt in other parts of the country. On the whole, Surat, except in its society, which is no where excelled in British India, appears to me an uninteresting and unpleasant city, and, in beauty of situation, inferior even to Broach.

The Education Society of Bombay have a school here, where a considerable number of Parsee, Mussulman, and Hindoo boys are instructed in writing, reading, arithmetic, and English.[1] They read the Scriptures, as a text-book, without objection, and their progress seemed highly creditable. Some of the boys were of good families. The schoolmaster is an old soldier, but the chief conductor of the school is Mr Jefferies the Chaplain.

April 17.—We left Surat in a large lateen-sailed boat with twelve rowers, for the mouth of the Taptee, where the Vigilant Company's ketch was waiting to receive us. The bar at the mouth of the river is broad, and sometimes said to be formidable to boats. When we passed there was a considerable swell, but the surf by no means high or dangerous. The Vigilant we found a vessel of about sixty tons, very neat and clean, with a good cuddy, and two small cabins partitioned from it; she carried six little carronades, and had a crew of twenty men; twelve sepoys, who form a part of its establishment, had been removed, to make room for us, on board the two country boats which received our luggage and horses. The serang was a Mussulman, a decent and intelligent

---

[1] The Bombay Education Society had been established in 1815, largely through the efforts of Archdeacon Barnes.

man, and the crew, though not very nimble or alert in their movements, were, to all appearance, steady, and tolerably acquainted
with their business. In other respects the bark was a bad one; a
heavy sailer, rolling and pitching severely, and a bad sea-boat,
having the scuppers of her deck so low in the water that on shipping
a sea, the crew had no resource but baleing. The wind, which had
been for some time unfavourable, blew almost a gale from the
S.W. and we remained at anchor the whole of the day, tossing
and pitching very uncomfortably.

Early next morning we dropped down with the tide for a few
miles; and, the wind drawing round a little more to the north as
the sun rose, we made a pretty good run to the parallel of Damaun,
a Portuguese settlement, at the foot of some high hills, and thence
to within sight of the yet higher range of 'St John'. We ran on
through the night.

At breakfast on Wednesday the 19th, we passed the mountains
of Bassein, exhibiting, besides some meaner elevations, one very
high hill of a table form, and another not quite so elevated, rising
in a conical peak. Thence we coasted the islands of Salsette and
Bombay, both rocky, and in some parts considerably elevated, but
with the high mountains of the Concan seen rising behind both.
Though at a considerable distance from the shore, we passed a
vast number of bamboos, planted as fishing-stakes, and a fleet of
boats, which, like all others which I have seen on this coast, had
large lateen sails. They were extremely picturesque; and though,
apparently, not very manageable, made their way fast through
the water: they could not tack, but wore with great celerity and
accuracy; and, though their gunwales were often scarcely above
the water, impressed me with the idea of their being good sea-
boats, and good sailers. Their style of rigging differs from that
of the Mediterranean, in that they have seldom more than two
masts, of which the hinder is much the smallest. They have also a
bowsprit, and their sails, instead of being a right-angled triangle,
have the foremost angle cut off, so as to bring them nearer the
principle of a lug-sail. They are very white, being, I believe, made
of cotton. As the sun set we saw the Bombay light-house, and,
about midnight, anchored in the mouth of the harbour.

Glossary

Bhat bard
Bheestie, bihishti water-carrier
Bhooly, bowlee, bhudki, bavali well

Chahtah, chhata umbrella
Chobdars attendants carrying silvered sticks
Chuprassee, chaprasi messenger
Clashees, khalasis tent-pitchers
Cofilah, kafila caravan
Cutcherry, kachahri court-house
Cutwal, kotwal urban police-chief

Dandy, dandi boatman
Daroga police superintendent
Decoit, dakait robber
Dewan, diwan minister; agent
Dhooly, doli a litter
Duffildar, dafadar non-commissioned officer
Dustoory, dasturi commission

Faqueer, fakir religious mendicant
Firmaun, farman order

Ghat steps for descending to river; hill
Ghee, ghi clarified butter
Gomasta, gumashta agent
Gool, gul water-channel
Gooroo, guru Hindu religious teacher

Hackery light carriage
Hajee, haji one who has made pilgrimage to Mecca
Hanjar, khanjar curved dagger

Havildar non-commissioned officer
Howdah, hauda seat on elephant

Imam prayer-leader at mosque

Jaghir, jagir assignment of rent-free land
Jeel, jhil lagoon
Jemadar, jamadar village headman; junior officer; servant

Khamdar, kamdar governor, agent
Khânsaman house-steward
Khelât, khilat dress of honour
Killadar, kiladar commandant of fort
Kincob, kamkhab gold brocade

Manjee, manjhi steersman
Mohout, mahout driver of an elephant
Moonshee, munshi teacher
Moulah, mulla learned Muslim, teacher
Moulavie, maulavi one learned in Muslim law
Musnud, masnad cushions arranged as throne
Mut, matha Hindu monastery; obelisk

Nautch, nach-girl dancing girl
Nullah, nala watercourse
Nuzzur, nazar present

Pergunna, pargana district subdivision

Glossary

Poojah, puja   Hindu religious ceremony
Potail, patel   village headman
Punkah, pankha   fan
Purwunna, parwana   official order

Ryot, raiyat   peasant

Saees, syce, sais   groom
Serai, sarai   inn
Sircar, sarkar   House-steward, accountant; Government
Sittringee, shatranji   striped carpet
Soubahdar, subadar   commanding officer

Suwarr, sowar   cavalry soldier
Swamee, swami   Hindu holy man or monk
Syud, saiyid   one claiming descent from the Prophet Muhammad

Tatty, tatti   mat
Thakoor, thakur   chieftain
Thannadar, thanadar   police official
Tonjon   sedan-chair
Tussuldar, tehsildar   minor official

Vakeel, vakil   ambassador, representative

Select Bibliography

A. WORKS BY REGINALD HEBER

Narrative of a journey through the Upper Provinces of India, from Calcutta to Bombay, 1824–5, (with notes upon Ceylon); an account of a journey to Madras and the Southern Provinces, 1826; and letters written in India (ed. Amelia Heber), 2 vols., London, 1828.

The poetical works of Reginald Heber, London, 1841.

A charge delivered to the clergy of the Diocese of Calcutta, London, 1827.

Hymns, written and adapted to the weekly Church Service of the year (ed. Amelia Heber), London, 1827.

The personality and office of the Christian Comforter asserted and explained, in a course of sermons preached before the University of Oxford in the year 1815 (the Bampton Lectures), Oxford, 1816.

Sermons preached in England (ed. Amelia Heber), London, 1829.

Sermons preached in India (ed. Amelia Heber), London, 1829.

The whole works of Jeremy Taylor, with a life of the author, and a critical examination of his writings, 15 vols., London, 1822.

B. OTHER WORKS

Bearce, G. D. *British attitudes towards India 1784–1858,* Oxford, 1961.

Cholmondeley, R. H. *The Heber letters 1783–1832,* London, 1950.

Cnattingius, H. *Bishops and societies,* London, 1952.

Corrie. *Memoirs of the Rt. Rev. Daniel Corrie, LL.D.,* by his brothers, London, 1847.

Gibbs, M. E. *A history of the Anglican Church in India,* Delhi, 1971.

Heber, A. *The life of Reginald Heber, D.D., Lord Bishop of Calcutta; with selections from his correspondence, unpublished poems, and private papers; together with a journal of his tour in Norway, Sweden, Russia, Hungary and Germany, and a history of the Cossaks,* 2 vols., London, 1830.

Hough, J. *The history of Christianity in India,* Vols. IV and V, London, 1860.

Kaye, J. W. *Christianity in India,* London, 1859.

Le Bas, C. W. *The life of the Rt. Rev. Thomas Fanshaw Middleton, D.D.,* 2 vols., London, 1831.

Smith, G. *Bishop Heber,* London, 1895.

C. ARTICLES

Quarterly Review. No. LXX, Mar. 1827; No. LXXIII, Jan. 1828.

Edinburgh Review. No. XCVI, Dec. 1828.

Index

Index

Chunar, 5, 113, 132

Church Missionary Society, 5, 7, 9–10, 18, 24, 25, 28, 29, 33, 37, 45, 49, 130, 146, 306

Churches, consecration of, 9, 31, 86, 315

Cleveland, A., 97–103, 107

Coleridge, S. T., 21, 22

Colquhoun, Sir R., 223

Convicts, 47–8, 49; *see also* Prisons

Cooke, Miss M. A., 49n.

Corrie, Archdeacon, D., 5–6, 10, 27, 39, 68, 69, 98, 104, 106, 112, 113, 130, 131, 146, 153, 155, 161, 169, 170, 178, 246, 248

Cossacks, 15, 17, 162, 268

Cotton, 74, 77, 79, 193, 199, 201, 255, 311, 315

Dacca, 27, 29–30, 35, 68, 76, 79–89, 117, 156, 158; Nawab of, 80–5, 88–9, 172, 176

Deb, Radha Kanta, 65–6, 68

Delhi, 26, 30, 31, 36, 155, 224–39, 240, 242; Humayun's Tomb, 225, 227–8; Jami Masjid, 225, 229, 251; Kutb Minar, 236–7; Red Fort, 225, 226, 230–5, 264, 273; Safdar Jang's Tomb, 237

Dinapur, 5, 37, 120–4

D'Oyley, Sir C., 117, 120, 136

Duncan, J., 7, 36, 154

Dungarpur, 280–1, 294

Dutch, 79, 314

Edinburgh Review, 21, 29, 35

Education, *see* Schools

Elliott, C., 228, 230–5, 238–9

Elphinstone, M., 305, 315

Evangelicals, 1–9, 18–19, 25

Fatehpur Sikri, 30, 251–5

Faridabad, 239–40

Fort William College, 5, 181

Franklin, W., 103, 106n., 114, 162

Frazer, W., 130, 132, 137, 138

Freemasons, 66

French, 53, 79, 248–9, 314–15

Gaikwar, 30–1, 289, 290, 291–6, 298–9

Garos, 107

Ghazi-ud-din Haidar, 145, 171, 175–91, 193

Ghazipur, 125–9

Ghosal, Jai Narayan, 36, 130n.; Kali Sankar, 130–1, 134

Graham, Capt. J., 100, 101, 103, 104, 106

Grant, C., 3, 5, 35

Greeks, 79, 84, 86, 153, 313

Grey, Sir C. E., 21

Gujarat, 7, 12, 30–1, 36, 37, 269, 287–317

Gurkha War, 26, 30, 185, 215, 220, 261

Gypsies, 107–8, 211, 259

Hakim Mehdi Ali Khan, 184–5

Hastings, Marquess of, 7, 9, 26, 30, 65, 100, 101, 102–3, 145, 154, 184, 185, 187, 224, 257

Hastings, Warren, 7, 145, 154

Hawtayne, 50

Heber, Amelia, 17, 24, 37, 104

Heber, Reginald: Bampton Lectures, 20; Bible Dictionary, 20; birth, 13; and Byron, 21; character, 31, 36–8; consecration of, 26; Continental tour, 14–17; death, 38; education, 13–14; Hodnet, Rector of, 17; hymns, 20; and Sir W. Jones, 17; *Palestine*, 14, 21–2; poetry, 14, 22–3; political views, 20–1; *Quarterly Review* articles, 17, 21, 23; religious views, 1, 17–20, 28, 29, 33–5, 36–7, 121, 146–7, 200–1, 259–60, 288–9, 308–11; and St Asaph, 17, 20; and Jeremy Taylor, 20

Heber, Richard, 13

Himalayas, 203–6, 217, 218, 222

Hinduism, 1, 2, 3, 8, 46, 53, 62–3, 69–70, 132–4, 137, 138, 139–40, 142–4, 265–6, 268–9, 274, 276, 303n., 308–11; astronomy and cosmography, 96, 142–3, 221–3 (*see also* Meru; Observatories); Heber's views, 19, 33, 37, 128, 134, 281, 288–9, 308–11; Holi, 278; human sacrifices, 128, 266; Janmasthami, 116–17; *Puranas*, 67, 115, 221, 223n.; *Ramayana*, 46n., 159–61; *Vedas*, 140, 221; *see also Sati*; Swami Narayan

Holkar, 30, 256, 278, 281–2

Home, R., 179, 182

Hospitals, 122, 311

Howrah, 45

Humayun, 225, 227–8

Indian Bishops and Courts Act, 27

Indigo, 35, 51, 71, 72, 77, 78, 79, 121

Index

Index

Police, 87n., 91, 111, 129, 147, 173, 198, 227, 243, 271
Portuguese, 2, 79, 101, 317
Pretyman, Bishop, 38
Prinsep, J., 131, 138, 143
Prisons, 87–8, 98, 129, 221, 265

Quarterly Review, 21, 35, 36–7

Rajmahal Hills, 95, 97, 216
Rajputana (Rajasthan), 26, 30, 38, 250–86
Raper, Col. F. V., 262
Ricketts, M., 169, 171, 175–8, 181–2, 187, 197, 199
Rohilkhand, 30, 197–212, 256, 297
Roman Catholics, 2, 19, 58–9, 248, 311, 313
Romer, J., 313
Roy, Baidyanath, 64
Roy, Ram Mohan, 8, 12, 57, 130n.
Rudarpur, 206, 211–12
Russia, 14–17, 31, 165, 298; *see also* Cossacks

Saadat Ali, 171, 174, 175, 182, 183, 185, 186, 191
Sakrigali, 98
Salmon, Capt. W. B., 168, 169
Sati, 2, 8, 55–7, 65, 126–8, 141, 146, 245, 303n.
Schools, 2, 4, 7–8, 11, 31, 45n., 50, 57, 65, 69, 112, 122, 123, 146, 304, 316; girls', 7, 49–50; Jai Narayan Ghosal's, 36, 130–1, 137–8; for Paharis, 99–102, 107
Scott, Sir W., 21, 95n., 100n., 170, 232n., 265
Serampore, 2, 51–2; missionaries, 2, 3, 5, 6, 29, 56
Shah Jahan, 36, 225, 226, 229n., 235, 247–8
Shahjahanpur, 197–8, 200
Shams-ud-daula, *see* Dacca, Nawab of
Shastri, Gangadhar, 291, 297
Shaw, Col. T., 102
Shishgarh, 203–4, 207
Shore, F. J., 35
Sibpur, 11, 48n.
Sikandra, 30, 245–6, 252
Sikraul, 130, 147
Sikre, 242–3
Silk, 92, 93
Sindhia, 30, 60, 256, 278, 281, 294

Singh, Gurman, 208–9
Skinner, Col. A., 224, 239, 266
Slavery, 47
Smith, Dr, 239, 241, 257, 267, 270, 283–4, 285–6, 290, 300
Society for the Promotion of Christian Knowledge, 1, 2, 7, 10, 11, 18, 24, 25, 28, 50
Society for the Propagation of the Gospel, 9, 10, 11, 18, 25, 28, 107n.
Southey, R., 21, 22, 24, 137n., 262n.
Stowe, M., 30, 68, 83, 86
Sugar, 35, 77, 193, 199, 255, 283, 289
Surat, 31, 35, 312, 313–17; Nawab of, 314, 316
Swami Narayan, 36, 303–4, 305–11
Syrian Churches, 28–9

Tamilnad, 2, 11, 38
Templer, J. W., 109–10, 112–13
Terai, the, 30, 204–12
Textile industries, 29, 35, 79, 92, 139, 156, 228–9, 315
Thomason, T., 6, 10, 113
Thornton, John, 14–16
Tibet, 202, 217
Tiruchchirappali, 38
Titagarh, 48–9, 55, 61
Traill, G. W., 213, 221–3
Tranquebar, 2

Udaipur, 268, 270–1, 274, 280
Utilitarians, 7

Vaccination, 106

Wallich, N., 48–9, 55, 246
Warner, E. L., 91–2
Wazir Ali, 81, 174
Wellesley, Marquess, 4, 154, 314n.
Wer, 258–60
Wilberforce, W., 2, 3, 6, 18
Wilford, Col. F., 223
Williams, J., 289, 290–3, 295–300
Williamson, T., 300–1, 303–4
Wilson, Mrs. M. A., 49–50
Women in India, 8, 68, 127–8, 174–5, 178–9, 221, 248, 283–4; *see also Sati*; Schools
Wynn, Sir C. W. Williams, 24, 27

Zamindars, 62, 90, 91, 97, 98, 100, 102, 103, 110–12, 119, 185–90, 193, 195, 198, 200, 244, 256